SCIENCE, TEC

MW01156825

This book provides a comprehensive introduction to the
human, social and economic aspects of science and technology. It examines a broad range of issues from a variety of
perspectives, using examples and experiences from Australia
and around the world. The authors present complex issues
in an accessible and engaging form. Topics include the responsibilities of scientists, ethical dilemmas and controversies,
the Industrial Revolution, economic issues, public policy,
and science and technology in developing countries. The
book ends with a thoughtful and provocative look towards
the future. It includes extensive guides to further reading, as
well as a useful section on information searching skills. This
book will provoke, engage, inform and stimulate thoughtful
discussion about culture, society and science. Broad and
interdisciplinary, it will be of considerable value to both
students and teachers.

Martin Bridgstock, David Burch, John Forge, John Laurent
and Ian Lowe are all in the Faculty of Science and
Technology at Griffith University, Queensland, where they
have been teaching an introductory course in science,
technology and society for upwards of fifteen years. All are
highly respected in the field as researchers, teachers and
writers, and between them they have published over a dozen
books and 500 articles.

SCIENCE, TECHNOLOGY AND SOCIETY

An Introduction

MARTIN BRIDGSTOCK, DAVID BURCH,
JOHN FORGE, JOHN LAURENT
AND IAN LOWE

CAMBRIDGE
UNIVERSITY PRESS

PUBLISHED BY THE PRESS SYNDICATE OF THE UNIVERSITY OF CAMBRIDGE
The Pitt Building, Trumpington Street, Cambridge, United Kingdom

CAMBRIDGE UNIVERSITY PRESS
The Edinburgh Building, Cambridge CB2 2RU, UK   http://www.cup.cam.ac.uk
40 West 20th Street, New York, NY 10011–4211, USA   http://www.cup.org
10 Stamford Road, Oakleigh, Melbourne 3166, Australia

© Martin Bridgstock, David Burch, John Forge, John Laurent and Ian Lowe 1998

This book is in copyright. Subject to statutory exception
and to the provisions of relevant collective licensing agreements,
no reproduction of any part may take place without
the written permission of Cambridge University Press.

First published 1998

Printed in Australia by Brown Prior Anderson

Typeset in New Baskerville 10/12 pt

National Library of Australia Cataloguing in Publication data

Science, technology, and society: an introduction.
Bibliography.
Includes index.
ISBN 0 521 58320 9.
ISBN 0 521 58735 2 (pbk.).
1. Technology – Social aspects – History. 2. Science –
Social aspects – History. I. Bridgstock, Martin. II.
Title.
303.483

Library of Congress Cataloguing in Publication data

Science, technology, and society – an introduction/
Martin Bridgstock ... [et al.].
p.   cm.
Includes bibliographical references and index.
ISBN 0-521-58320-9 (alk. paper) – ISBN 0-521-58735-2 (pbk.: alk. paper).
1. Science – Social aspects. 2. Technology – Social aspects.
3. Science and state. 4. Technology and state.
I. Bridgstock, Martin, 1948–
Q175.5.S3738 1998
303.48'3–dc21   97–30209

A catalogue record for this book is available from the British Library

Contents

Figures

Tables

Contributors

MARTIN BRIDGSTOCK has a background in sociology, and has researched and published in the areas of ethics and misconduct in science. He is currently a senior lecturer in the School of Science at Griffith University and a Scientific and Technical Consultant for CSICOP, the American sceptical organisation. In 1986 he co-edited (with Dr Ken Smith) the book *Creationism: An Australian Perspective*. This book, deeply critical of creation science, went through several reprints and played a substantial part in preventing creation science being taught in Queensland schools.

DAVID BURCH is a political scientist and is currently senior lecturer and Director of the Science Policy Research Centre at Griffith University. He is the author of *Overseas Aid and the Transfer of Technology* (1987), an editor of *Globalization and Agri-Food Restructuring* (1996), and has published numerous articles on aid and on technology and rural social change in Australia and the Third World.

JOHN FORGE is a philosopher of science with a PhD from University College London. He is a senior lecturer in the School of Science at Griffith University, and has published widely in the philosophy of science and on issues concerned with nuclear weapons and science and ethics. He has been Senior Visiting Fellow at the Center for Philosophy of Science at Pittsburgh on three occasions. He edits the journal *Metascience*.

JOHN LAURENT is a lecturer in the School of Science at Griffith University. He is interested in the history of ideas, including evolutionary theory, and in economic history. His previous publications include (with Margaret Campbell) *The Eye of Reason? Charles Darwin in Australasia* (1987); *Tom Mann's Social and Economic Writings* (1988) and (with

Philip Candy) *Pioneering Culture: Mechanics' Institutes and Schools of Arts in Australia* (1994).

IAN LOWE is a Professor in the School of Science at Griffith University, and former Director of the Science Policy Research Centre. He is a former director of the Commission for the Future, and edited *Teaching the Interactions of Science, Technology and Society* (1987). Professor Lowe has published, broadcast and spoken widely on issues concerning science and technology policy, energy and the environment. In 1991 he presented the ABC's Boyer Lectures on the topic *Changing Australia*.

Preface

This book sprang from two different sources, both related to our positions as academics teaching Science, Technology and Society in the Faculty of Science and Technology at Griffith University. In the first instance, the imperatives of providing undergraduate students with a broad view of the relationships between the sciences, technology and the larger society seem to become more pressing as the years go by: industrial empires rise and fall, computerisation transforms the nature of work, and biology cuts ever closer to our concepts of who we are and why we are here. As a society, we have a fairly simple choice. We can ignore these changes and attempt to cope with them as they appear. Or we can seek to understand what is happening and to exert some measure of control. Our view is clear: we favour the latter option. The second reason for writing the book was the need to fill a gap in the market. Although many excellent books and papers exist for our area, we have not found a single work which covers the material we want students to understand, at the level which seems appropriate. So, after a good deal of thought, we decided to write our own.

At its most basic level, this book seeks to show undergraduate students (and first-year students in particular) what science, technology and society is all about. It presupposes no study in or knowledge of the area, and is pitched at a level which most students should find clear and comprehensible. However, the book also recognises that students often become interested in some aspect of Science, Technology and Society and wish to pursue studies at a more advanced level. To assist with this, there is an extensive further reading section at the end of each chapter and an appendix concerned with seeking further information on any topic. Because of these, we hope that the book will be of use to many people beyond the introductory level. Naturally, we have not covered everything. However, we have tried to indicate the neglected areas and where interested students may go for more information.

From the time we began writing to the time the book appeared, more than two years elapsed. Inevitably, in a project of this complexity, many misunderstandings and errors occurred. We are grateful to the staff of Cambridge University Press Australia – notably Philippa McGuinness and Jane Farago – for their helpful and constructive efficiency. Our thanks also go to Janet Mackenzie, the copy editor, who has played a major part in giving the book greater clarity and coherence. We would also like to express our thanks to the Royal Australian Chemical Institute for permission to reproduce their ethical code in Chapter 4, and the National Australian Bank *Quarterly Summary* for permission to reproduce two diagrams in Chapter 7.

MARTIN BRIDGSTOCK, DAVID BURCH, JOHN FORGE,
JOHN LAURENT AND IAN LOWE

PART ONE

Scientific and Technological Communities

CHAPTER 1

Introduction

Martin Bridgstock, David Burch, John Forge, John Laurent
and Ian Lowe

What is Science, Technology and Society, and why should anyone want
to study it? In particular, why should science students have an interest in
the subject? Many science degrees have a unit or two concerned with it,
and some have several. It is natural for students to wonder why. Would
it not be more sensible for, say, chemistry students to study as much
chemistry as possible? There are many reasons why students, whether
scientists or not, should study science and technology in their social
aspects. First, we need some background and understanding of the
significance of science and technology in the recent past, and their
importance in the modern world.

The importance of science and technology

Most people would agree that science and technology are of great
importance in the world today. Some highly developed countries, such
as Sweden and Switzerland, spend 2 or 3 per cent of their gross domestic
product (i.e. the total wealth a country produces) on science and
technology. As we shall see in the next chapter, Australia spends about
$5 billion a year (about 1.34 per cent of its gross domestic product), but
is not considered a big investor in the area. These large sums tell us that
decision-makers in government and industry are strongly convinced of
the importance of developing science and technology.

It is equally clear that science can alter our entire conception of
ourselves and our place in the universe. The most famous instance of
this was the series of events known as the Scientific Revolution. During
this turbulent time in the sixteenth and seventeenth centuries, Galileo
and other scientists began to argue that the Earth was not at the centre
of the universe, but whirled on its own axis, and orbited around the Sun.

Later, Darwin argued that humans arose as the product of natural processes, not divinely wrought miracles.

This century, the surprises have kept coming. Physicists now believe that, at base, the universe is probabilistic, and that it arose as the result of a huge explosion, the Big Bang. Also, plate tectonics has revealed that the continents upon which we live are not stable, but drift across the Earth and crash into each other. As we write this text, it seems possible (though not certain) that the remains of simple life have been discovered from the planet Mars. Whatever the future holds, it seems certain that science will play a major part in shaping our view of the universe—and of ourselves.

It is in conjunction with technology, though, that science has had its most dramatic effects. In the nineteenth century, science-based technology began to transform whole industries. In this century, it has made warfare far more dangerous—indeed, a major nuclear war could wipe out all human life—and has changed virtually all aspects of our lives. We have seen the rapid onslaught of computerisation and telecommunications. This has created a world-wide net of communication, and also wiped out employment for many millions of people throughout the world. Modern pharmaceuticals can cure diseases which terrified our forefathers, and yet other diseases arise, sometimes from the effects of the drugs themselves.

Clearly, these changes are important, and the workings of the science and technology which produce them must be understood. However, it is dangerously easy to take notice of only one aspect of what is happening: to enjoy computers and their games and ignore the unemployment created by computers; or to take antibiotics for infections and neglect the evolution of 'super-bugs' which are resistant to them. More important, perhaps, it is easy to overlook the fact that science is always the product of human activity. This is one reason why it is important to study Science, Technology and Society. We are all familiar with terms such as the 'progress of science' or the 'onward march of technology', and we tend to forget that all scientific knowledge has been produced by people thinking, believing, arguing, and sometimes making mistakes. It follows that human beings can always decide what research is done, and what is done with the results: science and technology are not the product of some unstoppable force, but are human products which both shape, and are shaped by, the society from which they emerge. For this reason, we all need to have some understanding of the links between science, technology and society, whether we are practising scientists or simply people who, every day and in many ways, experience the effects of science and technology.

For young people undergoing a university education, there are other reasons why the study of Science, Technology and Society can be valuable. As we noted earlier, the advent of modern technology has transformed whole industries and has even changed our ideas of work. The familiar situation of receiving an occupational training that would last a whole lifetime has now passed, and it is expected that many people will have to train and re-train several times in a working life in order to maintain their level of skills and their employment. In this rapidly changing work environment, flexibility and adaptability are important attributes, and science students with some background in Science, Technology and Society are often valued because of their broader view and their capacity to locate their scientific work in a wider context. This might be important, for example, when attempting to evaluate the social impacts of a project, or when applying for funds for a research proposal which has to demonstrate some social benefit as well as scientific originality.

In addition, many science graduates follow careers which do not require a detailed scientific understanding. Within a few years of graduation, many are working in areas such as local government, business and retail work. Their scientific training has not been wasted, because it can be useful in a wide range of work. Employers can make more of graduates with a broad range of skills and knowledge, and the flexibility and breadth gained from studies in Science, Technology and Society can be of great assistance as students seek work.

Finally, we believe that there is a responsibility for all people to have some awareness of how science and technology work, for the reasons we have discussed already. Science and technology are changing every aspect of our lives, all the time. No one in the contemporary world is untouched, and the greater our understanding of what is happening, the greater our ability to ensure that science and technology are used in ways which benefit the human race, rather than leading to our destruction.

Some basic terms

As with other words describing human activity, the basic terms *science* and *technology* cannot easily be defined. H. G. Wells once said that, with the aid of a good joiner, he would undertake to defeat any definition of a chair offered to him. In the same way, any definition of science or technology is likely to come adrift somewhere. Therefore, we will not offer hard and fast definitions, but will instead make some straightforward points which we understand about science and technology.

Science is our most effective way of understanding the natural world. All science involves some form of observation or experiment, and some sort of theorising about how to explain the evidence collected. The *Concise Oxford Dictionary* defines *science* as 'systematic, organised knowledge', and this systematic nature sets science apart from other types of understanding. In addition, science is concerned with evidence and with theory. Scientific evidence often comes from experiments, though some sciences, such as astronomy and geology, do not do experiments. To explain the evidence, theories are put forward, and further evidence is often sought, to see whether the theory accords with additional observations. The exact relationship between theory and evidence is extremely complex, and at this stage we simply note that science involves both. For those interested in the nature of science, Alan Chalmers (1982) has written a good introduction, dealing with the ideas of important philosophers of science such as Popper, Kuhn and Feyerabend.

Technology is even more difficult to outline than science. Many people regard technology as simply applied science. In their view, scientists produce knowledge and then technologists turn it into important products and devices, such as computers and spacecraft. In our view, this approach is too narrow. As we shall see in this book, science did not begin to be systematically incorporated into our production systems until the middle of the nineteenth century. If technology is simply 'applied science', we would have to conclude that there was no technology before that. In fact, quite complex and sophisticated technologies were needed to build the pyramids of Egypt, the Great Wall of China, and the ancient irrigation systems of India and Sri Lanka (Ceylon). Such knowledge was based on craft rather than science, with knowledge being slowly accumulated and applied (often through trial and error) and passed on from one generation to the next.

Broadly, we regard technology as a body of skills and knowledge by which we control and modify the world. More and more, technology is being influenced by scientific knowledge, with spectacular results. Technology has always been important in human affairs. Military technology, such as the bow and arrow and the armour worn by knights, has enabled kings to carve out huge empires. The technology of shipbuilding and navigation enabled Britain to conquer a quarter of the world. We should also notice that, from this viewpoint, medicine is a technology. It enables doctors to intervene in the human body through drugs or surgery.

An important term, cropping up again and again in the literature, is R&D. This stands for 'research and development'. Defining it is complex, and there is at least one manual on the topic (OECD 1970). Broadly, however, it refers to all activity concerned with developing new scientific knowledge, and new products and processes. For nations, it is a measure of the effort being put into science and technology.

A key point in Science, Technology and Society studies is that these activities are not isolated. They are all carried out in social, political and economic contexts. Therefore, if we are to understand what is happening in the modern world, we must understand how science influences the larger society. We must also understand how the larger society influences science.

In addition, there is another way in which the word *society* can be applied to science and technology. Scientists and technologists do not work in isolation. They work in universities, firms or research groups, and the functioning of these groupings is also a legitimate focus of study. Questions about ethics and conduct within these groupings, how they should be financed and how they are best organised, are also matters which researchers in Science, Technology and Society can ask about. You will notice this division in the book: Part One deals with matters pertaining to scientific and technological communities, the second part with relationships between science and technology and the wider society.

The origins of Science, Technology and Society studies

Any discipline has a history, involving founders and important scholars, and Science, Technology and Society is no exception. Although most work has been done since World War II, views of the relationships between science, technology and society go back for many centuries. Some of these are only incidental. For example, Plato, in the fourth century BC in the *Gorgias*, recognised the value of engineers, but went on to protest about their low status in ancient Greek society (Salomon 1973:6). Probably the first attempt to outline the ideal relationships between science, technology and society, though, was published in 1527 by the British lawyer and thinker Francis Bacon, in his book *The New Atlantis*. Bacon told of an imaginary voyage to a small island in the South Seas, where a civilisation was based upon science and technology. 'The end [i.e. goal] of our foundation is the knowledge of causes, and secret motions of things; and the enlarging of the bounds of human empire, to the effecting of all things possible' (quoted in Salomon 1973:7). In Bacon's imagination, scientists are accorded the same honours as royalty, and carry out their work in an organisation (called 'Solomon's House'), making scientific discoveries, and turning these discoveries into technology. This was a remarkable vision, long before science had demonstrated that it could influence technology in major ways (see Chapter 7 for more details). It is not surprising, therefore, that the vision had some important omissions. For example, Bacon did not provide any finance for his scientists and technologists. In modern terms, the R&D budget was zero!

It took many centuries for events to catch up with Bacon's vision. Thinkers in the Enlightenment, during the eighteenth century, laid out a program for extending knowledge and repelling superstition (Goodman and Russell 1991). Scientific academies were founded in Europe, many with the aim of promoting the useful advancement of knowledge (e.g. Merton 1968). During the French Revolution, the philosopher Condorcet advocated the realising of Bacon's vision on democratic lines (Salomon 1973:13). However, it was not until the present century, under the stimulus of war and political upheaval, that the discipline of Science, Technology and Society was launched.

Politics has played a crucial part in the Science, Technology and Society movement. One of the earliest efforts arose out of the experience of the 1917 revolution in Russia and the establishment of a (supposedly) socialist state. Marx and Lenin argued that a socialist state like the Soviet Union represented a higher stage in social development than the liberal democracies of the West. One part of this theory was the materialist interpretation of history, which held that all significant social and intellectual change is caused by change in the productive forces of the economy. Of course, this places technology at the very heart of historical change.

This approach was also applied to science, and the Marxist view of science became known to scholars in the West through a conference on the history of science, called Science at the Crossroads, which was held in London in 1931. Notable among the Soviet delegation was a historian named Boris Hessen, who gave a paper entitled 'The Social and Economic Roots of Newton's *Principia*' (Hessen 1931). The *Principia* is Sir Isaac Newton's famous book, in which he put forward his three laws of motion, his law of gravity and much more. Hessen argued that Newton was led to address certain sorts of problems because their solution would lead to advances in technologies that were important to the dominant social forces of the time. These technologies included advances in navigation, mining, and the development of weaponry.

Although the Soviet Union collapsed in 1992, for a long time many Western thinkers were impressed by the communist experiment. In particular, it was noted that science and technology were an important part of communism: the state financed large scientific and technological projects and did not leave developments to chance.

Perhaps the most influential of these thinkers was the physical chemist J. D. Bernal, of London University. After visiting the Soviet Union in 1934, he concluded that science in Britain should be organised, like that in the Soviet Union, to solve pressing economic problems. He wrote a book called *The Social Function of Science*, which appeared in 1939. The key point of this book is that science is not primarily a search for the understanding of the universe; rather, it has a social function. This function is the improvement of the lot of humanity. Much of the book—naturally, with many references to the Soviet Union—is a plan for the direction and use of science in the national interest. There was a fierce reaction to this: many scientists felt strongly that science could not be directed, and in the United Kingdom after World War II (1939–45) the Society for Freedom in Science was formed to combat what they called 'Bernalism'.

War has also had a major impact on the analysis of the role of science and technology in society. Of particular importance was the development of the atomic bomb. As Chapter 3 recounts, the American Manhattan Project was set up in 1942, in conditions of complete secrecy, with the aim of making the first atomic bombs. Late in the war, the Japanese cities of Hiroshima and Nagasaki were destroyed by these bombs, forcing Japan to surrender. Many scientists who were engaged on the project later expressed regret at their involvement in the Manhattan Project. For the next fifty years, too, the rest of the world saw the production of huge numbers of nuclear weapons in the Cold War arms race between the United States and the Soviet Union, and lived with the prospect of total destruction.

Thus, at the end of World War II, Bernal's argument was clearly true, at least in its essentials. Governments knew that, for their countries to progress, they had to support scientific research and technological development. As a result of this, governments began to plan for science and technology.

Perhaps the most dramatic of these developments took place in the United States. A distinguished scientist, Vannevar Bush, was asked to report on a suitable plan for science after World War II. Bush recommended the setting up of a National Research Foundation—which later became the National Science Foundation. He also wrote a report, *Science, The Endless Frontier* (Bush 1945), which advocated the setting up of a national policy concerned with science.

The development of government science policy (as it came to be called) was mainly concerned with the use of limited funds for the best effect. After the war, spending on science was growing exponentially, with the money spent doubling roughly every fifteen years. This could not continue, as eventually science would consume all of the government's budget. Governments had to make choices about what to fund and what not to fund, and they had to develop criteria to help them make choices. They also needed to be able to measure the effectiveness of their decisions. This has restarted the debate about the freedom of science which first surfaced as a response to 'Bernalism'. Two key questions are whether governments or scientists are best equipped to decide what should be funded in science, and how 'success' is to be judged.

More recently, Science, Technology and Society has come to embrace another area of study, known as technology assessment, and concerned with the impact of large-scale technologies on society. As technology becomes bigger and more complicated—with nuclear power stations, jumbo jets and supertankers—it follows that the impacts are felt far and wide if something goes wrong, even if it is only a minor problem. The nuclear disasters at Chernobyl (1986) and Three Mile Island (1979) are good examples. It is now clear that the likely impact of technologies should be assessed before they are introduced. Researchers in this field look at emerging technologies and try to ensure that positive outcomes are exploited and negative effects avoided. An extension of this is environmental impact assessment, which examines the effects of major developments on the physical environment.

From this brief discussion of how Science, Technology and Society arose, you will see that the discipline has emerged as a composite of a number of study areas. Some of these have been briefly discussed, and others, such as 'Ethics and Science' and 'Science and the Economy', are discussed elsewhere in this book. All the different approaches have some things in common: they are all concerned with science and technology in a social context, in which science and technology both shape, and are shaped by, the society in which they are performed. This basic approach is reflected throughout the book, and in the themes which arise from it.

Themes

This book is organised round two major themes. As you read each chapter, you should think about what has been said, and how it illustrates and extends the ideas implicit in the themes.

The first theme is this: *Science and technology are important in the world, and growing more so, and this presents both problems and opportunities to humanity.* The brief outline of Science, Technology and Society, above, shows how science has increased in importance. Chapter 6 on the Industrial Revolution discusses the importance of technology in this monumental event. The first part of Chapter 7 shows how science for the first time began to influence industrial technology. The discussion of science policy in Chapter 9 examines the ways in which governments have sought to use science.

The second theme is: *How we treat and use science and technology affects what is produced and what effects it has.* As Chapter 3 points out, research and development are organised in several different sectors, and these focus on producing different types of knowledge. In addition, as Chapter 8 argues, industrially useful innovations are taken up and used by industry: a useful invention which is not exploited has no economic consequences. You should find this theme appearing in other guises throughout the book as well.

Structure

We argued above that the term *society* can be considered as applying either to the scientific community, or to the wider society, which includes us all. Part One of the book adopts the former perspective. Chapter 2 is a guided tour of modern science. The main types of science—academic, industrial and government—are examined, and some explanation made of why each exists, and how they work. Then Chapter 3 takes up the issue of how far scientists are ethically responsible for the work they do. The conclusions lead on to Chapter 4, which examines a range of examples of dubious or unethical conduct in science.

Once we accept the obvious point that science is a human activity, then it is reasonable to ask: what happens when the inevitable disagreements arise? Chapter 5 investigates what sort of controversies arise within science, and how they may be settled. It also looks at how science becomes involved in larger controversies, and how these are resolved. Two quite different issues—continental drift and a medical research scandal—are examined in some detail.

Part Two of the book takes the broader view of the term *society*. In Chapter 6, John Forge examines the process of the Industrial Revolution. This event has transformed the world, and it is important to understand what happened and why.

Science and technology now take up a substantial part of the world's wealth, and are important factors in the future of all nations. Chapter 7 studies the impact of science upon industry, as it first occurred in the British alkali industry in the nineteenth century. Then the role of science and technology in the Australian economy is considered, and compared with two other advanced nations, Japan and Sweden.

Given this importance of science and technology to the economy, it is natural that economists have tried to understand exactly what is happening. Chapter 8 deals with the economics of science and technology. Some important questions are posed about how science and technology relate to modern economies, and some tentative answers given.

Because science and technology cost so much money, and governments fund a sizeable proportion of this, it follows that governments feel a need to make decisions about the scale and direction of that funding. In addition, governments must also make choices about which technologies will be used, and how. Chapter 9 reviews the process of making public policy for science and technology. By looking at a series of recent—and contentious—decisions, Ian Lowe illustrates the general argument that science and technology are increasingly being steered toward the short-term economic goals of the government of the day.

Some of the most spectacular events of our day are occurring in Third World countries. In Chapter 10, David Burch reviews the role of science and technology in the development of the Third World. Looking over developments of the last thirty years, this chapter considers the role of indigenous technology, and the transfer and impacts of Western technologies, and also the role of appropriate technology. It also draws on the lessons learned from the diverse experiences of China, India, South Korea, and other countries.

Finally, Ian Lowe describes how the world is being dramatically shaped by new technology, and discusses the complex problem of trying to use science and technology to develop a preferred future. Chapter 11 builds on the material in the earlier chapters to show how crucially the social dimensions of science and technology influence the future of humanity. We must move away from passive acceptance of these things as determined, and examine our own role in the future.

Science, Technology and Society is a vast field, and this book can do no more than outline some of its main features. At the end of each chapter are suggestions for further reading, aimed at leading the reader deeper into the subject. In addition, at the end of the book is an appendix (Appendix 1) which explains how to obtain further information on any subject raised in this book, or any related matter, through the use of modern databases and computer searching techniques. A second appendix deals with the important subject of referencing.

It is important that the reader should be able to investigate independently, because we have not been able to cover all the relevant fields of study which could be included. We have not, for example, devoted much attention to the important area of medicine and health care, nor to recent issues relating to the environment. In addition, we have largely neglected the rapidly growing area of gender, science and technology. This latter needs a little explanation. The themes in this book highlight the importance of science and technology, and also stress that how they are used has important consequences. Feminists have pointed out that scientists and technologists are virtually all male, and that the decision-makers (politicians and managers, for example) are also overwhelmingly male. Therefore, it is reasonable to ask how far this affects the nature and impact of both science and technology. The omissions—of health, the environment and gender issues—do not mean that we do not consider these questions important, only that we have neither the time nor space to include them.

Further reading

Since Science, Technology and Society is a large, diverse area, you will probably be more interested in some parts of it than others. The chapters in this book will direct you to reading relevant to their subject matter. Here, we will look at the overall perspectives.

Those interested in the history of Science, Technology and Society should read, or at least dip into, *The Social Function of Science* (Bernal 1939). Hessen's work is important and interesting and can be found in Bukharin (1931). An early document in the debate on freedom and planning from the freedom camp is J. R. Baker (1939). Bush's report is not freely available but it is discussed in Rose and Rose (1970) and also Greenberg (1969). Both of these books are good on the origins of Science, Technology and Society. Finally, with regard to the early teaching of the subject, the reader might like to consult some of the study guides put out under the rubric of SISCON, or Science in Social Context. These guides were published by Butterworth in London in the late 1970s. Jan Todd's recent book touches on another area: how technology is transferred between nations, and focuses upon Australia (Todd 1995).

It is always useful to look at other textbooks. The book by Ziman (1976) is rather old, but is an interesting look at Science, Technology and Society through the eyes of a distinguished physicist. The view of Easlea (1980) is about as far from that of Ziman as it is possible to get, but both were scientists. The books by Lowe (1987), McGinn (1991) and Webster (1991) are also worth a look. Perhaps the best text of all, though it is rather old, is the large reader by Spiegel-Rösing and de Solla Price (1977). On almost any topic, it is worth checking through the index of this work to see if anything is relevant. For a sweeping, advanced and up-to-date survey of the field, the 800-page handbook of Jasanoff and her colleagues (Jasanoff *et al.* 1995) is the ideal work.

Like any field of study, Science, Technology and Society develops through articles in journals and magazines. *The Bulletin of the Atomic Scientists* is readable and important: it was founded by scientists concerned about the nuclear arms race, and is informative about science, technology and weaponry. *Daedalus* and *Minerva* often have useful articles about history and current trends in science and technology. These journals are all from the United States. *Prometheus* is Australian, and dwells upon economic and policy aspects of science. *Search* is also Australian, and leans more towards environmental matters, while the British journal *Social Studies of Science* is more sociological, and the intellectual arguments there rage very hot.

The important US scientific journal *Science* often has reports on relevant issues. The magazine *New Scientist* is useful as a general source of information on current developments, and frequently discusses their social implications.

References

Baker, J. R. (1939), 'Counterblast to Bernalism', *New Statesman*, 440: 174.

Bernal, J. D. (1939), *The Social Function of Science*. London: Routledge, 1939.

N. Bukharin (ed.) (1931), *Science at the Cross-roads*. London: Frank Cass.

Bush, V. (1945), *Science, the Endless Frontier*. Washington, DC: US Government Printing Office.

Chalmers, A. (1982), *What Is This Thing Called Science?* St Lucia, Qld: University of Queensland Press.

Easlea, B. (1980), *Liberation and the Aims of Science*. Edinburgh: Scottish Academic Press.

Goodman, D., and Russell, C. A. (1991), *The Rise of Scientific Europe, 1500–1800*. Sevenoaks, Kent: Hodder and Stoughton.

Greenberg, D. (1969), *The Politics of Pure Science*. Harmondsworth: Penguin.

Hessen, B. (1931), 'The Economic Roots of Newton's *Principia*', in Bukharin (1931): 151–212.

Jasanoff, S., Markie, G. E., Peterson, J. C., and Pinch, T. (eds) (1995), *Handbook of Science and Technology Studies*. London: Sage.

Lowe, I. (ed.) (1987), *Teaching the Interactions of Science, Technology and Society*. Melbourne: Longman Cheshire.

McGinn, R. E. (1991), *Science, Technology and Society*. Englewood Cliffs, NJ: Prentice-Hall.

Merton, R. K. (1968), 'Science and Economy of Seventeenth Century England', in Merton (1968), *Social Theory and Social Structure*. New York: Free Press: 661–81.

OECD (1970), *The Measurement of Scientific and Technical Activities*. Paris: Directorate for Scientific Affairs.

Rose, H., and Rose S. (1970), *Science and Society*. Harmondsworth: Penguin.

Salomon, J. J. (1973), *Science and Politics*. Cambridge, Mass.: MIT Press.

Spiegel-Rösing, I., and De Solla Price, D. (eds) (1977), *Science, Technology and Society*. London: Sage.

Todd, J. (1995), *Colonial Technology: Science and the Transfer of Innovation to Australia*. Cambridge: Cambridge University Press.

Webster, A. (1991), *Science, Technology and Society: New Directions*. London: Macmillan.

Ziman, J. (1976), *The Force of Knowledge*. Cambridge: Cambridge University Press.

CHAPTER 2

The Scientific Community

Martin Bridgstock

What's the go of it? What's the *particular* go of it?
James Clerk Maxwell,
Physicist.

This chapter aims to give you some idea about the world-wide scientific community and what makes it work. As the quote from Maxwell suggests, we will not be concentrating upon facts and figures, but upon the basic organisation of science, and its particular 'go', the way it works.

More than fifty years ago, the sociologist Robert K. Merton (1942) outlined a theory of how the scientific community works. Merton saw science as a self-regulating community of researchers, governed by a strong and distinctive ethos. This ethos involved the sharing of information, scepticism about results until evidence was produced, and a strong belief in the pursuit of truth. Merton was a shrewd observer of humanity, and was fully aware that many scientists pursue careers for their own self-interest. However, he argued, the ethos of science bound scientists to conform to the rules and expectations of science. In addition, scientists constantly scrutinised each other's work, ensuring that standards were maintained. Merton's ideal should be borne in mind as we investigate the scientific community.

The first point to make is that science is a varied activity, even within one country, as Figure 2.1 illustrates. It is based on official Australian statistics, and shows three important things about science in this country. It shows where the largest amounts of money come from to support science, where that money goes, and where the scientists are. We saw in Chapter 1 that R&D involves more than science. However, these figures give a broad outline of what is happening.

One point is that science is a substantial activity. Although Australia is

15

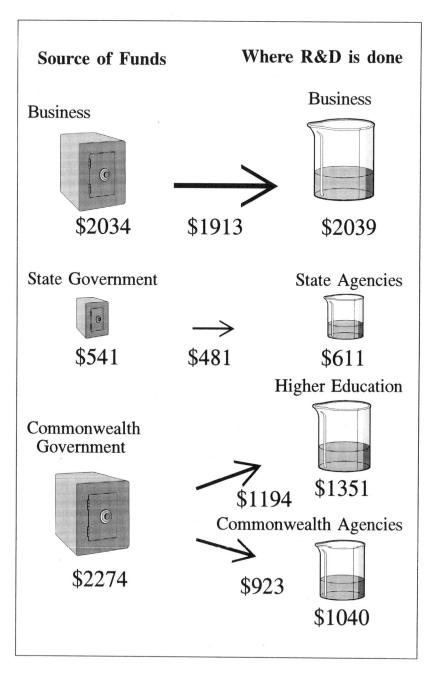

Figure 2.1 Main suppliers, recipients and flows of R&D funding in Australia, 1990–91 (amounts in millions; amounts less than $100 million have been ignored). *Source:* DIST 1994.

a small country in world terms, it still spends about $5 billion per year on science and related activities. According to Unesco (1995), it employs about 68,000 people as scientists, engineers and support workers. In rich countries, science and technology usually absorb an expenditure of 1–2 per cent of all the wealth the country produces. This point will become important later in the chapter. After all, if science is not cheap, then it is logical for governments to be concerned about the wisdom of spending the money, and the return science gives for that investment.

It is clear from the left side of Figure 2.1 that, with minor exceptions, money for science comes from two sources. Governments—state and federal—provide a little more than half the total expenditure, while business enterprise provides the rest. When we look at where the money goes, there are three main types of organisation that undertake scientific research. Naturally, nearly all of the money provided by business enterprise goes to its own laboratories. Governments also fund their own laboratories, such as the CSIRO and assorted state government laboratories. However, there is another sector as well. Academic science, funded almost entirely by the Commonwealth government, does about one-quarter of the science in Australia.

As a first step, then, we can conclude that—in Australia at least, and perhaps in most countries—science is done in one of three settings. There is academic science, done in universities and similar organisations. There is business, or industrial science, done by scientists working for corporations and similar enterprises. And there is government science—whether at the state or Commonwealth level—done in places like the CSIRO.

In Australia, government policy has often resulted in closer collaboration between these different types of activity. For example, the CSIRO is now expected to raise much of its funding by collaborating with the business sector. Following Maxwell's question, above, it is reasonable to ask what is the '*particular* go' of these different types of science. Why are they done in different places, and does anything different drive them? To answer these questions, we shall begin by looking at the behaviour and motivation of scientists in academia.

The strange nature of academic science

We may define academic science simply as that science which is carried out in academic institutions. These are often called universities, though Massachusetts Institute of Technology in the United States, and the Royal Melbourne Institute of Technology do not have this title. Academic scientists often combine the roles of teaching and research, though there are full-time researchers in universities.

There are two key terms in considering academic science: the research *paper*, which is usually published in a scientific *journal*. A paper is simply a research report, often couched in dry scientific language which only other scientists can understand. Scientific journals are not the big scientific magazines—such as *New Scientist* and *Scientific American*—but highly specialised publications, mostly devoted to publishing research papers. In contrast to *New Scientist* and *Scientific American*, journals report scientific results to other scientists. Perhaps the three most prestigious journals in the world are *Nature, Science,* and the *Proceedings of the National Academy of Sciences.* The first one is British, the other two American. Tens of thousands of others are published across the world.

A crucial feature of scientific papers is that they are *refereed*. This means that, when a paper is submitted for publication in a journal, it is not simply up to the editor as to whether it is printed. Instead, the paper is sent to several expert referees for comment and evaluation. On the basis of their reports, the editor then decides whether or not to publish the paper.

On the face of it, academic scientists behave in some strange ways. They place great stress upon publication in refereed scientific journals. Each year, most scientific departments and centres publish a research report, which consists mostly of lists of the papers they have published. Discussing science with academic scientists soon reveals that the number of papers published matters very much. For example, at one conference, a well-known researcher was introducing a scientific speaker from Eastern Europe, of whom most of the audience had never heard. To reassure the audience about the speaker's excellence, he began by telling them: 'He's a really good researcher. Published about twice as many papers as I have.'

Clearly, publishing is important to scientists. And yet, there is a strange paradox about academic scientists and their publications. Scientists spend many years in training to do research. On top of these years of training, a scientist may take months to carry out a particular piece of research. Some experiments are difficult and complex to set up. Others involve the painstaking collection of hundreds of observations. At the end of years of training, and months of toil, a scientist may have accumulated some worthwhile results. So, naturally, the scientist writes up the results in the form of a scientific paper and sends it to the editor of a suitable journal. Here is the strange feature. No matter how important the results, nor how prominent the journal, the scientist is not paid for a paper which is published. Indeed, in many journals, scientists are actually charged for the publication of their work.

Why is this so? If scientific knowledge is valuable, why are scientists not paid for their contributions? And, if they are not paid, why are they so anxious to publish? The answer lies in the nature of the academic science community. Scientists advance in academia through promotion within their organisations, or through being appointed to better research positions in other places. For example, a scientist may begin life as a research assistant in Sydney, move to a lecturer's position in Brisbane, and culminate her career by being appointed as a professor in Melbourne.

The key to promotion through the academic system in science is, in large measure, success in journal publication. Broadly speaking, the more papers published by a scientist, and the better the quality of those papers as judged by other academics, the more likely the academic is to be promoted within the academic system. The Americans have coined a brutal phrase for this pressure: 'publish or perish'. In modern academia, either scientists produce research papers and publish them, or they are eventually eliminated from the system.

As a young student, the author of this chapter happened to meet a senior professor from the Massachusetts Institute of Technology, one of the leading scientific institutions in the world. Being simple-minded, the student said to the professor: 'What happens if one of your young lecturers is good at teaching, but no good at research?' The terse reply came: 'He goes.' The student continued, 'And what happens if he's good at research, but no good at teaching?' The reply came, as terse: 'He stays.' It is hard to summarise the importance of research and publication more succinctly.

Besides employment, scientists can be rewarded—in ways both tangible and intangible—for their successes. The greatest reward which a scientist can receive is the Nobel Prize in one of the scientific fields. Accompanied by a substantial sum of money, it constitutes the peak of a scientist's career. Other awards—such as the Garfield Medal—are also highly valued.

In addition to prizes, scientists can receive a number of other rewards. These can include promotion, honorary degrees, and admission to the Academies of Science in various countries. A far more modest reward is a simple citation in a scientific paper. A scientist who writes a paper might explain that he is using the scientific method pioneered by Jones to test the theory of Smith, using a mathematical refinement proposed by Brown. In each case, a reference (see Appendix 2 at the end of the book) states exactly where work on these topics is to be found. Scientists take referencing very seriously. Since their contributions to knowledge are what entitles them to employment and promotion, they are usually anxious to ensure that they receive their due (Merton 1957).

This emphasis on research in modern academia has imposed some strains. Academic scientists, for example, may feel pressured to neglect their teaching duties and concentrate upon producing papers. They may be unwelcoming, or unavailable, to students with problems, or for any activity which does not help them increase their publication list.

It also follows that students at the undergraduate level probably do not have much idea about how science is actually done. Although they learn a good deal of science, do lab experiments and the like, they usually do not read or submit journal articles, nor do they make discoveries. Instead, they study established knowledge, packed down and condensed into textbooks and lectures, which is quite different from what is done at the research front (Cole 1992).

Another consequence is the pressure upon many scientists to get money for research through the grants system. Science, as we have seen, costs money, and academic scientists are constantly on the look-out for sources of finance. They need not only scientific equipment, but also skilled research assistants and, often, chemicals and other supplies, and perhaps computer support as well.

Applications to the major research funds in Australia—such as the Australian Research Council and the National Health and Medical Research Council—are extremely competitive, with less than one application in five being successful (Rip 1994:13). If one talks to scientists, one often finds that being successful in grant applications is almost as important as publishing papers. Once one has the appropriate equipment, it is almost a simple matter to produce publishable papers (McCain and Segal 1977).

The Dutch student of science, Arie Rip (1994), has commented upon a 'cycle of credibility' which scientists follow in their careers. In order to be considered seriously for research grants, they must have demonstrated a good record of published papers. However, they must have money in order to publish those papers. Therefore, for successful researchers in science, there is often a careful use of resources to generate an impressive list of papers, which can in turn be used to generate still more income. We shall look at some of the ways that academic science is changing later. For the moment, let us examine some of the consequences of this system.

Consequences of the 'publish or perish' system

One consequence of this system is that scientists are motivated, in academia, both to produce and to publish scientific knowledge as fast as they can. In industrial science and military science—see below—scientists may well produce knowledge, but it is not usually published: no corporation wants its rivals to know what its discoveries are!

As a result, there are races in science to make important discoveries. Imagine two teams of scientists—perhaps in different countries—each trying to solve a particular problem in science. They know that whoever solves the problem first will gain international recognition and perhaps a Nobel Prize. The loser will be recorded as confirming the result, but that is all. Naturally, there is great pressure upon the scientists to solve the problem first (Merton 1957).

There are many recorded instances of these processes in science. Perhaps the most famous one is in the book by J. D. Watson (1970), *The Double Helix*. Shortly after World War II, Francis Crick and James D. Watson, two scientists in Cambridge, UK, were trying to unravel the basic structure of DNA. They were motivated to hurry by the knowledge that Linus Pauling, the great American scientist, was also trying to solve the problem. Other cases are easy to find, such as that in the book *Anatomy of a Scientific Discovery* (Goldberg 1989).

A second consequence of the 'publish or perish' system is that, inevitably, a hierarchy develops among scientists. The noted researcher and historian, Derek de Solla Price (1965) has shown that about half of all the work in science is published by about one-tenth of the scientists. Further, this highly productive 10 per cent also dominates the most important work. As you might expect, the most successful scientists gravitate towards the most prestigious universities, where the best jobs are to be found. Thus, a self-reinforcing process tends to be set in motion, where a handful of institutions are noted for their outstanding work in science. In the United States, these elite institutions include Harvard University, Johns Hopkins, Berkeley and the Massachusetts Institute of Technology. In the UK, Oxford and Cambridge have long been supreme, though they are rivalled by Imperial and University Colleges, London.

The Australian situation is somewhat less clear. A group of universities called the Group of Eight (the Universities of Melbourne, Sydney, Adelaide, Queensland and Western Australia, plus the Australian National University, the University of New South Wales and Monash University) have tried to assert their supremacy as research institutions, but this has been strongly disputed by other researchers (Toohey 1996). Although some universities do more, and better, research than others, no clear-cut group of elite institutions has developed.

A third consequence of the 'publish or perish' system is that most scientists find that the formal publication system—papers in journals—simply cannot keep them up to date with work in their field. A paper may take a year to be refereed and published, and so be hopelessly out of date by the time other scientists read it. This leads logically to a less formal system of communication, through conferences and correspondence. In this way, scientists can keep in touch with each other and the latest developments (Hagstrom 1975:30).

A mass of other consequences also follow from the nature of the academic system of science. These will be mentioned briefly. First, the pressure to produce results in academia creates the temptation to fabricate results. This is dealt with further in Chapter 5. Second, as the Internet and World Wide Web increase in importance, scientists seeking the fastest possible interchange of information are likely to rely more and more on these electronic sources. However, it is still not clear whether a paper published on a Web site, for example, or in an electronic journal, has the same status as a paper in a conventional journal.

Traditionally, universities have stood for independent thought and argument (Lowe 1994). As industrial money has flowed into academia, it has become clear that pressures exist for academics to mute their criticism (Bridgstock 1996; Gibbs 1996). As industrial money becomes more important to scientists, the question of loyalties and values becomes more pressing. Finally, as science develops, experiments and research projects often require more than one scientist. De Solla Price (1965) showed that multiple authorship is becoming more common in many sciences, and papers with dozens of authors are not unknown (Ziman 1976). It is not clear whether this move toward multiple-authored work means that better science is being done (Bridgstock 1991), though some experiments, especially in areas like high-energy physics, are probably impossible without a large number of collaborators (Swatez 1970). A brief summary of this kind cannot give the full flavour of the academic science system. Readers are urged to obtain a good account of scientific work (e.g. Goldberg 1989; Charlesworth et al. 1989) to gain a fuller insight into how research is done.

The academic science system is not static. Some of the changes will be reviewed at the end of this chapter, but some can be indicated here. Gradually, as all Australian academics are finding out, there is a greater stress upon teaching in universities. The days when a scientist—or any academic—could gabble through badly prepared lectures, then gain promotion by spending every available minute on research, are drawing to a close. This change is occurring partly because governments are insisting that universities justify the money which is spent on them, in terms of good-quality learning by students (e.g. Reid 1996). Another reason for this change is that more students are paying at least part of their education costs, and they seek out the institutions which deliver the best education. This is especially true for foreign students, who have to pay full fees.

Another important development concerns the flow of money to do scientific experiments. Science, as we have seen, is not cheap, and left to itself it would continue to grow at a steady rate. Governments have therefore encouraged scientists to collaborate with each other, with other institutions and with industry, in order to carry out research more cheaply (ASTEC 1991:43). There has also been a greater stress upon making research more useable and more suited to serving 'practical' ends. This greater involvement between different sectors and different institutions will be dealt with later. It clearly has the potential to transform the nature of academic science.

Science in business organisations

It is easy to overlook the sheer quantity of research and development which is carried out in business—usually industrial—organisations. One reason for this can probably be traced to the media, where scientists—whether academic, industrial or government employed—are often called 'Professor', which is an academic rank. Table 2.1 should dispel some of these illusions. It shows the investment in research and development (R&D) in a range of developed countries. As you can see, in most countries more than half of all the R&D is funded by the business sector and, presumably, it serves the goals of commerce. In several developed countries, over 60 per cent of the R&D is funded by business. Business in Australia contributes less than half the total expenditure on R&D.

Although commercial R&D is a relatively small sector in Australia, it is growing fast. Table 2.2 compares the state of business R&D in several

Table 2.1. Overall and business investment in R&D, 1981–91, as percentages of gross domestic product (GDP)

Country	Total R&D as % of GDP	Business R&D as % of GDP	Business R&D as % of total R&D
South Korea	1.86	1.56	83.9
Japan	2.87	2.22	77.3
Switzerland	2.86	2.13	74.5
Germany	2.66	1.61	60.5
Sweden	2.9	1.75	60.3
Singapore	0.9	0.49	54.4
Taiwan	1.69	0.88	52.1
USA	2.75	1.39	50.5
Canada	1.5	0.62	41.3
Australia	**1.34**	**0.53**	**39.6**
New Zealand	0.88	0.29	32.9

Source: Adapted from DIST 1994:10.

developed countries. The growth is compared both for the money which business allocates to R&D, and for the work actually performed. Apart from a few Asian 'tiger' economies, Australia's sector is growing the fastest. Why is this so? Why has Australia such a modest business R&D sector, and why is it growing so fast?

The reason for Australia's small business sector lies in the way that the country was created. Modern Australia began as a dumping-ground for British convicts, and then became a collection of British colonies. For over a century Australia's main exports were agricultural; wool, wheat, meat, and the like. Then, after World War II, Australia developed a large mining industry. Primary products boosted the country's wealth to high levels (e.g. Home 1988).

What had happened to Australia's industry while this was going on? Slowly, especially during the 1920s and 1930s, Australian manufacturing began to appear. However—and this is a key point—it generally did not seek to compete with industry in other countries. Instead, Australian industry was heavily protected by tariffs, taxes levied on imports, so that it could sell its goods on the home market (Kelly 1992:6). The hope was that eventually Australian manufacturers, developing efficiency behind the tariff walls, would begin to sell their goods abroad. The reality is that the industries developed in an inefficient fashion.

One important trend helped to convince Australia's leaders that Australia was developing in an inappropriate way. The price of commodities—raw materials of various kinds—declined gradually over several decades before 1980 (Harrison, 1983:307). This condemned a number of poor countries in the Third World, who relied solely on one

Table 2.2. Growth in business R&D, 1981–91, as funded by business, and as performed in business enterprises

Country	Growth in business R&D	Growth in R&D performed in business enterprise
South Korea	29.3	31.6
Singapore	22.3	23.8
Taiwan	16.4	16.5
Australia	**14.2**	**13.1**
Canada	5.4	5.8
New Zealand	7.7	5.0
Germany	5.1	4.2
USA	4.0	3.6
UK	4.2	2.8

Source: Adapted from DIST 1994.

crop, to terrible poverty. Australia was never a poor country, and it never depended completely upon one commodity. However, changes were clearly needed, and from the early 1980s they appeared. Tariffs were greatly reduced, and tax incentives were introduced to encourage Australian firms to invest in R&D. These incentives were a 150-per-cent tax write-off for any money which firms spent on R&D. This sounded spectacular, but in practice, it amounted to about a 15-per-cent subsidy for firms to do research (ASTEC 1991). Gradually, over a number of years, science and technology improved in Australian firms, and new firms sprang up based on new technologies. Although Australia is still well behind other developed countries, there seems little doubt that its position is changing for the better. Recent reductions in the tax subsidy, and some cuts to the scientific budget, may change this in future.

What is special about industrial R&D?

On the face of it, research and development in industry might seem similar to that in academia. Similar equipment is used, and many of the procedures are the same. However, the closer we look, the more differences appear. First, as we have seen, academics are under great pressure to publish their results and so further their careers. By contrast, industry rarely allows its scientists to publish.

The reasons for this difference are obvious. No corporation, if it has made a potentially valuable discovery, wants its competitors to know about it. Industrial secrets are an important feature of R&D. Instead of rushing to publish results, firms hurry to lodge patents, thus establishing their rights as discoverers of the process. In some cases of fast-moving technologies, firms may even avoid patenting altogether, because a patent has to describe the process in detail, and the firm making the discovery does not want competitors to learn what it is doing (Rogers 1982).

A second consequence is also obvious. All R&D carried out in industry has, as its eventual goal, the improvement of the firm's economic position. This may be in the form of better products or cheaper methods of production. Thus a great deal of industrial R&D focuses on the solution of specific practical problems. That is, the research is of an applied or developmental nature, rather than a quest for knowledge for its own sake.

Table 2.3 compares the sectors in which R&D is done and the objectives for which it is carried out. It shows, for Australian R&D, that business research is completely concentrated upon the purpose of economic development. It follows logically that work done in industry will be applied in nature, and there is evidence for this (e.g. Marcson

Table 2.3. Purpose of R&D by sector of performance, 1990–91

Note: this table includes all Australian science, engineering, social sciences and humanities.

Socio-economic objective	Non-business sectors $Am	Business sector $Am	Total $Am	Business as % of total
Defence	235.1	0.0	235.1	0.0
Economic development	1383.3	2039.0	3467.3	58.8
National welfare	785.0	0.0	785.0	0.0
Advancement of knowledge	666.9	0.0	666.9	0.0
Totals	3070.2	2039.0	5109.2	39.91

Source: Adapted from DIST 1994:4.

1979:162). In the United States, some pure research is done in industry, and economists have spent a good deal of time and trouble trying to work out why this is so. After all, if academia has as its goal the production of knowledge, why not simply tap into whatever is provided freely from there?

This point has been the subject of much research (e.g. Pavitt 1987; Rosenberg 1990) Although pure scientific knowledge cannot be patented, a corporation which acquires such knowledge first may have an advantage in the race to new products and processes. Therefore, it is worth a corporation's while to invest in pure research. Second, as Rosenberg points out, even if a firm does not do much pure research, it needs a research capability in order to evaluate and exploit the knowledge of universities. Therefore, a research unit has value in this way too. For the most part, however, the R&D carried out in industry is applied in nature. There is usually a specific goal in mind, and teams of scientists and technologists collaborate to reach that goal. Often, there is intense time-pressure as well.

A key feature of industrial R&D is that, inevitably, management is in control of the process. Since the science or technology is a means to an end, it follows that management must know what is happening, and be able to control it. A good example of this is Tracey Kidder's award-winning book *The Soul of a New Machine* (Kidder 1982). The book tells the story of a group of programmers and hardware specialists who produced a new processor for a minicomputer. The management had complete oversight of the process, and used a range of strategies to keep the pressure on the young workers to produce results.

In general, the firms supporting R&D tend to be large, established corporations. The reasons for this are clear. Investment in R&D is long-term and risky. Only large corporations can take a sufficiently long, broad view, factoring in likely short-term losses, in order to achieve their aims. Overwhelmingly, the firms doing research are household names such as IBM, Boeing, BHP, and the like. There are exceptions to this. In the early days of the microcomputer industry, many of the leading firms were small, and yet they had some of the highest R&D expenditure of any sector of the economy. However, as they have settled down into a steadier pattern of growth, large firms such as IBM, Intel and Apple have tended to dominate research in the field.

In addition to normal R&D, firms are also anxious to know what their competitors are doing and planning. Therefore, a form of research called 'reverse engineering' is prominent, especially in the more competitive, highly technological industries (Cotgrove and Box 1970). This consists of taking apart one's competitor's products and seeing exactly how they work, what new technology they incorporate, and whether anything useful can be borrowed.

A problem might strike a thoughtful reader here. We have seen that, in academic science, scientists have a strong motive to contribute knowledge as quickly as possible to the common pool of understanding. In this way, a huge reservoir of knowledge exists which can be used by people working in different scientific areas. In industry, though, there are strong disincentives: firms do not want their knowledge spread round, and usually insist that their employees sign non-disclosure agreements to prevent knowledge leaking out. Why, then, does industrial knowledge not stagnate into a number of isolated pools, with much duplication of effort and no communication between them?

There seem to be a number of answers to this question. It is surprising how little research has been done on industrial science, given its great importance. However, a number of possible answers exist, and they all seem to relate to the circulation of scientific knowledge. One mechanism for circulating information was discovered by the researcher T. J. Allen (1977), and dubbed by him the 'technological gatekeeper'. These gatekeepers are usually senior researchers within industrial organisations. They have a strong interest in keeping up to date with relevant scientific and technological developments, and also in passing on such information to people within their own organisations. Allen found that information flowed from journals and other sources to the gatekeepers, and from them to people within the organisation who, the gatekeepers thought, might be able to use it.

Independent research has confirmed the existence and functioning of gatekeepers in industrial organisations. It is clear, however, that the gatekeepers' function can only be a limited one. The information they pass on is unlikely to be of a secret nature, and consequently it is probably of minor importance. However, there are other means by which information circulates. We have already seen that reverse engineering is one means by which firms learn about each other's products. The disadvantage, of course, is that such information is always out of date: by the time the product is on the market, the firm that made it is moving on to new developments.

An immediate means of circulating information is through the movement of people. From time to time, people leave one job—voluntarily or otherwise—and move to another. It is natural, although often against contracts, that they carry important information with them, which may be useful in their new work (e.g. Pavitt 1987).

Working in industrial R&D: strains and satisfactions

During the 1960s, a profoundly misguided strand of research existed regarding scientists in industry. Scientists, it was argued, face an intrinsically frustrating time in industry. True scientists have a strong natural desire to pursue knowledge, and to follow their own research interests wherever they might lead. By contrast, industrial scientists are under the control of management, and can find themselves moved from project to project, never being allowed to settle and really follow research through (Kornhauser 1962).

Two British sociologists, Steven Cotgrove and Stephen Box, set out to investigate this view. To their surprise, their discussions with industrial scientists revealed no such dissatisfaction, and it took considerable research to indicate what was happening (Cotgrove and Box 1970). Among science graduates, Cotgrove and Box discovered, there were indeed some who strongly wished to pursue the expansion of knowledge for its own sake, and who believed strongly in the publication of scientific knowledge for all to read. Cotgrove and Box termed these 'public scientists'. However, a substantial number of scientists, while they enjoyed doing science and solving problems, felt no particular need to publish the results. Since their satisfaction was a private one, these were termed 'private scientists'. Finally, yet other graduates simply regarded science as a job. These, the researchers termed 'organisation scientists'. For this latter group, the key points were that science was a reasonably pleasant, well-paid occupation: if a better one appeared, they would probably take it.

With a good deal of complication, Cotgrove and Box found that public scientists went overwhelmingly into academia, while the other two types of scientist went into industry. This, of course, minimised the possibilities of conflict between the perspective of the scientists and the requirements of industry. Thus, a simple notion that scientists in industry feel constrained and restricted does not apply. It follows, of course, that the outlook and attitudes of scientists in the two sectors are likely to differ markedly. Those in academia are likely to be fascinated by the discovery of the details of the natural world, how it works and why it does so. They are also interested in the approbation of their peers— other scientists—and less interested in the practical applications of their work. Scientists in industry are more likely to be interested in the effects of their work. They enjoy solving practical problems and seeing the results of what they do.

This latter point is vital. Scientists who enjoy seeing practical consequences from their work may also, eventually, be interested in becoming involved in management themselves. Therefore, it is advisable for graduates contemplating an industrial career to be aware that, from the perspective of the recruiting firm, they are possible future management material.

Changes in Australian industrial science and technology

Australia, as we have seen, has an unusual background for a modern industrial state. It began as an exporter of agricultural goods—wool, wheat, meat, and the like—to industrial countries. When Australia began to develop industrially, in the 1920s and 1930s, a high wall of tariffs was erected to protect the new industries from competition. This led to inefficient, complacent local industries, producing goods of poor quality. Often these industrial firms also did little science and technological research.

As we have seen, things changed radically in the 1980s, when tariffs were reduced. Many older industries foundered—notably in the states of Victoria and South Australia—but the federal government, as we have seen, introduced measures to foster R&D. Over ten years, this tax break had a remarkable effect upon Australian industry. A whole range of new firms appeared, stressing high-technology industry and producing new products. It is not clear whether Australia will become a major manufacturing power, like Sweden and South Korea, but the turnaround is startling. The most dramatic changes have been in the fields of pharmaceuticals and computer software, though there are others.

Australian industry is currently in a state of almost continuous change. With parts of industry—the older parts, usually—in a state of contraction, and new firms springing up to cater for particular niches, the future looks exciting, and also dangerous.

Government science

We may define government R&D as science and technology which is not only funded by governments, but also carried out in government laboratories. It is tempting to regard government science as completely unnecessary. After all, if academia (and, to a lesser extent, industry) can do pure research to produce basic knowledge, and if industry can take knowledge and turn it into products and processes, what is the need for government science at all?

To grasp fully the need for government science, two useful concepts must be understood: *market failure* and *public goods*. The term *market failure* conjures up dramatic pictures in the mind: share prices crashing, stockbrokers rioting and perhaps committing suicide, and so on. It is really much less dramatic than that. Essentially, market failure describes circumstances in which the free market fails to allocate goods in the most efficient possible way.

As a simple example, imagine a piece of research which could yield valuable new products for the market. Unfortunately, the research is very expensive to do. What is more, when it is done, no firm doing the research will be able to make all of the new products: the costs are too great, or the expertise required is not to be found in any one firm. As a result, it is not worth the while of any firm to invest in the R&D, even though, considered as a whole, it will yield results far greater than the cost. The key argument here, clearly, is that in some circumstances, it would be better if some other party—the government—stepped in to do the research. Since research is not free, it would have to be paid for by some form of levy, or from general taxation. This is controversial. Some people—such as maverick Oxford scientist Terence Kealey (1996)—argue that all pure research can be done by industry. His arguments have been vigorously countered, however (e.g. Pavitt 1996), and generally, across the world, it is accepted that the market does not ensure that all necessary research will be done.

A second important concept is *public good*. This is not the same as the good of the public. A public good, in its pure form, has this characteristic: that use or enjoyment of it cannot be restricted to some people. Either everyone has access to the public good, or no one has. This peculiar property means that public goods cannot be bought and sold, like the things one sees in shops. In consequence, it means that normal commercial and market processes cannot deal with them.

Examples of public goods—although none follow the description completely—are easy to find. Clean air in a city is not something which can be restricted to a few: the air is clean either for everyone, or for no one. Freedom from invasion by foreign armies is not something which can be limited: either a country is secure, or it is not. Clean food and water, standardised weights and measures, currency that cannot be easily forged, freedom from the fear of crime in the city at night, are all things which cannot be restricted to a few people. Either everyone has them, or no one has them.

These two concepts, market failure and public goods, can be used to explain most governmental involvement in science and technology. For example, government environmental laboratories monitor the provision of such public goods as clean air, clean rivers and freedom from noxious levels of noise. The government food laboratory ensures that the public good of clean and wholesome food is obtainable. The national weights and measures laboratory monitors the use of standard measures—the litre, the kilogram, etc.—and ensures that we get what we expect when, for example, we buy a litre of milk. However, there are some problems. For example, in what sense can research in Antarctica be described as due to market failure, or to the concept of public good? Yet the Australian government supports several large research bases in the Antarctic.

The short answer is that politicians, quite naturally, use science in pursuit of their political goals. In the case of Antarctica, Australia claims about 40 per cent of the continent. Under the Antarctic treaty, in order to maintain this claim, Australia must support genuine scientific research. Therefore, it is perfectly logical for politicians to continue to support our—fairly expensive—effort in this area of research.

Australian government science has, in general, been an unusually large fraction of this country's R&D effort. As we have seen, one reason for this is that Australia's industry has tended, until recently, to be of a 'branch-office' variety, selling or packaging products which were researched, developed and manufactured in some other country. In addition, major parts of Australia's economy were composed of small farmers and graziers who needed the benefits of scientific research, but were unable to finance any themselves. Therefore, the government developed a tradition of stepping into these areas and carrying out research in the national interest.

By far the best-known government research organisation has been the CSIRO, funded by the Commonwealth government (see Chapter 7). Founded soon after World War I, this developed several dozen different divisions, each seeking to do research supporting some aspect of Australian industry. For the most part, this science was of an extremely high order, though a heated debate developed in the 1980s, as economist Stuart Macdonald (1982) alleged that it was not possible, from published documents, to tell whether the CSIRO was doing a good job or not.

Since the 1980s, as the world in general, and Australia as part of it, has swung toward free enterprise and the market philosophy, the CSIRO came under pressure to involve itself even more closely with industry. Instead of being almost entirely funded by government, it was required to find 30 per cent of its finances from external sources. These could be industrial consultancies, competitive national grants, or any other source. The CSIRO succeeded well in this way, although researchers found that the people within the organisation paid a considerable price in terms of strain and uncertainty (Leslie and Harrold 1993).

Changes in academic, government and industrial R&D

From the information already given, it is clear that vast changes are taking place in science and technology. The most marked change, especially in Australia, is that industrial research and development is growing rapidly—almost more rapidly than anywhere else in the world (DIST 1994). At the same time, government and academic research are being cut back somewhat, and researchers in these areas are being pressured to seek funding from the commercial sector.

For many people, this has been a stressful process (Leslie and Harrold 1993). However, for some scientists who knew nothing of the commercial sector, it has been both a revelation and a liberation. In the United States, the historian Henry Etzkowitz has documented the delight of many scientists as they discovered that they 'have a trade' and could sell their services to industry for mutual profit (Etzkowitz 1993; 1994).

An important work on this theme was written by policy expert Michael Gibbons and a team of academics (Gibbons *et al.* 1994). They postulated that a new form of knowledge was appearing, as a result of the breaking down of the barriers between the different sectors. The new knowledge, which they term 'Mode Two', was overwhelmingly applied in nature. Whereas traditional academic knowledge was—theoretically at least —evaluated by standards of truth and intellectual interest, the new knowledge is evaluated by standards of applied usefulness. These standards, of course, vary from situation to situation.

There is no doubt that Gibbons and his colleagues are at least partly right: knowledge generated for an industrial firm is almost certain to be evaluated using different criteria to, say, that which is used in an academic paper. On the other hand, Gibbons *et al.* also claim that the new knowledge is just as coherent as the old. This seems unlikely, on the face of it. After all, if one firm wants to get its production line going, and another wants to understand a new, important principle in micro-electronics, it is hard to see how they are using exactly the same criteria, and hard to see how one sort of knowledge is useful for the other firm's goals. Therefore, we may be moving into a scientific world in which there are different sorts of knowledge, useful to different people in different circumstances.

Gibbons *et al.* believe that this new type of knowledge will eventually absorb the older sort. In one sense, of course, this is bound to happen. If knowledge is becoming more heterogeneous, then academic knowledge is simply one sort of knowledge. On the other hand, it does stand out precisely because its criteria are at one end of a spectrum: it is abnormally deep, thorough, and not related directly to the interests of business firms. Therefore, although academia is merging into business to some extent, they are unlikely to become identical.

Science and war

We have not yet mentioned one of the most important and controversial aspects of science: its association with warfare. We shall see elsewhere (Chapter 6) that science began to play a large part in industry round about the middle of the nineteenth century. The transformation of the alkali industry convinced virtually everyone that science could be important in the world of practical affairs, and should be supported financially. As a result, government and industrial backing began to appear for science.

The nineteenth century was a relatively peaceful century—at least in Europe. There was a savage civil war in North America, and a massive series of battles as European countries conquered, or subordinated most of the rest of the world. However, Europe itself for long periods was at peace. This changed in the twentieth century, when the two most terrible wars in history erupted. As the major European powers struggled to destroy each other, the enhanced role of science became clear. World War I was known as the Chemists' War, World War II as the Physicists' War (Ziman 1976).

Perhaps the most notorious case of scientific involvement in World War I was that of the great German chemist, Fritz Haber. A fierce patriot, he placed his laboratory at the disposal of the Kaiser of Germany when the war broke out. The Kaiser made good use of Haber. Germany desperately needed nitrates—previously imported from South America—to fertilise its soil and make its explosives. Haber found a method of nitrogen fixation from the air, thus preventing Germany's early military collapse. Then, as the war bogged down to static trench warfare, he pioneered the use of poison gas. The story has been told in many places (e.g. Ziman 1976). If the German army had taken proper advantage of Haber's invention, Germany might well have won the war.

As it was, counter-measures appeared in a few weeks, and the opportunity was lost (Ziman 1976).

Scientists were totally involved in World War II, and many books have
been written on the subject. The most dramatic development, of course,
took place right at the end, when scientists took the initiative in telling
the American President Franklin Roosevelt about the possible development of an atomic bomb, vastly more powerful than any other explosive.
In a crash program, American and other scientists developed the
weapon and it was used upon two Japanese cities, bringing about a
Japanese surrender.

The rights and wrongs of the atomic bomb have been heavily debated.
John Forge considers some of them in the next chapter. Jungk (1958)
has chronicled the anguish of some of the scientists as they wrestled with
their consciences over the issue. It is remarkable, though, that most of
the scientists were not at all worried by the development of the weapon,
and, when it was used, simply felt that their efforts in the war had been
justified.

Earlier in the war, equally important developments had also taken
place. At one stage, the United Kingdom stood completely alone in
Europe against Germany. Its major ally, France, had been rapidly
defeated, and the German air force, the Luftwaffe, now attacked Britain
to bring about its surrender. The Royal Air Force was only a fraction of
the size of its enemy. However, an important invention enabled the
British pilots to hold the Germans at bay. A string of radar stations were
built around the British coast, enabling Britain's commanders to detect
German attackers and direct RAF fighters to intercept them. Effectively,
this doubled the size of the RAF, and was crucial to its victory (Ziman
1976). It is important to note that the use of radar was vital here:
German physicists knew all about the principles, but the British organised a radar detection system to defend their islands, with military and
scientific people working closely together.

A most remarkable contribution of science in World War II has come
to light only recently. During the war, the German armed forces made
heavy use of a coding machine termed Enigma, which they believed to
be unbreakable. It looked like a laptop computer, and coded typed
messages according to a complex, quickly changing scheme which, they
believed, no one could break without having the original machine.

In fact, British mathematicians, aided by information from Poland,
had broken the Enigma codes early in the war. As a result, British and
US commanders had a strong flow of information throughout the war
which the Germans believed was confidential to them. It seems clear
that, at least in the later parts of the war, this played a major part in the
defeat of both Germany and Japan (Hinsley and Stripp 1993).

After World War II, science became involved in warfare to an enormous extent. It was estimated that, in the 1970s, about half of all the science in the world was directly or indirectly involved in military purposes. This was principally because of the world-wide rivalry between the United States and the Soviet Union, known as the Cold War. Because of this arms race, enormous military capabilities appeared in the world. At the height of the Cold War, each of the major powers had the ability to wipe out all life on Earth many times over. This was not with nuclear weapons alone: highly dangerous chemical and biological weapons had similar capabilities.

The Cold War is now over. In the former Soviet Union, thousands of scientists have lost their jobs, and are having to turn their abilities to

Table 2.4. Proportion of government R&D spending with military objectives, and proportion of all R&D spending which is government targeted for military objectives (%)

1 Country	2 Proportion of government R&D spending with military objectives	3 Government military R&D spending from Column 2 as a percentage of all national R&D spending
Australia	8.9	3.6
Austria	0.0	0.0
Belgium	0.2	0.01
Canada	5.4	2.01
Denmark	0.6	0.2
Finland	2.1	1.0
France	33.6	17.4
Germany	8.5	3.5
Greece	1.4	0.5
Iceland	0.0	0.0
Ireland	0.0	0.0
Italy	8.5	4.7
Japan	6.1	1.0
Netherlands	3.4	1.5
New Zealand	1.6	0.8
Norway	5.1	3.0
Portugal	0.4	0.3
Spain	12.5	6.9
Sweden	23.5	9.3
Switzerland	20.0	2.4
UK	42.5	16.5
USA	59.0	24.8
OECD	36.0	14.0

Source: Calculated from Unesco 1995.

other uses. Some, apparently, are trying to sell weapons to other countries (Belyaninov 1994; Kapitza 1994). Things have been less severe in the United States, but many scientists have found themselves out of work. However, as Table 2.4 shows, some developed nations still spend a substantial proportion of their R&D budgets on military matters. Column 1 shows the proportion of the government R&D budget directed to military aims. A number of countries target a high proportion of their money in this way: notably the United States on 59 per cent, and the United Kingdom on 42.5 per cent. By contrast, some nations, such as Australia, Iceland, Ireland and Portugal, spend almost nothing on military R&D. Column 2 shows military-targeted spending as a proportion of the nation's total R&D budget. Almost certainly, this understates the true national military R&D budget: a company might do research to produce a new military device and then sell it to the government, for example. However, it does show that there are huge differences in what nations spend to develop weapons, and that in many important nations, military R&D is still a substantial proportion of the total effort.

The Cold War has left an alarming legacy. Millions of weapons are still in existence, and many of these have found their way into the hands of an assortment of freedom groups and terrorist organisations. It looks as if we shall be coping with the aftermath of the Cold War, and the involvement of science in it, for many years to come.

Summary and conclusion

In this chapter, we have sought to understand the '*particular* go'—the specific driving forces—of the different kinds of science. We saw that science can broadly be divided into three main areas—academic, industrial, and government—according to where the work is actually done. In addition, it is clear that science is not cheap. Even in a small country like Australia, billions of dollars per year are spent to support the work of tens of thousands of scientists.

Within each sector of science, different driving forces are at work: they select different scientific problems to study, and fund different work. This, of course, accords closely with one of the themes of this book. In academia, until recently, scientists were driven by the 'publish or perish' ethos: scientists were rewarded for producing original scientific work, published in refereed academic journals. In industry, by contrast, the firm's financial position is the key factor. Managers ensure that most of the work done is applied in nature, directly related to the firm's interests. As a consequence, by academic standards, the work may not be pursued to the same level or depth. On the other hand, there is more likelihood of something being produced, other than paper, at the end.

Government science is by far the most complex of the three sectors, as there does not seem to be a simple way of summarising why this large sector exists. Instead, there are a series of explanations. As ASTEC (1991) argues, some government research is done because of market failure: industrial firms simply cannot carry out some types of research, or else cannot capture enough of the benefits of it. Therefore, governments may do work to benefit that industry. In addition, governments may have certain research done because it contributes to the production of 'public goods'—goods and services which the public value, but which cannot be bought and sold in the normal commercial manner. Finally, there is simple national or political interest. It is in some nations' interest, for example, to do research in Antarctica because it gives them a voice when it comes to discussing that continent's future.

As we have also seen, the different research settings foster different types of scientific career, and produce different types of work. Not surprisingly, the majority of work done in industry is applied science, shading into technology and product development. In academia, despite changes, the research is still largely pure or basic in nature.

Judged by what we have seen, Merton's concept of a self-governing, autonomous community of researchers does not seem an adequate description of how science is done. Perhaps it is best to regard it as a kind of 'public morality' of science; scientists feel obliged to conform outwardly to an ethical, unselfish image, no matter what their own ambitions, objects and sources of funding.

As we also saw, however, things are changing rapidly. Governments are pressuring scientists in both academia and government laboratories to seek more of their funding from industrial sources. This in turn is rapidly changing the nature of all types of science. It will need a close watch, in coming years, to fully understand all the developments which occur.

Further reading

It is useful for any student of Science, Technology and Society to gain an understanding of how it feels to 'do' science or technology. Therefore, it is a good idea to read one or more histories of scientific break-throughs and incidents, to see how the scientists themselves saw things.

One of the best of these is the book by Jungk (1958). This delineates two different communities. The first, in Göttingen, Germany, in the 1920s, was the physics community which began to puzzle out the nature of the atom. The second, in the United States during the war years, built the atomic bomb. The contrasts between the two communities are beautifully portrayed.

The books by Goldberg (1989) and Watson (1970) also show scientists in action, and both are worth reading. On the side of industrial technology, the prize-winning book by Kidder (1982) shows the enormous stress that technologists can work under, as they race to produce a new type of computer. Finally, Charlesworth *et al.* (1989) took a different route, analysing one excellent scientific organisation in detail and writing about it vividly.

Price (1965) is readable, and was one of the founding works which began the discipline of statistically studying science. It is a vivid outline of some key ideas. Gibbons *et al.* (1994) have written a careful analysis of how science is changing, and how the different types of science are beginning to merge.

References

Allen, T. J. (1977), *Managing the Flow of Technology.* Cambridge, Mass.: MIT Press.
Australian Science and Technology Commission (ASTEC) (1991), *Research and Technology: Future Directions.* Canberra: Australian Government Printing Service.
Belyaninov, Kirill (1994), 'Nuclear Nonsense, Black-market Bombs, and Fissile Flim-flam', *Bulletin of the Atomic Scientists*, March–April: 44–50.
Bridgstock, M. W. (1991), 'The Quality of Single and Multiple Authored Papers: An Unresolved Problem', *Scientometrics*, 21, 1:37–48.
Bridgstock, M. W. (1996), 'Ethics at the Interface: Academic Scientists' Views of Ethical and Unethical Behaviour involving Industrial Links', *Industry and Higher Education*, October: 275–84.
Charlesworth M., Farrall, L., Stokes T., and Turnbull, D. (1989), *Life among the Scientists: An Anthropological Study of an Australian Research Community.* Melbourne: Oxford University Press.
Cole, S. (1992), *Making Science.* Cambridge, Mass.: Harvard University Press.
Cotgrove, S., and Box, S. (1970), *Science, Industry and Society.* London: George Allen and Unwin.
Department of Industry, Science and Technology (DIST), Science and Technology Policy and Programs Branch (1994), *Australian Science and Innovation Resources Brief.* Canberra: Australian Government Publishing Service.
Etzkowitz, H. (1993), 'Enterprises from Science: The Origins of Science-based Regional Economic Development', *Minerva*, 31, 3:326–30.
Etzkowitz, H. (1994), 'Knowledge as Property: The Massachusetts Institute of Technology and the Debate over Academic Patent Policy', *Minerva*, 32, 4:383–421.
Gibbons, M., *et al.* (1994), *The New Production of Knowledge.* London: Sage.
Gibbs, W. W. (1996), 'The Price of Silence', *Scientific American*, November: 10–11.
Goldberg, Jeff (1989), *Anatomy of a Scientific Discovery.* New York: Bantam Books.
Hagstrom, W. O. (1975), *The Scientific Community.* London: Feffer and Simmons.
Harrison, P. (1983), *The Third World Tomorrow.* London: Penguin.
Hinsley, F. H., and Stripp, A. (1993), *Code Breakers.* Oxford: Oxford University Press.
Home R. W. (ed.) (1988), *Australian Science in the Making.* Cambridge: Cambridge University Press.

Jungk, R. (1958), *Brighter than a Thousand Suns.* New York: Harcourt Brace.

Kapitza, S. P. (1994), 'Russian Science: Snubbed and Sickly', *Bulletin of the Atomic Scientists*, May–June: 47–52.

Kealey, T. (1996), 'You've Got It All Wrong', *New Scientist*, 29 June: 23–6.

Kelly, P. (1992), *The End of Certainty.* St Leonards, NSW: Allen and Unwin.

Kidder, T. (1982), *The Soul of a New Machine.* London: Allen Lane.

Kornhauser, W. (1962), *Scientists in Industry.* Berkeley and Los Angeles: University of California Press.

Leslie, L. L., and Harrold, R. I. (1993), 'Commercialization of Scholarship in Australian Universities', *Prometheus*, 11:95–108.

Lowe, I. (1994), *Our Universities are Turning us into the 'Ignorant Country',* Kensington, NSW: University of New South Wales Press.

Macdonald, S. (1982), 'Faith, Hope and Disparity', *Search*, 13:290–9.

Marcson, S. (1979), 'Research Settings', in Nagi and Corwin (1979): 161–91.

McCain, G., and Segal, E. M. (1977), *The Game of Science.* Monterey, Calif.: Brooks/Cole.

Merton, R. K. (1942), 'Science and Technology in a Democratic Order', *Journal of Legal and Political Sociology*, 1. Reprinted in Merton (1968), *Social Theory and Social Structure.* New York: Free Press: 604–15.

Merton, R. K. (1957), 'Priorities in Scientific Discovery: A Chapter in the Sociology of Science', *American Sociological Review*, 22:635–59.

Nagi, S., and Corwin, R. (1979), *The Social Contexts of Research.* New York: Krieger.

Pavitt, K. (1987), 'The Objectives of Technology Policy', *Science and Public Policy*, 4:182–8.

Pavitt, K. (1996), 'Road to Ruin', *New Scientist*, 3 August: 32–5.

Price, D. J. de Solla (1965), *Little Science, Big Science.* New York: Columbia University Press.

Reid, I. (1996), 'Brave New World of Quality Education', *Campus Review*, 2 August: 7.

Rip, A. (1994), 'The Republic of Science in the 1990s', *Higher Education*, 28:3–23.

Rogers, E. (1982), 'Information Exchange and Technological Innovation', in Sahal (1982).

Rosenberg, N. (1990), 'Why Do Firms Do Basic Research (With Their Own Money?)', *Research Policy* 19:165–74.

Sahal D. (ed.) (1982), *The Transfer and Utilization of Technical Knowledge.* Lexington, Mass.: D. C. Heath and Co.

Swatez, G. M. (1970), 'The Social Organisation of a University Laboratory', *Minerva*, 8:36–58.

Toohey, P. (1996), 'Misguided Desire for an Ivy League of Their Own', *Campus Review*, 21 August: 8.

Unesco (1995), *Statistical Yearbook 1995.* Paris: Unesco Publishing and Bernal Press.

Watson, J. D. (1970), *The Double Helix.* Harmondsworth: Penguin.

Ziman, J. (1976), *The Force of Knowledge.* Cambridge: Cambridge University Press.

CHAPTER 3

Responsibility and the Scientist

John Forge

Michael Polanyi, a chemist turned sociologist of science, tells an interesting story. He recounts that he and the philosopher Bertrand Russell were on the radio in Britain and were asked what practical applications might result from the Einstein formula, $E = mc^2$. Neither of these eminent gentlemen could think of any. The interesting thing about this tale is that it took place in April 1945, a bare three months before the first atomic bomb was dropped, but some forty years after the Einstein formula was discovered and expressed in the special theory of relativity. Polanyi told this story in an essay called 'The Republic of Science', first published in 1962, because he wanted to convince his audience that the practical outcomes of pure scientific research were often unforeseen, unforeseeable even, and certainly unintended (Polanyi 1969:58–9). If that were true, then it would not be possible to hold scientists *accountable* or *responsible* for their work outside the context of pure science. They would not be *answerable* in any way for where their work leads and what it enables others to do.

Would it not be better if the scientists were responsible for their work? Certainly, scientists like to claim credit when they do something which helps others. Medical research is one of the best examples. Gene therapy, for instance, is becoming widespread and effective, and it is now possible to treat a number of inherited genetic effects by introducing normal genes into the body (see Weatherall 1991 for many examples). These therapeutic techniques stem directly from pure scientific research, and scientists are happy to claim credit for them. Indeed, many scientists working in the area of the biological sciences argue that they should have funding for their research because of its medical applications. But the issue of funding should not be exaggerated, for it

40

is true that many scientists would be genuinely pleased to have done good and helped others.

There is, inevitably, another side. If scientists can claim credit when they do good things and help other people, then they must accept blame when they do bad things and harm others. But can science do bad things? To argue that it cannot is wildly implausible, for it would be necessary to show either that science-based technologies are always good for us, or that, for those that are not, scientists are somehow absolved of any blame. That second line will not do: responsibility cuts both ways, and if credit can be claimed in one instance, then blame must be accepted in another. As for the first line, it does seem that some specifically anti-personnel weapons, like small plastic landmines designed to maim and laser weapons designed to blind, are un-equivocally bad; hence it can be argued that the scientific research that went into making them should not have been done at all. This sort of responsibility is known as *moral* responsibility.

It is imperative in all of this to distinguish two quite different questions. For a particular example of scientific research that has as outcome a given technology, we can ask whether the overall effects are good or bad, right or wrong, and hence whether the scientists involved deserve our praise or blame. Or we can ask whether the scientists are responsible or accountable at all; can we *either* praise them *or* blame them? Clearly, if a team that invents the plastic for a mine is not responsible or accountable in the first place, then it cannot in any way be blamed for the children maimed in Angola or Cambodia. If respon-sibility is attributed, then the team can try—surely not successfully—to claim that it should have done the work because the mines helped to shorten the wars.

The main aim of this chapter is to argue that scientists are morally responsible for the applications of their research, but only under certain circumstances. This means that, in those circumstances, there is no such thing as research which stands outside society. In those circumstances, the scientist is responsible. What are the conditions which determine the situations in which scientists are responsible? That is what we must determine, and in that connection we must look at what Polanyi says about foreseeability. To this end it is useful to have a case study to refer to, and the Manhattan Project will do nicely. If we cannot attribute responsibility in this instance, we never will! So the chapter begins with a quick outline of the Manhattan Project, moves on to identify the con-ditions under which responsibility can be attributed, and concludes with discussion of the *neutrality* of science. The idea that science is neutral, or *value-free*, is bound up with the question of moral responsibility.

The Manhattan Project

The Manhattan Project produced three atomic bombs; one was tested in July 1945, and the other two were dropped on Japan one month later. The Manhattan Project designed and manufactured two types of atomic bombs: the Hiroshima bomb was a 'gun-barrel' bomb, in which two subcritical hemispheres of uranium-235 (U-235) were flung together by a chemical explosive charge to create a supercritical assembly. That is the 'obvious' way to make an atomic bomb. The Nagasaki bomb was more sophisticated and used plutonium. (References for this section are mentioned under *Further reading.*)

The operating principle of an atomic weapon is the divergent self-sustaining chain reaction, and the design brief for the bombmaker is to produce an assembly where this reaction can be realised. U-235 is a fissile material, which is to say that its nucleus can split into two (sometimes three) nuclear fragments, i.e. fragments which correspond to the nuclei of other atoms, and give out some energy. This energy comes from its mass, which is to say that it is liberated by the physical process described by the Einstein formula. The amount of mass converted into energy via each such fission reaction is tiny. However, the value of c, the speed of light, is large, and if enough uranium atoms can be made to fission, then the output of energy is impressive.

A U-235 nucleus will fission if it is hit by a neutron going at a certain speed, not too quick and not too slow. Neutrons live inside nuclei, and fission reactions tend to liberate neutrons. If every uranium fission produced one neutron, then, provided one had enough atoms, the reaction could go on indefinitely. But if each fission produces more than one neutron, then it is possible for the reaction to diverge, to get bigger. The resulting build-up of energy can be rapid, as individual nuclear reactions are very fast indeed. A number of factors determine whether the reaction as a whole will diverge: these range from the purity of the uranium-235, which must be highly enriched to increase the proportion of U-235 over the more common uranium-238 isotope to about 80 per cent, to the size and shape of the system. Thus, what constitutes a *critical assembly* is a function of purity, geometry and mass. For instance, a sphere of 80 per cent pure U-235 of 20 kilograms would be critical, whereas two 10-kilogram hemispheres would not be. Thus, a device which brings the two hemispheres together is the 'obvious' design for an atomic bomb.

The scientific research on which this design is based goes back to the beginning of the present century. The Einstein formula, already mentioned, was discovered in 1905. At that time the fact that atoms have nuclei was not known and neither had the neutron been discovered. Clearly, without these two pieces of knowledge, the Einstein formula could not have been used for the design of a nuclear weapon. The nucleus was discovered in 1911 and the neutron twenty-one years later. These two discoveries led, eventually, to the uncovering of nuclear fission, in Berlin at the end of 1938. One could say that the chain reaction which was produced in 1945 was preceded by a 'chain reaction' in the international physics community, with one discovery stimulating another.

Scientific discoveries can lead to applications that are totally unexpected. Before the discovery of the Einstein formula, no one thought that it would be possible to convert mass into energy. It was thought that mass was conserved in the universe, that there can be no increase or diminution of mass and hence that mass could not be converted in energy: the old idea was that mass is conserved, while now it is thought to be mass-energy that is conserved. After the Einstein formula, the possibility of converting mass into energy became known. Suppose we call this *theoretical possibility*: it is what scientific theory tells us is allowed *in principle*. Thus, it was necessary to know the Einstein formula, the existence of the nucleus and the existence of the neutron before the atomic bomb could be conceived as possible in principle.

What is possible in principle may not be possible *in practice*. For example, suppose uranium and plutonium, and all the other fissile materials, have properties which are incompatible with the practical realisation of a bomb. Suppose that whenever a neutron hits a nucleus it liberates only one more neutron; there could be no divergent chain reaction. Or suppose that the fission reaction was too slow. Or that the critical mass of U-235 was very small. In all of these scenarios the atomic bomb, while possible in theory, would not work in practice. So, how was the theoretical possibility of the bomb seen also to be practically possible?

In fact, before the Manhattan Project it was known that the bomb was possible in theory, but many doubted that it was practical. As it turned out, a remarkable paper was written by two German émigré scientists, Otto Frisch and Rudolf Peierls, which predicted some essential parameters, such as the mass of a critical assembly (sphere). These two physicists were worried that the Nazis might develop an atomic bomb. One was Jewish and the other had a Jewish wife, and both had left Germany for England in the 1930s. They understood how aggressive the Nazis were, and they wanted to use their scientific abilities to help the Allies. So they drew attention to what they thought was the practical possibility of the bomb: their calculations, which proved remarkably accurate, predicted that a very large explosion could be generated in a critical assembly of U-235. They sent a memorandum of their results, written in England in 1940, to the committee that was examining ways to use science in the war. It was not acted on for several months, but then, when its significance was realised, it was taken very seriously indeed. A great deal of further work was undertaken by the scientists of the Manhattan Project before the practical possibility of the bomb was assured, but what Frisch and Peierls did was to show that this work was worth doing.

Once the bomb was shown to be a practical possibility, there is a sense in which the scientific research was over. There remained the design, engineering, fabrication, development and finally the testing stages. The project could have failed at any of these points—what is possible in practice may not be *realised in fact*—but it did not. It is worth mentioning that one of the main design problems concerned the plutonium bomb. The gun-barrel method does not work for plutonium, and here the project nearly foundered. The trouble is that the hemispheres simply cannot be brought together fast enough to prevent pre-ignition, to prevent the reaction from beginning too soon and blowing the barrel to pieces. Some highly creative design work was needed.

The fissile bomb material must be kept in a subcritical state before detonation, when the assembly must be made supercritical as fast as possible. Suppose the material were fashioned into a hollow sphere, whose dimensions were such as to leave the material in a subcritical state. Then suppose that it were possible to implode the sphere by squeezing it with a shock wave generated by precise chemical explosives. Would that work for plutonium? Yes it would, and it produced two of the three Manhattan Project atomic bombs. The clever implosion design just described was devised by an American physicist called Seth Neddermeyer. Without his creative mind, Nagasaki might have been spared; and Hiroshima too, for it is unlikely that the United States would have dropped the bomb if it had had just one.

But drop the bombs it did. The decision was ultimately made by President Truman, and the last direct orders were given by the captains of the two B29 bombers, Colonel Paul Tibbets and Major Charles Sweeney, to fly their planes to Hiroshima and Nagasaki. But many other military, civilian and scientific personnel gave advice on matters ranging from target selection to the question as to whether the Japanese would give in. So let us leave the historical details behind us, having seen enough of them, and turn directly to the question of moral responsibility. In doing so we move from historical analysis to philosophical analysis.

Responsibility

To start, let us say this:

Proposition 1
A person is *morally* responsible for an act or decision which she makes intentionally, on condition that it is appropriate to praise her or to blame her for what she did or for what she decided.

We do not yet know exactly what praise or blame amounts to; they are evidently something to do with morality, but we have not yet been in a position to say just what it is to be moral. Proposition 1 has, in fact, the character of a *definition* because it tells us that morality has something to do with praise and blame. But it is not a definition of *moral* behaviour, because a person can be praised or blamed for all sorts of reasons: for scoring a goal, choosing a good wine, baking a horrible cake, and so on. No one likes a hard tasteless cake, and the cook may be criticised; but he has not, surely, committed a moral offence (unless, maybe, he did it deliberately to ruin a carefully planned dinner party). So, it is a particular *kind* of praise and blame that attaches to moral behaviour. However, the aspect of the definition which we want to focus on here is not the part about morality but the part about responsibility. And the definition seems to tells us this: if you did it, then you are responsible (MacKie 1977:208). That seems fair enough.

We can immediately draw one conclusion: science *in and of itself*, as a constellation of knowledge, theories, methods—science in the abstract, to use the language of Chapter 1—cannot be said to be responsible for, or implicated in, anything whatsoever. For instance, the formula $E = mc^2$ cannot do anything itself, except describe a pattern or law of nature. It is *we* human beings that do things, *we* cause things to happen, and *we* must accept responsibility for what we do.

Think for a moment how absurd it would be to 'evaluate' a law of nature. We can say that a law is useful, or, like Polanyi and Russell in 1945, that there is no apparent use for it; we can say that it is theoretically significant, or we can say that it has interesting applications in the laboratory; but we cannot say it is good or bad. It is not just silly to say that $E = mc^2$ is a bad law while $F = ma$ is a good law: it is nonsense. (Science in this sense is neutral.) So, from Proposition 1 we conclude that moral responsibility can only attach to the scientist, to the person, not to science in and of itself. So the question of the moral responsibility of science quickly reduces to the question of the moral responsibility of the scientist, as it should do.

Proposition 1 cannot, however, be accepted as it stands; it is only a first attempt. For suppose our subject is coerced into doing something under dire threat, or is drugged, or goes mad, or is just having a really bad day. Is she still responsible? It is quite easy to give a general principle to cover these situations, but quite hard to put that principle into practice. The principle is this: if our person, call her P for short, is both rational and free to act as she will, then Proposition 1 applies. (With regard to rationality, it is easiest here to think of rationality as means–ends or instrumental rationality, or 'purposive' rationality; see Weber 1947:115.)

Rationality and freedom to act

P is rational if she selects a means that is likely to bring about the end she has in view. For the moment we can assume the end is given, but evidently instrumental rationality can only govern the selection of ends in a given case when those ends stand as the means to a more distant goal. The selection of one's ultimate goals is then not a matter for instrumental rationality—in fact it is to do with one's *values*. On the assumption that the end is given, for instance that it is to drop an atom bomb on Hiroshima, then the rational person selects the means that is likely to achieve that end more or less efficiently: for instance, fly there directly in a plane, avoid enemy fighters, don't go in bad weather, get a good bombardier, etc.

Instrumental rationality seems to be just what we are looking for, because we are investigating the conditions under which P is responsible for doing something. And this is what instrumental rationality is about: if P consciously selects a given means to an end, call it X, then she must want X to take place, exist, or whatever. (It is assumed here that only rational action is fully intentional action.) Colonel Tibbets wanted the bomb to explode over Hiroshima, which is why he did what he did. And what one consciously and deliberately wants to do, and then does, one is responsible for.

To continue, we may note that one notion of madness is complete irrationality: seeming always to select means that lead *away* from the (apparent) ends in view. If Colonel Tibbets always flew his planes upside down when the bomb doors were open, he would have had a short career in the air force. If his court martial agreed that he truly believed that that was the best way to release the bombs, and that he was not a pacifist in disguise, then he would get medical help and not a gaol sentence. Indeed, criminal law provides us with many examples and precedents that are relevant to this topic.

For example, typically, a jury has to decide two things: did the defendant do it, and if so, did he intend to do it. The defendant may be convicted on the first ground, but not the second, like the late Ronnie

Kray. He killed people in the East End of London in the 1950s, but he was assessed as insane (compare MacKie 1977:213). One might say that, although Kray killed people, he didn't mean to do it. Similar sorts of things can be said when someone is heavily drugged. If Colonel Tibbets were a guinea-pig for hallucinogenic drug tests—which the CIA did indeed conduct on service personnel in the 1950s—then he would not, at the same time, be a good choice as a pilot. Even if he could have understood the order 'Go bomb Hiroshima', it is unlikely that he would have been able to find the way there on LSD.

We might be tempted to the view that rational action is a necessary, though not sufficient, condition for ascribing moral responsibility. That is to say, everything which conforms to Proposition 1 must also embody rationality. The converse is not the case, because P might show the highest standards of rational behaviour in baking her cake, but that is really not something important enough for moral deliberation. But we should resist the temptation of that view. P could be coerced into doing something that she knows full well leads to X, which she believes to be wrong, but the alternative, Y, is even worse, even worse for her, that is. If she is tortured by the secret police, should she give away the hiding-place of her fellow freedom-fighters who are struggling against a repressive regime? It would be hard to blame her if she could not hold out.

So we need to build in the idea that the actions and decisions were undertaken *voluntarily*—alluded to in our principle by the words 'free to act'. No one made Seth Neddermeyer come up with the implosion design for the plutonium bomb, no one held a gun at his head: he did it of his own free will. The situation was a little different for Frisch and Peierls, especially for Frisch, who was Jewish. They wrote their memorandum in 1940, not 1944 after the tide had turned in the war. They felt Hitler had to be prevented from using an atom bomb which his clever scientists might well make for him. The Soviet scientists who worked on the atomic bomb after the war were in a different situation again. The first Soviet test was witnessed by Beria, Stalin's feared secret police chief, and had the test not worked he would have had the scientists shot (Rhodes 1996:366).

It must be said that these notions, of rational action and voluntary behaviour, are by no means trivial. They have exercised philosophers for many a long year. We cannot, therefore, expect to find some quick and simple resolution to all such questions as we have just raised. Let us say, then, that the actions and decisions we want to capture in Proposition 1 are a subgrouping, or subclass, of those that are both rational and voluntary. Notice that we still need rationality: we cannot make do with just free or voluntary action. Ronnie Kray might not have been a rational killer, but he did it voluntarily.

With all that in mind, we can re-formulate our condition:

Proposition 2
A person is *morally responsible* for an act or decision which she makes rationally
and voluntary, on condition that it is appropriate to praise her or to blame
her for what she did or for what she decided.

Let us try to be even more specific, and consider the *kinds* of actions
and decisions, as opposed to the circumstances under which they are
carried out, that we are interested in.

Cause and responsibility

One reason why the dropping of the two atomic bombs was so
momentous is that they affected such a lot of people; never before had
two bombs killed so many people. Not for nothing are nuclear arms
called weapons of mass destruction. Moral responsibility arises only
when our actions and decisions affect others. If our subject P gets up at
midnight for a cup of tea, that is not a morally significant action since it
concerns only herself. Again, this is necessary but not sufficient, because
some of the things we do which impinge on others are too trivial to
attract praise or blame—whatever morality is, it is 'weighty'.

(Notice one thing: those who are affected have been termed *others*,
not *other people*. While all of our examples so far have been of actions
affecting people, this does not necessarily mean that moral consideration extends only to people. Indeed, moral consideration, or moral
considerability as philosophers sometimes call it, is the complement of
moral responsibility: moral responsibility focuses our attention on the
subject, the person who did it, while moral consideration directs us to
the *object*, to the other who gets done to. We need to mention the
other here, but not say just who the other can be, in order to mark out
the domain of moral responsibility. The domain of its complement,
i.e. the domain of moral consideration, is a hot topic, of which more in
the next chapter.)

The concept of *cause* therefore seems to be relevant here. Colonel
Tibbets caused the explosion over Hiroshima by ordering the bombardier to arm Little Boy, as the uranium device was whimsically called,
and telling him to take over the navigation of the plane. The bombardier caused the explosion by arming and releasing Little Boy, and
the navigator caused it too, by charting the course from the home base
on the island of Tinian to Hiroshima. The aircrew would have done
none of these had they not been ordered to do so, via a long chain of
command stretching down from the highest authority of the President

himself, and they could have done nothing had the ground crew not fuelled and loaded the plane.

All of these people caused the killing of the city of Hiroshima. None of them did it individually; for instance, it is manifestly incorrect to say that Tibbets did it all on his own. This was a complicated operation, with lots of people involved. The concept of cause can be used here to flesh out what we mean when we talk about actions affecting others; we might well mean that subjects can be morally responsible when they cause things to happen to others.

First, we need to establish a statement of *causation*:

Proposition 3
If C is a cause of X, then if C does not happen, neither does X.

This seems to be what we want, for we want to capture the idea that Tibbets and the others were all causally involved with the dropping of the bomb. For if just one of those people failed to do something, do C, then the bomb would not have been dropped on Hiroshima (unless, of course, someone else did C).

Proposition 3 allows us to define *causal responsibility*:

Proposition 4
P is causally responsible for X, if C is a cause of X, and if P brings about C.

'Bringing about' really just means 'does': flies the plane, arms the bomb, gives the order, etc. Now, and here is where things get interesting, the causal connections, the *causal net* as some like to call it, are manifold in time and space.

Seth Neddermeyer did research into implosion techniques at the Manhattan weapons lab in Los Alamos in 1944. That design was used to make the 'Fat Man' bomb dropped by Major Sweeney. Without Neddermeyer, no Fat Man and hence no bombing of Nagasaki (unless of course someone else had been clever enough to come up with that design). Neddermeyer, as a matter of fact, produced one vital node in the causal net that led to Nagasaki; so according to Proposition 4, he was causally responsible. Some of the lesser lights at Los Alamos might not have done work essential to the production of Little Boy and Fat Man. It would certainly be difficult to reconstruct the whole net, but such a net did exist, and we can point to some vital nodes therein.

What about Einstein? He actually did two things: namely, discovered $E = mc^2$, and wrote to President Roosevelt telling him that a bomb might be practically possible. We know the former was a vital node, but it is impossible to tell if the latter was. In 1905 Einstein was in the same position as Polanyi and Russell were in 1945, that is to say, in a state of complete ignorance with regard to the practical application of his work. Indeed, the formula was an unintended consequence of the special theory of relativity. Einstein was not trying to establish mass-energy; he had other aims. This gives us an important clue about the connection between causal and moral responsibility, and it is this:

Proposition 5
P cannot be morally responsible for certain consequences of her actions if she was not in a position to know what these consequences would be.

What does it mean to say that P 'was not in a position to know'? That is a matter of degree: Einstein was clearly not in a position to know about the bomb in 1905, while Colonel Tibbets clearly was. For many of the vital causal nodes in between, it is not clear whether the actors were in a position to know or not. It seems that each particular instance, both in connection with the Manhattan Project and in other cases in which science interacts with society, will have to be treated on its own merits.

There can be no precise criterion for applying Proposition 5; but even so, there are some rules of thumb. A scientist who is aware that something is possible in principle, that it is theoretically possible, who chooses to investigate whether it is possible in practice, is in a better position to know about consequences than a scientist who works on basic theory. So again, it is more plausible to attribute responsibility to Frisch and Peierls than to Einstein. The former believed that their research might show that the bomb would work. They knew *in general* where their work might end up. Once the design process has begun, where people like Neddermeyer come in, the end comes into clearer focus; once this happens, the case for attributing responsibility becomes correspondingly stronger. Thus, the distinction between the types of research illustrated by the Manhattan Project is a guide to the application of Proposition 5.

Finally, taking our clue from Proposition 5, we can express all our ideas in the following statement.

Proposition 6
P is morally responsible for X only if she is causally responsible for X, if she was in a position to know that X would come about, if what she did was freely undertaken and if she was fully rational.

Again, this is a necessary condition for moral responsibility, because the things which P causes to happen, like the dirty cup left over from her midnight visit to the teapot, are not morally significant. But all we were trying to do here was to work out what sorts of things to which moral responsibility attaches. Proposition 6 does that.

The 'republic of science' fights back

In 'The Republic of Science' Polanyi claimed, among other things, that scientific research is motivated not by any practical considerations but by the pure search for knowledge. Indeed, Polanyi argued that it must be so, because scientists are just not able to foresee the practical effects of their work (Polanyi 1967:59). We've just been talking about that and we agree that Einstein could not know about the bomb. But Neddermeyer did. Do we say, then, that Neddermeyer was not doing science? Or that he was doing applied rather than pure research? Or what? This matter is crucial for the whole question of the ethics and morality of scientific research, because if scientists really cannot know where their research is going, then they cannot be held responsible for what they do. But surely we *want* them to be responsible. An enterprise which produces nuclear weapons cannot be conducted by people who refuse to acknowledge what they do.

(Remember that we are not in the business of actually praising or blaming yet, but we are in the business of assigning 'praise-or-blame'. And we want to assign it to pure science, the engine-room of technology. Why? Partly because of what we have said above, because we have a theory about moral responsibility which implicates, for good or bad, science and scientists. Besides that, we want to minimise the bad effects of science and maximise the good ones, because we want to be optimistic that, on the whole, science and morality can be compatible. So we want to convince scientists to accept responsibility for their work in the belief that they are, on the whole, decent people like the rest of us, who would refrain from doing the wrong thing if they could.)

It is not, however, possible to draw a sharp distinction between pure and applied science, such as Polanyi seems to want, as the following example shows. There was a theoretical division at Los Alamos headed by Hans Bethe, who was to win a Nobel Prize for theoretical physics. Other Nobel Prize–winning theoretical physicists, like Richard Feynman, worked with Bethe. They performed calculations that solved questions about the parameters of bomb design—on such technical issues as the fission cross-sections of U-235 and plutonium. That work represents 'pure' scientific knowledge, knowledge about how things are in the world quite apart from their applications. That same work, done in different circumstances, could have been published in a scientific journal and might have lain there neglected and unread. But *unless* that were true, unless pure research described how things are, it could have no application in technology. (More will be said on this topic in Chapter 6, when the relation between science and technology is examined in more detail.)

Thus, one cannot insulate pure research by arguing that it is different in character from applied research. That argument won't wash. But the republic of pure science can fight back in other ways. There are in fact another two well-known arguments, 'arguments from neutrality', that seek to insulate the pure scientist. They are reformulated here, as A and B, to apply specifically to our case study. To conclude this section we will have a look at them.

Argument A

1. Things like bombs have good and bad uses.
2. Therefore, a bomb in itself is neither good nor bad.
3. Therefore, goodness and badness attach to uses, not to technology.
4. If technology is neutral, so is science.

If someone presents us with a sequence of statements or *premises* designed to persuade us of the truth of a conclusion, and we don't want to accept the conclusion for some reason, then there are two ways we can proceed: we can see if the conclusion really follows from the premises, or we can reject the premises as false. What does 'follow' mean here? It means that *if* the premises are true, then the conclusion must be true, and the argument is then valid. The argument 'All pigs lay eggs, Jane is a pig, So Jane lays eggs' is clearly valid, but of course its main premise is false. This means that the two ways in which one can dispute a conclusion, challenging the validity of the argument or denying the truth of the premises, are independent. With this in mind, what about A?

Is A1 true? Do bombs really have good uses? Suppose Hiroshima and Nagasaki prevented a million civilian deaths in the invasion of the Japanese mainland, which was the official justification for the use of the atomic bomb. In that case there would have been a *justification* for using the bombs, but it cannot be said that the use was good. Killing innocent people cannot ever be good, unless 'good' is defined away as 'justified' or 'the lesser of two evils'. Bombs are specifically designed to kill and destroy; they *embody* that purpose. It is never good to kill and destroy. Most people—there are some notable exceptions—believe that it is sometimes necessary and justified to kill and destroy, but again that does not mean it is ever good. So A1 is not true.

Even if A1 were true, A2 would not follow. Suppose there was something that was totally evil or totally bad—there is surely nothing like this we are familiar with, but we could imagine some terrible fictional devil who is totally evil. Then killing that creature with a bomb might be considered a good use. But if that were so, it would not follow that the bomb itself was 'neutral'. Rather, for once, something whose essential purpose was killing and destroying, something inherently wrong, actually had a use that everyone agreed was good. In spite of itself, the bomb did good.

We have pretty much disposed of the argument. But it is worth saying something about the conclusion. The three premises are supposed to establish the truth of the first part of the conclusion, that technology is neutral. The last part of the conclusion then states that science is neutral. The conclusion itself is a sort of mini-argument, but it is not really spelt out. Why, if technology is neutral, should science be as well? The idea seems to be that there is no other source of value for science than through technology. In and of itself, independently of its applications in the 'external' context, science has no value. Is that right? This is the cue for the next argument.

Argument B

1. The same science, for example nuclear physics, can be used to generate different technologies, like atomic bombs and nuclear power stations.
2. Therefore, even if technology were not neutral, science would be.

B1 is true: the same basic scientific principles can be used to generate different technologies. We have agreed that technologies are themselves value-laden, and that for those which produce bombs and the like these values are strongly 'negative', with the products in question being unequivocally bad. Now, while we would not necessarily say that nuclear power stations are altogether good, they are certainly not in the same league as atomic bombs. Our judgements about value will therefore be different for power stations. So not only can the same science give rise to different technologies, but judgements about the values inherent in these technologies can be markedly different. All this supports the view that scientific knowledge itself is neutral; it has no value in and of itself.

Does this mean that, after all, Polanyi is right and that those engaged in pure research are doing something that is neutral and hence that they have no responsibility whatsoever? When Neddermeyer was designing implosion assemblies and when Fermi was designing nuclear reactors, they were using essentially the same scientific principles with different aims in mind. Maybe the principles they were using were value-neutral, but the aims were not. There is a difference between the principles themselves considered as theory, and the *uses* to which they are put. The latter are presented in a context with all the attendant effects, intentions and values, and whenever a scientist works in such a context she must shoulder responsibility.

The only scientists who are entirely free from moral responsibility for the knowledge they produce are therefore those who work on discovering or extending fundamental theory, for it is only then that the effects and applications are entirely unknown and unforeseen. However, these scientists are a tiny minority. Nearly every scientist at work today is making use of accepted scientific principles to work out some specific problem, and most have a very good idea what the solution will be like. It is often only a detail—a number, perhaps, or a mechanism or a pathway—that is unknown. Maybe that solution will have no practical application but maybe it will, and the lesson of this chapter is that the morally responsible scientist will try to look ahead and see what those applications might be.

Conclusion

We hope you are convinced that nearly all scientists must accept responsibility for the ways in which their work affects society as a whole. If these effects are deemed to be good, to be beneficial to people, then no doubt scientists will be happy to answer for them. As mentioned already, scientists like to be represented as conferring benefits, from AIDS-fighting drugs to hardy plant varieties to new fuels, and many other things besides. But when it comes to military technologies, to persistent and polluting pesticides, to nuclear power stations (perhaps), there is a tendency for the scientist to hide behind the general, the businessperson or the politician, and to say that what is wrong depends on how the science is used. That will not do; as we remarked above, responsibility cuts both ways.

The next logical step is to see how the moral responsibility of science is to be discharged. That is a difficult and complex issue, because it is not obvious what a moral code for science should look like. However, in the chapter that follows we will address that issue.

Further reading

Polanyi's essay 'The Republic of Science' (Polanyi 1969) is certainly worth reading. The topic of responsibility goes back a long way, in fact to the fourth century BC. The classic discussion is in Book Three of Aristotle's *Nicomachean Ethics* (Aristotle 1962); it is very short, and recommended to the interested reader. John MacKie (1977) is a sensible and influential philosopher, who gives a good discussion of the conditions under which we can attribute moral responsibility. Peter Singer's *Practical Ethics* (Singer 1993) is a much-read text on ethics. It is accessible and would be recommended without qualification if it were not for the fact that Singer does push his own line, consequentialism, rather hard. For the Manhattan Project, Rhodes (1986) is an excellent book: it is the rare combination of a good scholarly book and an exciting story. Schroeer (1984) is good too, but more technical. Smyth (1989) is interesting: in 1946 Smyth published *Atomic Energy for Military Purposes*, and it was realised almost immediately that it gave away much too much information. Soviet spies eagerly bought copies! Surprisingly, there are not many books that focus on the moral responsibility of science. Beach (1996) is more about the conduct of research itself, but is worthwhile none the less. Erwin *et al.* (1994) is a collection of papers, some of which are excellent, and the same goes for Shea and Sitter (1989).

References

Aristotle (1962), *Nicomachean Ethics*. Trans. M. Ostwald. Indianapolis: Bobbs-Merrill.

Beach, D. (1996), *The Responsible Conduct of Research*. Weinheim, Germany: VCH.

Erwin, E., Gendin, S., and Kleiman, L. (1994), *Ethical Issues in Scientific Research*. New York: Garland.

MacKie, J. (1977), *Inventing Right and Wrong*. Harmondsworth: Penguin.

Polanyi, M. (1969), 'The Republic of Science', in M. Grene (ed.), *Knowing and Being: Essays by Michael Polanyi*. Chicago: Chicago University Press: 49–72.

Rhodes, R. (1986), *The Making of the Atomic Bomb*. New York: Simon and Schuster.

Rhodes, R. (1996), *Dark Sun: The Making of the Hydrogen Bomb*. New York: Touchstone Books.

Schroeer, D. (1984), *Science, Technology and the Nuclear Arms Race*. New York: John Wiley.

Shea, W., and Sitter, B. (eds) (1989), *Scientists and Their Responsibilities*. Canton: Watson.

Singer, P. (1993), *Practical Ethics*, 2nd edn. Cambridge: Cambridge University Press.

Smyth, H. (1989), *Atomic Energy for Military Purposes*. Stanford: Stanford University Press.

Weber, M. (1947), *The Theory of Social and Economic Organisation*. New York: Free Press.

Weatherall, D. (1991), *The New Genetics and Clinical Practice*, 3rd edn. Oxford: Oxford University Press.

CHAPTER 4

The Rights and Wrongs of Science

Martin Bridgstock

Science has been getting some bad press over the last decade or two. More and more scientists have been accused of behaving badly. In some cases, they have been accused of mistreating human or animal subjects. In other cases, they have falsified their findings, or simply accepted behaviour by other people which was clearly wrong. As John Forge argued in the last chapter, it is reasonable in many circumstances to regard scientists as responsible for the effects of their conduct, and in this chapter we shall see what that conduct was, and what the consequences were.

To think about right and wrong conduct in science, we have to know two things. We have to know what the conduct is, and we have to know by what standards to judge it. As we shall see, this is often very difficult. This chapter will take you through some cases in which scientists behaved very badly. We shall look at some of these, and ask why they did so. In other cases, there is fierce debate about whether they did right or wrong. We will look at the arguments on both sides.

The great sociologist Robert K. Merton regarded science as a self-policing system. In his view, apprentice scientists are rapidly educated in what is, and is not, acceptable behaviour in science. Further, once they are working in science, their conduct is constantly under scrutiny. He wrote: 'Scientific inquiry is in effect subject to rigorous policing, to a degree perhaps unparalleled in any other field of human activity' (Merton 1973:311). With this in mind, the history of bad conduct in science comes as quite a shock.

We begin with some work which is so bad that it is questionable whether it can be called science at all. Certainly, this mass of crimes—for crimes they were—are the worst perversion of science which has ever existed. What we learn from Nazi science may help us to understand more recent cases.

The 'science' of the Nazis

Dr Mengele approaches a wooden cage in which two small children are imprisoned. He points to one of the children and orders that the child be brought into the examining room. The child is laid onto the examination table naked. Its mouth is gagged and eyes are blindfolded. Assistants hold the child down onto the table on each side. The doctor steps forward with his scalpel and makes a long incision into the child's leg along the tibia. He then begins to take scrapings from the bone. When he is finished, the leg is bound up and the child is returned to the cage ... nothing is given for pain. [Vigorito 1992:12]

This terrible passage comes from the memoirs of Sara Vigorito, who suffered in the Nazi concentration camps under the 'mad doctor', Josef Mengele. She was not alone. About 1500 pairs of twins and tens of thousands of other people also suffered, and most of them died. One of the most notorious experiments took place in the Dachau concentration camp. People were immersed in icy water, and they were carefully monitored until they finally died. There was no anaesthetic, nor any attempt made to ease their suffering at all. This experiment has come back to haunt us, as we shall see later.

These crimes were part of the massive tragedy which took place in Europe before and during World War II. Hitler and his Nazi party regarded some races as inferior to others. The Jews were considered the worst, but Russians and Poles were also believed to be subhuman. This deprived them of human status. In addition, some groups had no right to life. These included Gypsies, homosexuals, and the mentally subnormal. Because of this policy, a huge 'industry of death' appeared in Europe in the 1940s. Trains were chartered and millions of people moved to concentration camps. In some camps people died of starvation, cold or disease. In others, people were herded into huge gas chambers to be killed.

To some scientists, the Nazi concentration camps were a huge temptation: here were people who could be experimented on with none of the normal problems. In addition, to scientists who had joined the Nazi party, there was a positive duty to assist the Nazi cause. The freezing experiments were wanted by the German air force, to see what would happen to airmen who ditched into cold seas. The experiments involving lethal injections were simply to find the best ways of killing concentration camp inmates.

It is tempting to think of the Holocaust as so abnormal that we can learn nothing from it. In addition, it all took place fifty years ago. So why not forget the whole thing? In fact, there are good reasons to remember what happened. As we shall see, some of the Nazi experiments continue to cause controversy today. In addition, the Nazi atrocities in science are not unique. During the Japanese occupation of the Chinese province of Manchuria, from 1931 to 1945, similar atrocities were carried out, mostly upon Chinese prisoners. These have only recently been brought to light, and are chronicled in Harris's book, *Factories of Death* (Harris 1994).

First, let us dispose of the idea that the Nazi scientists were all sadists or madmen. Some were, undoubtedly, but even those who suffered under Mengele did not think of him as mad:

> Mengele loved precision and order and these rated above everything else ... he was extremely intelligent and although his victims feared him, he was never thought of as a monster ... there were times when he abruptly left the room when confronted with the wailing of child victims ... almost as if he felt that he might be moved with pity and discontinue his experiments ... somehow he had been trapped within himself and in his own selfish goals ... and he had slipped over the edge and made science his god. [Vigorito 1992:12–13]

There were certainly sadists and lunatics among the Nazi doctors, but quite a number of them had good qualifications, and were well-regarded in science. Yet they carried out some of the most hideous atrocities ever performed in the name of science.

The Tuskegee project

The story of the Tuskegee project is a peacetime horror story. Tuskegee, a small town in the American state of Alabama, was the scene of a scientific scandal which became public in 1972. Essentially, 399 men infected with syphilis, were denied treatment—or even knowledge of their illness—for more than forty years while the progress of the disease was monitored. What was more, this was done by doctors and scientists working for the US Public Health Service (Jones 1981).

To appreciate the horror of this, we should know a little about syphilis. It is a sexually transmitted disease; before modern antibiotics, it was far more frightening than AIDS is today. This is because syphilis is transmitted more easily: almost any unprotected sexual act, or kissing, or other sorts of body contact will pass on the syphilis infection. Once a person is infected, the first sign is a small sore, called a chancre, which usually appears on or near the genitals. Then, for a number of years, little seems to happen. There may be the odd skin rash or mild fever, but the victim usually feels quite well. This quiet stage—termed latency—is the time when the disease is becoming established in the body. It is drilling into the bones, the liver and other organs.

After some years, the victim enters the tertiary state. Sores and tumours appear, growing and coalescing into ulcers. The bones may deteriorate, and the nose may eventually disappear, leaving a single hole for nose and mouth. The disease may penetrate the eyes, causing blindness, and the brain, causing insanity. It may also kill, by attacking the heart. Before the appearance of modern antibiotics, it is hardly surprising that syphilis was regarded as the 'carnal scourge'.

To deal with the end of the story first, Senator Edward Kennedy held an inquiry into the Tuskegee experiment. Eventually compensation was paid to the eighty-six men still alive, and to the relatives of the deceased. Tragically, some of the men never understood what had been done to them.

How did it happen?

Until 1940, syphilis was a difficult illness to treat. For centuries mercury had been used, but it was very expensive. In 1906 the German chemist Paul Ehrlich had discovered Salvarsan-606, a chemical which could kill syphilis. However, it was an arsenic derivative, and almost as dangerous to the patient as the disease itself. For poor people before 1940, there was effectively no treatment for the disease.

The inhabitants of Tuskegee were certainly poor. The area is in the rural part of Alabama, one of the poorest of the United States. In addition, until the 1960s, Alabama was one of the hardest-line segregation states: blacks were excluded from virtually all political office, and higher education. In Tuskegee, the black men were illiterate and ignorant. A good deal was known about the effect of syphilis before the Tuskegee project began. In the 1890s, a study of Norwegian men had demonstrated the devastating effects that the disease could have. However, some American doctors in the Public Health Service believed that syphilis in black men could have different effects. Black people's nervous systems were believed to be cruder than white people's. A similar study on blacks seemed a good idea.

In the 1920s the doctors located 399 men in Tuskegee who had syphilis. They located some others who were free of the disease, for comparison. The lynch-pin of the study was a black nurse named Rivers. She kept track of the men and took them for their regular examinations at the Tuskegee Institute. The men were not told of the nature of their diseases, except sometimes that they had 'bad blood'. They submitted to an annual examination. In return they got a square meal, treatment for diseases (except syphilis, of course) and a free ride in Nurse Rivers's car. They also knew that, when they died, they would receive free burial.

Few of the men could have afforded to see a doctor, but in case any of them did, the local doctors were given a list of the infected patients. Any who consulted a doctor were to be referred back to Nurse Rivers (Jones 1981:134). During the early stages of the project, there was effectively no cure for syphilis. However, some sharp questions could be asked about the ethics of the project even at this stage. The most obvious is: why were the men not told about their disease? They would not understand the details, but some possible future sexual partners might have been saved from infection. In addition, are not human subjects of research entitled to be told what is happening?

The Tuskegee experiment took a nastier turn in 1942 when the United States entered World War II. At about the same time penicillin, a cheap antibiotic which could cure syphilis, became widely available. All of the men could be called up, to face a medical inspection. In a short time, doctors working for the army might diagnose all of the subjects as suffering from syphilis, and cure them with shots of penicillin. The Tuskegee researchers found an answer. The chairman of the state draft board was contacted, and he arranged that none of the men were called up; thus none of them could be diagnosed with, or cured of, syphilis. It is clear that, at this stage, the Tuskegee experiment changed its nature. Until about 1942 it had essentially been monitoring incurable people, albeit depriving them of information. It now became an active effort to stop these men being treated for a curable and fatal disease.

It is easy to see the Tuskegee experiment as racist. After all, the doctors were all white and the subjects were all black. However, it is more complicated than that. Nurse Rivers, the centre of the project, was black. In the 1950s, something happened which was even stranger. After the war, the white doctors in the area were gradually replaced by black ones. The Tuskegee researchers approached the new black doctors and asked them to cooperate—remarkably, all of them did so!

We must understand that it was not a secret project: papers describing the findings of the studies appeared in medical and scientific journals. A total of seventeen scientific and medical papers appeared on the topic. It was not until the late 1960s that one doctor finally blew the whistle. Peter Buxtun, a worker within the Public Health Service, became suspicious. His initial protests got nowhere, so he gave the story to the newspapers. Senator Edward Kennedy became involved, and the fate of the Tuskegee project was sealed.

Before assessing the Tuskegee experiment, it is worth noting what it discovered. The men with syphilis did indeed suffer much more than those without: their death rate was three times as high, and they suffered far more from a range of illnesses and symptoms, especially heart and circulation trouble. However, no dramatic results appeared: nothing new was learned about the action of the disease. It is also worth noting that the study, as a scientific experiment, did not stand up well. Over the years, a substantial number of the men left the state, to visit relatives or to seek work. Some had medical treatment while out of state, thus rendering the study invalid: it was not a study of untreated syphilis!

Why was the Tuskegee study ethically wrong? As we saw, until about 1940 there was no proper cure for syphilis. Given the attractions of the study, the researchers might have been able to persuade many of the men to participate, even if they told them the whole truth. The meal, the treatment for other diseases and the promise of free burial were considerable inducements. However, the men were kept in ignorance. There is a clear problem with this: subjects of experiments should be told what is happening. Further, if the men had been told—even in simple terms—of the situation, many further infections might have been avoided. An advisory panel set up in 1971 commented: 'The most fundamental reason for condemning the Tuskegee study is ... that [the subjects] were never fairly consulted about the research project, its consequences for them and the alternatives available to them' (Katz 1992:249). We can also ask: would any of the doctors like to be studied in this way? Would they like to be kept in ignorance of a fatal infectious disease, even if nothing could be done to cure it? Almost certainly, the answer would be no.

About 1940, penicillin became available. A few injections could have cured each of the men. The Tuskegee study now appears in a new, and much more malignant, light. It was now actively preventing these men from being cured, fostering suffering and death in the name of science. As we know already, it is too simple to regard the Tuskegee study as pure racism. A black nurse was at the centre of the project and black doctors cooperated with it. As we have seen, the Norwegian study had examined white men infected with syphilis. The justification for the Tuskegee project was a school of thought which held that black people were fundamentally different from white: more animal-like and more child-like, with a coarser nervous system. Of course, this *is* a racist viewpoint. To these researchers, it would seem logical to compare the effects of syphilis on blacks and whites.

Despite this reasoning, there are some problems with the science involved. People in the southern United States live in a different climate and eat different types of food from those in Norway. Logically, a proper study would compare black and white people in the same area. Alternatively, black people in some part of the United States similar to

Norway should be selected. Of course, these were not feasible courses of action, and so blacks in Tuskegee were studied because they were available. It seems clear from this that an element of racism did lie at the heart of the Tuskegee project. Even if we do not regard the idea of blacks and whites being different as racist, the failure to study whites in a similar way is a clear sign that something was amiss.

As the project continued, it seems to have taken on a life of its own. Doctors and researchers learning about the project simply assumed that it was 'all right' and remained silent about its questionable ethical aspects. Perhaps this is the most important point about the Tuskegee study. An open discussion at any stage of the project would probably have concluded that it was, at least, suspect. The role of the whistle-blower is often important in these matters. This is the person who sees that something is wrong and does something to make the matter public. Whistleblowers may begin by complaining to people involved in the project. If that fails, they go further afield, perhaps complaining publicly or to politicians. This was the role played by Peter Buxtun.

Of course, whistleblowers are not welcome in organisations where something wrong is happening. They have suffered terribly in some cases. It follows that whistleblowers must receive some kind of protection for their courage. Processes must be clearly laid down so that complaints can be made and investigated.

The National Women's Hospital case

Astonishingly, another case parallels the Tuskegee case. It took place in Auckland, New Zealand, where the National Women's Hospital has an international reputation for excellence. Among other things, it tests and treats women for the dangerous disease of cervical cancer. Because cervical cancer is widespread, and can be fatal, it is important that it be detected early, before it begins to do major harm. Across the world, it is accepted that the best way to predict cervical cancer is to take a small smear of cells from the cervix (the area where the womb joins the vagina) and examine them under a microscope. Certain abnormalities in the cells—called *carcinoma in situ*, or CIS—are generally accepted as danger signs. A woman with CIS is normally treated to remove the abnormal cells, and so stave off cervical cancer.

However, one small group of doctors, led by Associate Professor Herbert Green at the National Women's Hospital, did not accept that CIS was a danger sign for cervical cancer. Green believed—probably rightly—that too much surgery was performed upon women. He also regarded CIS as a benign occurrence, posing no danger. Therefore, over many years, Professor Green and his team monitored the women with abnormal cells, but did nothing further. Fierce battles took place between doctors and researchers at the hospital, though these were all in private. Green's opponents published an article in a medical journal arguing that his method was endangering people's lives (McIndoe *et al.* 1984). This caught the attention of two feminists, Sandra Coney and Phillida Bunkle, and in 1986 they wrote an article in a popular New Zealand magazine on this topic (Coney and Bunkle 1987). The inference was that a number of women—perhaps twenty-six—had died as a result of the non-treatment of CIS.

Naturally, there was a great uproar, and Coney and Bunkle were fiercely attacked by doctors, patients and politicians alike (Coney 1988). Eventually, a Royal Commission was held, which broadly supported the criticisms of Coney and Bunkle (Cartwright 1988). This case will be discussed further in the next chapter.

Discussion of the two cases

The similarities between the Tuskegee project and the National Women's Hospital case are, on the face of it, considerable. In both cases, people did not receive the accepted treatment for a given condition. In both cases they were not told about this, and in both cases there is evidence that they suffered accordingly. However, there are some important differences. Nobody disputes that syphilis is a terrible disease, and that leaving it untreated will cause death. However, Professor Green did not accept the connection between CIS and cervical cancer. Therefore, from his viewpoint, the women were not ill and required no treatment.

Professor Green was virtually alone in this view. To quote from one of the expert witnesses at the Royal Commission:

> Green's iconoclastic views were well known as a result of his publications, as a result of his participation in international meetings and his speaking tours during his sabbatical leaves and because he was the only author to continue to espouse that view. [Coney 1988:169]

Now, was Professor Green entitled to treat patients in a way which he thought right, but which no other expert in the world agreed with? Further, was he entitled to do this without telling the patients? Would Professor Green, or any of us, want to be treated in a way that virtually all of the medical profession condemns, especially if we are not told that our treatment is so controversial? The answer to this question is fairly clear. Thus, although the National Women's Hospital case resembles that of the Tuskegee project, it is really somewhat different, and raises different issues.

How should we think about right and wrong in science?

This section should give you some useful ideas for thinking about right and wrong in science. It is nowhere near a complete discussion—some extra books are listed at the end of the chapter—but you should find it helpful. A good start when considering rights and wrongs is to consider a principle known by the awkward name 'universalisability'. This is exemplified by the so-called Golden Rule of many religions, namely that you should always act towards others as you would hope they would act towards you. The advantages of this are obvious: it is hard to imagine most of the murders and brutalities in history taking place if people had used the rule.

The Golden Rule is a good place to start, but it has its problems. As George Bernard Shaw pointed out many years ago, people have different tastes. How does the Golden Rule apply, for example, to a religious fanatic? He is quite prepared to die, and sets out happily to kill his enemies. What is needed are some acceptable forms of conduct, that go beyond a particular individual's tastes, that can be raised to universal principles. But there are other issues besides; for instance, where are the boundaries which determine whom we should act towards in a moral way? Dr Mengele regarded the people he experimented on as less than human. He did not accept that human rights and considerations should be extended to them. As we shall see, one of the most difficult areas concerns animals: exactly how far should rights and considerations be extended to non-human species?

Mengele's actions were clearly morally unacceptable, as were those of the Tuskegee researchers. How would they react, one wonders, if doctors examined them, but did not tell them that they had a fatal disease, and did not treat them for it? Further, what would they think if those doctors then took active steps to prevent them from being treated by anyone else? There would probably be major lawsuits and huge compensation pay-outs.

Philosophers often say that there are two types of approach to deciding what is right and wrong—and hence they believe that these should inform our choices about what sorts of actions and behaviours are to be universalised. The two approaches are called *consequentialist* and *non-consequentialist* (surprise!), which for our purposes can be regarded as equivalent to the *deontological* approach. The intimidating names conceal two simple ideas, and we use them both in our daily thinking.

Consequentialism begins with the view that acts are not right or wrong in themselves, but only because of their consequences. Thus, when we are working out what is the right thing to do, we should examine the total consequences—for everyone, not just ourselves—and choose the act that has the best overall consequences. The most influential form of consequentialism is *utilitarianism*. This argues, in its simplest form, that our acts should be aimed at maximising the happiness and well-being of the greatest number of people.

There is no doubt that something like utilitarianism does affect the way we think about right and wrong. We probably all condemn a drunk driver who speeds through quiet streets. However, our condemnation grows to horror if that driver runs down a young child. Objectively, the driver was equally wrong in the two cases, but we take a much more serious view of an action if it has horrible consequences than if it has not. Many utilitarians apply their arguments to *rules* of conduct, not to individual acts. Thus, they postulate that we should adopt rules of conduct which maximise the general benefit, rather than evaluating every act from scratch. As far as drunken driving goes, obviously the best rule is to drive carefully and minimise the chance of injuring anyone. Thus, rule utilitarianism yields far more sensible and practical results than does applying utilitarianism to individual acts.

The other perspective has the general name of *deontology*. It begins with the view that actions are in themselves good or bad, whether or not they have bad consequences. For example, religious believers often regard acts in this way. If you believe that God forbids or demands certain acts, then there is nothing more to be said: those acts are clearly bad, or good. The consequences of the acts are not of interest, only the fact that God has spoken about them. Other deontological views are not religiously based. For example, contractarianism regards our behaviour as being bound by a series of contracts or agreements. If we live in a country, then we are bound by its laws. Therefore, driving drunkenly is a breach of our contract, and so wrong in itself.

It is easy to set up situations in which either of these perspectives leads to problems, sometimes even to absurdities. The simplest form of utilitarianism, as we have seen, treats the same action differently depending upon its consequences. Many deontological positions can also leave us in difficulties. A total pacifist would not lift a finger, even if his family were being attacked in front of him. To many people, this is courageous but ridiculous.

In fact, the two positions are not as far apart as they might seem. Utilitarians do not simply make up rules to advance human happiness out of nowhere; they firmly believe that some actions are right and others wrong, and argue from that to the general good. And, often, deontologists believe that their actions, if done by everyone, would greatly increase the well-being of people. The pacifist believes that a war-free world would be a much happier one. The devoutly religious person believes that humanity will do best by doing God's will, and so on. So, although the two approaches are formally different, they often lead to similar solutions to problems.

Let us be clear that this is not a full and proper survey of ethical principles: it is a brief, partial sketch of a few useful ideas. We will keep returning to these ideas through this chapter. They are valuable ones in sorting out why we might regard certain actions as right or wrong.

We have already seen that Mengele's actions fail the test of universalisability. How do utilitarianism and deontology see them? Well, there is no doubt that Mengele's actions caused hideous suffering. In addition, by relegating thousands of humans to subhuman status and then exploiting them for science, he set out on a course of action which could only, and vastly, increase the sum of misery in the world. On utilitarian grounds, Mengele stands condemned. From a deontological perspective, the only question is, what criteria do you use? By almost every moral and religious code that humanity has devised, mass murder and torture of the kind Mengele carried out is condemned. Thus, on either utilitarian or deontological grounds, Mengele's travesty of science is totally unacceptable. Mengele's actions were wicked in themselves, and they caused great hardship.

On the other hand, a more recent dilemma has been posed by Dr Robert Pozos, a well-regarded researcher at the University of Minnesota in the United States. Dr Pozos was considering using the Nazi data on freezing people to death to advance his research on hypothermia (Pozos 1992). Potentially, such research could be life-saving, but should Dr Pozos use data obtained in such a scandalous way? Some opponents of using the data have argued that the data is not reliable anyway (Berger 1992:115). Others have argued that nothing obtained in such a wicked fashion should be used (Kor 1992:7). In fact, Pozos discovered that many people had already referred to the data. His innovation was to raise the matter explicitly. There is no simple answer to this problem but, on balance, our culture seems to lean toward a utilitarian view and to favour using the data.

Stanley Milgram's obedience experiments

Our last case concerning experiments on humans is different. It has been defended as strongly as it has been attacked. What is more, it throws light upon a question which keeps recurring as one contemplates the earlier experiments: how could people have done these things to each other?

Imagine that you see an advertisement in a newspaper. A prominent university offers you a generous amount of money for an hour of your time. You gather that it is an experiment to do with memory and learning. You answer the advertisement and turn up at the university laboratory. You meet a man who has also answered the advertisement. He is a little older than you, and you get on well. The experimenter arrives: he is a cold, scientific man in a white coat. He tells you that the experiment is to do with punishment and learning. One of you will be the teacher, the other the learner. You are selected to be the teacher. You see the man taken into an adjoining room. He is strapped to a chair and an electrode attached to his arm. He can move one hand, enough to press a few buttons on a small keyboard before him.

The experimenter takes you into the laboratory. He seats you before a small panel, on which you can set problems for the man next door and see whether he makes the correct responses. Looming over you is a huge electric shock machine, with switches numbered from 15 volts, in 15-volt steps, up to 450 volts. You notice labels over some of the higher voltages, saying things like *Extreme intensity shock* and *Strong shock.* The experimenter tells you that the aim of the experiment is to test the effects of punishment on learning. You are to set the learner problems, and if he gets a problem wrong, he is to receive an electric shock. Because the effect of the shocks decreases, each shock must be 15 volts bigger than the one before. You look along the switches: 300 volts, 315 volts, 330 volts ... How far will things go?

The experiment begins. At first the learner does well, but he begins to make mistakes, and you give him small shocks, gradually growing into larger ones. At about 75 volts he grunts with discomfort, and at 120 volts he calls out that the shocks are really hurting. At 150 volts he shouts that he no longer wants to be part of the experiment. At 270 volts he is screaming in pain. At 300 volts he goes completely silent: he does not respond either to the problems or to the shocks. You consult the scientist, who is watching you closely. He assures you that the shocks may be painful, but do no damage. He tells you to go on with the experiment. What do you do?

Of course, this experiment is a complete fake. It has nothing to do with memory, learning or punishment. The man strapped in the chair is an actor, and is receiving no electric shock at all. The whole aim is to see how far you will go in giving electric shocks in exchange for a small amount of money, and because a man in a white coat tells you to. Most people believe that they would refuse to give the shocks quite early: usually below 150 volts. The reality is different. About 60 per cent of people give the full 450 volts of electricity. The experiment has been carried out in many countries, with similar results.

The experiment is controversial, for several reasons. One suspects that it brings us face to face with something about ourselves that we would rather not know. Most of us think that we make up our own minds about how to behave. The notion of ourselves as submissive creatures, willing to give up our own judgement so easily, is unacceptable to many people.

There are other reasons why the experiments are unacceptable. They inflicted great hardship upon people undergoing the experiment. When the research began, Milgram and his colleagues expected people to turn the switches up to a certain voltage, and then stop. However, as Milgram describes, things took a quite different course:

> Subjects were observed to sweat, tremble, stutter, bite their lips, groan and dig their finger-nails into their flesh ... Fourteen of the 40 subjects showed definite signs of nervous laughter and smiling. The laughter seemed entirely out of place, even bizarre. Full-blown, uncontrollable seizures were observed for 3 subjects. One occasion we observed a seizure so violently convulsive that it was necessary to call a halt to the experiment. [Milgram 1970:293]

The experimenters have been accused of causing unnecessary suffering, as well as deception. Milgram has defended himself vigorously from these charges. After each experiment, the subjects were carefully debriefed. They were introduced to the person they thought they had been torturing, and reassured that he was completely unhurt. Whatever they had done in the experiment, they were reassured that their behaviour was completely normal. Several months later, each subject received a follow-up questionnaire. Milgram reports that over 80 per cent of the people were glad that they had taken part in the experiment. In addition, nearly three-quarters, 74 per cent, said that further experiments should be made of the same type (Milgram 1974).

The other question is whether Milgram should have used deception in his experiments. Many ethical codes require experimenters to tell their subjects what they are doing. For example, Paragraphs 2 and 4 of the Nuremberg Code (1949:181–2), which appears at the end of this chapter, might leave us uncertain. They require that experiments should 'yield fruitful results for the good of society' and 'avoid all unnecessary physical and mental suffering and injury'.

There is no doubt that Milgram's experiments told us something new and important about ourselves. Did it justify the suffering? On balance, Milgram's experiment is thought to be unethical, though the value of its results is undisputed.

Two important things emerge from Milgram's study. The first is that we know a little more about human beings. We know that most of us have within us a strong urge to obey those in authority. Judging by the stress experienced by people in Milgram's experiments, it is difficult for us to disobey authority, even when we are being told to do something terribly wrong. Of course, when people in authority tell us to do something, usually there are good reasons—or at least the action is not clearly wrong. However, if we are to guard against terrible aberrations like the Tuskegee experiment, we must also, somehow, organise things so that people can take action if they see something happening which is unethical. The second point is that ethical codes are helpful, but they do not solve the problem. The subjects knew that shocking people was wrong, but they went ahead in Milgram's experiment anyway. Even if an ethical code denounces something clearly, it may not be obeyed. And often—as with parts of the Nuremberg Code—it is not clear whether something is unethical or not.

The key lesson which emerges from Milgram's experiment is that we must design our organisations with regard to human frailty. We must make it possible for the anguished—and often feeble—voice of opposition to evil to emerge, and to question complacent authority which is heading toward evil. These principles are just as important in the area of animal experimentation.

Animal experimentation

Animal experimentation is a far more difficult area than the use of human subjects. As we have seen, the key point for humans is that they can give informed consent. However, animals never can: no animal understands what an experiment is. How, therefore, do we decide when, if ever, it is ethical to experiment upon them? As science—and particularly biology—has expanded, the scale of animal experimentation has become huge. Finding a vaccine for poliomyelitis involved the use of 2.5 million animals, mostly monkeys (Blum 1994). What are the ethical issues in this area?

Those objecting to animal experimentation fall broadly into two categories, which can be termed *animal welfare* and *animal rights*. The animal welfare movement has existed for more than a century. It does not dispute that animal experiments are needed, but argues strongly that they should be minimised, and that suffering should be cut to the least possible. This movement has had considerable success. Ethics committees exist to supervise experiments, and to ensure that cruelty is minimised. The other wing of the movement—animal rights—is considerably more radical. It argues that animals have rights in the same way that humans have. In consequence, animal experimentation is morally wrong and indeed is abominably cruel.

The most important figure in this movement is the Australian philosopher Peter Singer. Singer is not active in the animal rights movement, but his book *Animal Liberation* (Singer 1975) laid its intellectual foundations. Singer argues that some animals, such as the higher apes, can be called 'persons'. They are aware of themselves as individuals, and they know that they have a past and a future. This entitles them to equivalent rights with humans. As a result, says Singer:

> In our present state of knowledge, this strong case against killing can be invoked most categorically against the slaughter of chimpanzees, gorillas and orangutans ... A case can also be made, though with varying degrees of confidence, on behalf of whales, dolphins, monkeys, dogs, cats, pigs, seals bears, cattle, sheep and so on—even perhaps to the point at which it includes all mammals. [Singer 1993:132]

Singer's argument is a *utilitarian* one. Having defined these animals as persons, suffering is minimised and happiness maximised by giving them immunity from horrible experiments and artificial death. With regard to animal non-persons who can feel pain, Singer argues that their suffering should be minimised as far as possible.

There is an obvious argument against this, but it backfires badly. Humans are more intelligent than other animals. Singer agrees with this, but points out that some humans are not intelligent. Examples are mentally handicapped adults and babies. If we extend rights to these and not to animals who are persons, argues Singer, then we are guilty of 'speciesism'—an equivalent to racism.

Of course, many people disagree with Singer's view. The simplest reason for disagreement is to adopt a deontological posture. Humans, even the mentally subnormal ones, are different from animals. One motivation comes from the Bible, where humanity is given dominion over all animals. However, one can easily believe that humans are fundamentally different from animals in other ways, and so are entitled to rights which animals are not. Still, Singer's view is coherent and powerful. It has influenced many people toward a radical view of animal rights. If animals have rights equivalent to human rights, then it follows that experimenting on them is equivalent to experimenting on a baby or a mentally subnormal person. Most of us would regard this as an outrage.

The animal rights movement has carried this argument to its conclusion, and some of its adherents regard scientists who experiment on animals as murderers and torturers. They are as determined to stop the experiments as if the subjects of the experiments were indeed humans. Naturally, scientists and other supporters of experimentation have argued back strongly. They have pointed to the great benefits which animal experimentation has brought to humanity; safer products, better drugs and surgical techniques, and so on. They have also pointed out the inconsistency of people strongly opposing animal experiments, yet wearing items like fur coats and leather shoes.

Another problem for animal liberationists is: where do you stop? It is easy to become angry about experiments on furry animals like chimpanzees and cats. What about ants and cockroaches, though? Do the liberationists use insecticides to keep these creatures out of their houses? There are many ways that animal liberationists can counter these arguments. Peter Singer's stance is one such way, although the line between 'persons' and 'non-persons' does seem difficult to draw. Others accept all the problems, and try to work out solutions. Some animal liberationists, for instance, accept plant rights as well. They may refuse to eat carrots (which involves killing a plant) but will eat tomatoes (because that is simply the fruit of a plant). Most other people have no patience with such fine distinctions, but seek for simpler answers.

Animal liberationists have tried to gain their ends by political and moral pressure. However, a fringe have gone much further than this. Laboratories have been raided and smashed, animals have been freed, and researchers have been threatened and attacked. Of course, the more respectable people in the movement have opposed this extremism. In response, scientists have developed powerful pressure-groups, to argue their case strongly (Blum 1994).

It seems unlikely that this dispute will disappear, or be solved by some sort of compromise. The differences are deep and philosophical, and the stakes are high. For scientists and their supporters, animal experimentation is a vital way of gaining knowledge, and may well benefit humanity greatly in the future. For their opponents, each experiment is an outrage equivalent to torturing a human being. No comprehensive solution is in sight, but scientists are already doing some obvious things to minimise the conflict. In general, experiments on animals in Western countries are now examined by ethics committees, to assess their justification and to make sure that any suffering is minimised. However, it is certain that this issue will continue to pose profound problems for many years to come.

Rights and wrongs in scientific work

So far, this chapter has dealt with major and spectacular controversies in science. Since there are millions of scientists in the world, and only a small number of major controversies, it is unlikely that most scientists have anything to do with them. However, at the day-to-day level, ethical problems still arise. In this section, we will look at some of the most common, and see what usually happens.

As we saw in Chapter 1, a majority of scientists world-wide work in commercial organisations, and we shall consider some of the ethics there shortly. Some of the most spectacular problems arise in academic science. This is the most studied area, and is a good place to start. In principle, academic science is a self-regulating professional system. Scientists produce knowledge and, if it is acceptable to journal referees, it is published. Once a scientist has a sufficient record of published papers, promotion and other forms of recognition will be awarded. The reality, of course, is less clear. Science is a career, and ambitious people are tempted to cut corners and perhaps behave improperly to achieve success. Let us look at some of the ways in which this can happen.

Fraud

There is a constant temptation on the part of scientists to claim results which were in fact not produced by experiments. This can happen if a cherished theory is not supported by evidence, or when someone is under such pressure—with a job at stake—that she feels she has no choice. The example of William Summerlin (Broad and Wade 1985:153) is a good example. Summerlin seemed to have made a break-through in research on the transplanting of organs. His boss, a hard-driving researcher, trumpeted his results across the nation, but Summerlin was unable to produce the results expected. Eventually he crudely faked results, and was caught.

More disturbing are cases such as those of John Spector and John Darsee (Broad and Wade 1985:63, 13). In both cases these young researchers built up huge lists of publications, and seemed set for brilliant careers in science. Spector, at Cornell University, was known as a brilliant experimentalist, and appeared to be discovering a mechanism by which cancers worked. Darsee published nearly 100 papers and abstracts in a year at Harvard University. However, fellow researchers became suspicious of their high productivity, and eventually, after extensive investigation and controversy, both researchers lost their jobs.

Ethically, there is little doubt that scientific fraud is unacceptable. However, an important point emerges from reading these cases: it is very hard to bring a scientific fraud to book. In many cases, it required sustained efforts by a whistleblower before anyone took any notice.

Plagiarism

Plagiarism is the taking of work—and credit for that work—from its rightful owner. Sometimes this is simple theft, sometimes it is more like extortion. As an example of the former, consider the case of Helena Wachslicht-Rodbard. This young researcher wrote a paper and submitted it to an important journal. After a reasonable interval, comments came back from referees indicating that, with some revisions, the paper might be acceptable (Broad and Wade 1985:161).

Dr Wachslicht-Rodbard was revising the paper when another paper in a journal caught her eye. Whole sections of her paper, her data and even her ways of phrasing things, had been taken and published elsewhere. Naturally, she complained, but it took months of badgering senior scientists before anything was done. One of the reasons for this was the standing of the authors. One, Vijay Soman, was a young researcher, but the other, Philip Felig, was a professor at Yale University Medical School, and a major scientist.

It took months of effort from Helena Wachslicht-Rodbard before the truth finally came out. The younger scientist, Soman, had written the paper based on Wachslicht-Rodbard's data, and Felig knew very little about it. His name was added because of their working relationship. This is termed 'honorary authorship', and is also counted as dishonesty in science, though many people do not regard it as serious. Soman left his job, and Felig lost a good deal of prestige through the incident. Perhaps the worst sufferer was the victim. Helena Wachslicht-Rodbard lost all interest in doing science, and left the profession.

Plagiarism can also take the form of extortion. Imagine a junior research worker—perhaps a research assistant—who has done all the work for a paper. If that research assistant suddenly finds that her boss has put himself as senior author on the paper, claiming credit which is not his, what can she do about it? Her contract may expire at the end of the year, and her boss will not renew it if she makes a fuss. According to some observers, this sort of unfairness is quite common in science, as scientists try to carve out reputations for themselves as first-rate researchers (Manwell and Baker 1981).

Other doubtful activities: the grey areas

It is not clear exactly where the boundaries of good and bad science are. In this section we will look at a few questionable types of behaviour. Some scientists regard these as wrong, others as perfectly acceptable. Imagine a scientist has done a series of experiments. Out of fifteen results, fourteen make good sense. The fifteenth is an odd result which makes no sense. This sort of thing is fairly common in science. Equipment can be unreliable, and the scientist is often looking for effects right at the limits of what can be seen. What can be done? Many scientists would simply drop the strange result, and act as though there were only fourteen experiments. Others would regard this as fraud, and insist on including the extra result, even if it made an otherwise good paper less convincing (Bridgstock 1993). What do you think?

As we have seen, scientists desperately need money to buy equipment, hire assistants and the like. If no money is available, laboratories will grind to a halt. Therefore, scientists develop skills and tricks to get money from the research organisations. One such trick is this: by putting in extra effort, get ahead of where the grant-giving organisation thinks you are by a whole series of experiments. You can then apply for money to do research which has already been done.

This strange-sounding procedure has huge advantages. You can give up-to-date progress reports on your research, and you can positively guarantee that, at the end of the project, there will be results to report. Meanwhile, of course, the money is being used to do still other research, so that the process can be repeated. As a result, the researcher is assured of a supply of funds, and the funding organisation is happy (if ignorant) because it is getting results for the money. On the other hand, this tactic is essentially dishonest, and unfair to other researchers who do not have a series of experiments up their sleeves (Bridgstock 1993).

Many other tricks and stratagems are used in science. Their details are not important: the aim always is to further the scientists' career, and to give some security in a difficult, uncertain profession. Who decides whether these tricks are acceptable? In theory, other scientists do. In reality, until recently, nobody seemed to worry too much! As we have seen, it was difficult to bring to light cases of quite blatant fraud. How much harder would it be if the misconduct was of such slight character that many people would not worry about it anyway! It follows that there is a broad grey area in science: many things are unclear.

Rights and wrongs in commercial science

Producing the 'right' results

The situation in industrial science—where most scientists work, worldwide—is even less clear. Of course, the ultimate aim of all science in business is to help the company commercially. If research promises to make profits for the company, money will be provided to do it. If not, then it will not. It follows that, in business, there may be pressure upon scientists to produce certain results, and dire consequences if the results are not produced.

What sort of pressures are these? Imagine firms which have to do research on the safety of their own products: drug makers are the obvious examples, but also car manufacturers, children's clothing makers (for fire safety standards) and many others. The makers of these products are legally required to make safety tests on their products. If the products don't pass the safety tests, they cannot be marketed. At the least, expensive modifications may have to be made.

The expenditure involved in bringing a product to market is awesome. For example, in the drug industry, it costs about $US100 million (about $A133 million) to bring a new drug to the market. That is a lot of money to lose if the safety tests don't work out! It is no wonder that, in some branches of industry, scientists have been told to produce the required results. Sometimes this is not done directly. Scientists do the safety tests and arrive at unsatisfactory results. They write a report and submit it to management. The report is returned with a statement that it is unsatisfactory and the research must be done again. Nothing is actually said, but the hint is fairly strong.

It might look as if there is a fairly simple answer to this. Have independent companies or researchers do the safety tests. However, it is not that simple. In drug research, the independent companies or researchers may be partly reliant upon the drug companies for funds. Thus, there is a pressure upon the testing scientists to produce the 'right' results, just as there was pressure upon the scientists within the firm to do so. This has caused major scientific scandals (e.g. Bell 1992:194).

Circulation of information

There are many other areas in which commercial scientists may feel pressure to break rules, just as there are in academic science. We shall look at one other important one: the question of whether to break confidentiality. It was clear in Chapter 3 that corporations and business firms use scientific knowledge to make money. It follows that they will want to keep useful information to themselves.

Clearly, commercial secrecy is an important feature of science in industry. It extends far beyond simply not telling other people about industrial secrets. It also means keeping quiet about research projects which were not successful. After all, if a company has spent money finding that a certain avenue of research is not useful, why should it save other firms that same expense? Thus, firms tend to impose a blanket ban upon communication with other corporations.

However, business firms do find it advantageous to keep an eye on what their rivals are doing. They get access to their patents, and buy and take apart their new products to see how they work. As we saw in Chapter 2, this latter practice is called reverse engineering. It is not an attractive feature of the modern world, but it is not illegal, and not clearly unethical.

Another way that information travels around is, simply, in people. Scientists and engineers move from firm to firm seeking better work. Or they may be retrenched from one firm and go to work for another. In these cases, of course, they carry all the knowledge from their previous jobs with them.

Managers are very aware of how much they may lose through employees switching jobs. Virtually all firms have non-disclosure agreements, which employees sign when they are hired. In addition, as soon as an employee is fired, or resigns, access to the firm is cut off. Often the former employee cannot get into the company buildings, but has to wait outside while personal effects are brought out. Despite all this, there is no doubt that information is passed around through people changing jobs. Of course, once a person starts with a new company, any previous loyalties may be forgotten. Some firms make it quite clear that they expect a new employee to talk about anything which has been done in the previous job. Others expect hints. The ethics of carrying information in this way, or expecting it to be carried, have been discussed a good deal, with no clear outcome (Hughson and Kohn 1980).

Things can become much more devious, as managers seek to discover what their competitors are doing. It has been known for a 'disgruntled employee' to leave one firm, and to seek employment with another. She then becomes a mine of information for the new firm, telling them about her previous employer's plans, secret findings and new developments. After the new employer has invested much time and money in the new areas, the employee quits: she was a plant all the time, sent to mislead the new firm (Rogers 1982).

Another method through which information is acquired is sometimes illegal: industrial espionage. People can be hired to acquire information about rivals' plans. It may be as simple as photographing their factories, to see what can be gleaned from the buildings they are putting up. Or it may be profoundly illegal, involving break-ins, theft of computer disks and telephone tapping. There is no doubt that huge amounts of this—thoroughly illegal—work does go on.

Codes of conduct, enforcement and whistleblowing

Scientists, and people concerned with science, have been aware of these problems for many years. A key question is, what to do about it? Clearly, relying on people's consciences will not work. Several steps suggest themselves. As we will see, these steps may help, but there is no chance of ensuring that science will always be carried out in an ethically correct fashion. A first, obvious step is for scientists to have some sort of an ethical code, which spells out exactly what is acceptable and unacceptable conduct. Several codes of this kind exist, and two are in an appendix at the end of this chapter.

Without doubt, some of the provisions of these codes clarify matters. For instance, the prohibition upon deceiving subjects, or keeping them in ignorance, seems to rule out the Tuskegee project and the National Women's Hospital case completely. It should also make us think carefully about the Milgram experiment. However, while the codes help, they do not sort the matter out completely.

One problem is simply this: who enforces the codes? Other professions solve this problem directly. For example, in medicine there is a court which hears complaints against doctors. The court—usually called a tribunal—has the power to admonish doctors (tell them off), fine them, or prevent them from working as doctors. This happens because, by law, professions such as doctors and lawyers can work only if they are on a list of approved practitioners. Since the court can strike them off the list, it has real power.

No such list exists in the case of scientists. Scientists work for a whole range of organisations, including universities, government organisations and businesses. There is no approved list of practitioners. Typically each sort of organisation has its own disciplinary proceedings and its own rules—if any—for what is right and wrong. Thus, a scientist who has been sacked from a university might be hired by a business firm and continue to work as a scientist.

In contrast to the ethical systems in medicine and law, the scientific system is patchy and sometimes does not work at all. Scientists who behave unethically may be called to account—by their employers or the grant-awarding bodies—or they may not. It depends upon the circumstances. In addition, as we have seen, in many cases it is whole organisations, not individual scientists, who go off the ethical rails. The Tuskegee project shows a whole organisation behaving badly over many decades.

One good idea is to ensure that people who blow the whistle on ethical breaches are not penalised. In many parts of the world, laws are now in effect which shield whistleblowers from retaliation, so that employers cannot victimise or harass people who have revealed unpleasant things which have been going on. One other point is also worth noting. It is not enough to set up an ethical code and leave it: science is constantly changing, and the changes often call for constant revisions to the ethical code. For example, a century ago most science was carried out by individual scientists, and little money was involved. Now science is often carried out by large teams, with many technical assistants and vast sums of money. Thus, it is clear that ethical codes should be under constant review, and there should be processes of updating them as science changes and new ethical problems appear.

Summary and conclusion

Let us begin with one or two simple facts. Scientists have, alas, been involved in some actions this century which, by any reasonable standards, are quite wrong. It was criminal and wicked for Josef Mengele and the Nazi scientists to torture unwilling victims in the Nazi concentration camps. It was also clearly wrong for the doctors involved in the Tuskegee project to keep people in ignorance of their illness, and even more so to prevent them from receiving treatment.

Stanley Milgram's obedience experiments are interesting for two different reasons. They can be argued about on ethical grounds. Milgram had to deceive his subjects to make the experiment work, and there is no doubt that the experiments did cause emotional suffering to many people. The experiments are also interesting because they throw some light on how people can behave as they did in the Nazi and Tuskegee experiments. There is, in most people, a strong streak of obedience, a willingness to go along with authority, even if that authority is pressing for something which is ethically wrong. We should bear this in mind when we are thinking about how to stop unethical behaviour.

Human experimentation is one area where feelings run high, and where different ways of thinking clash. We saw this clearly in the case of Dr Pozos's dilemma; should he use data from the Nazi experiments? Apart from questions about how credible the evidence is, the moral question remains. As we saw, a utilitarian viewpoint enables one to argue about the benefits and costs of using the data. On the other hand, deontological viewpoints may be simply incomprehensible to each other.

Apart from human experimentation, the area which raises the most questions is that of animal experiments. As we saw, feelings run high between scientists arguing for the necessity of animal experiments and animal rights groups, who believe that animals do have rights and that experiments violate these rights. This gap can be at least partly closed by careful ethical supervision of all experiments.

Bearing Milgram's experiments in mind, it is easy to see why people rarely blow the whistle, and often suffer badly for their courage when they do. Something can be done about this. First, in every area where ethical questions may arise, there should be codes of practice, so that scientists can find out what they should and should not do. Second, there should be clear-cut procedures by which whistleblowers can raise issues of concern.

Further reading

It would be helpful to read at least one account of a scientific scandal, to fully understand exactly what happened. The reader by Caplan (1992) has a number of powerful pieces in it. Harris's book, about the similar atrocities which took place in Manchuria during the Japanese occupation, despite its lurid title, is a thoughtful, carefully written scholarly work (Harris 1994). The account by Jones (1981) of the Tuskegee scandal is also well worth reading. The book by McNeill

(1993) is perhaps the best on the topic of human experimentation: it discusses some cases, and also the safeguards in various countries. A good discussion of ethics in the social sciences comes from Homan (1991). Regarding matters of fraud and plagiarism in science, there is no one best work. The book by Broad and Wade (1985) is sensationalist, and questions most of the prevailing assumptions about how the scientific community works. The book by Bell (1992) concentrates upon the interface between science and politics, and the consequent misconduct which may arise. By contrast, the work of Crossen (1994) focuses upon sponsorship of research, and the 'manufactured truth' which may emerge.

References

Bell, R. (1992), *Impure Science.* New York: John Wiley and Sons.

Berger, Robert L. (1992), 'Comments on the Validation of the Dachau Human Hypothermia Experiments', in Caplan (1992): 109–33.

Blum, D. (1994), *The Monkey Wars.* New York: Oxford University Press.

Bridgstock, Martin (1993), 'What is Scientific Misconduct?', *Search*, 24:73–6.

Broad, William, and Wade, Nicholas (1985), *Betrayers of the Truth.* New York: Simon and Schuster.

Caplan, Arthur L. (ed.) (1992), *When Medicine Went Mad: Bioethics and the Holocaust.* Totowa, N.J.: Humana Press.

Cartwright, S. (1988), *The Report of the Committee of Inquiry into Allegations concerning the Treatment of Cervical Cancer at National Women's Hospital and into other Related Matters.* Auckland: Government Printing Office.

Coney, Sandra (1988), *The Unfortunate Experiment.* Harmondsworth: Penguin.

Coney, Sandra, and Bunkle, Phillida (1987), 'An Unfortunate Experiment at National Women's', *Metro*, June: 46–65.

Crossen, C. (1994), *Tainted Truth.* New York: Simon and Schuster.

Harris, S. (1994), *Factories of Death.* London: Routledge.

Homan, R. (1991), *The Ethics of Social Research.* London: Longman.

Hughson, R. V., and Kohn, P. M. (1980), 'Ethics', *Chemical Engineering*, 22 September: 132–47.

Jones, James H. (1981), *Bad Blood: The Tuskegee Syphilis Experiment.* New York: Free Press.

Katz, J. (1992), 'Abuse of Human Beings for the Sake of Science', in Caplan (1992): 235–70.

Kor, Eva Mozes (1992), 'Nazi Experiments as Viewed by a Survivor of Mengele's Experiments', in Caplan (1992): 3–8.

Manwell, C., and Baker, C. M. A. (1981), 'Honesty in Science', *Search*, 12, 6: 151–60.

Merton, R. K. (1973), *The Sociology of Science: Theoretical and Empirical Investigations.* Chicago: University of Chicago Press.

McIndoe, W. A., McLean, M. R., Jones, R. W., and Mullins P. (1984), 'The Invasive Potential of Carcinoma in Situ of the Cervix', *Obstetrics and Gynaecology*, 64:158–62.

McNeill, Paul M. (1993), *The Ethics and Politics of Human Experimentation.* Cambridge: Cambridge University Press.

Milgram, Stanley (1970), 'Obedience to Authority', in L. Hudson (ed.) *The Ecology of Human Intelligence.* Harmondsworth: Penguin: 284–300.

Milgram, Stanley (1974), *Obedience to Authority*. London: Tavistock.
Nuremberg Code (1949), 'The Nuremberg Code' in *Trials of War Criminals before the Nuremberg Military Tribunal under Control Law No. 10*, vol. 2. Washington, D.C.: US Government Printing Office: 181–2.
Pozos, Robert S. (1992), 'Scientific Inquiry and Ethics: The Dachau Data', in Caplan (1992): 95–108.
Rogers, E. (1982), 'Information Exchange and Technological Innovation', in D. Sahal (ed.), *The Transfer and Utilization of Technical Knowledge*, Lexington, Mass.: D. C. Heath and Co.
Singer, Peter (1975), *Animal Liberation*. New York: New York Review.
Singer, Peter (1993), *Practical Ethics*, 2nd edn. Cambridge: Cambridge University Press.
Vigorito, Sara Seiler (1992), 'A Profile of Nazi Medicine', in Caplan (1992): 9–13.

Appendixes

Below are printed two ethical codes, from widely differing bodies. The first, the Nuremberg Code, was formulated soon after World War II, largely in response to the atrocities which had been committed. Naturally, it laid heavy stress upon human experimentation. Homan (1991) discussed some of the weaknesses of this code.

The second code is from the by-laws of the Royal Australian Chemical Institute. Since many chemists work in industry, and almost none do experiments upon people, it is far more concerned with proper conduct towards clients, employers and the general public.

The Nuremberg Code (1949)

1. The voluntary consent of the human subject is absolutely essential. This means that the person involved should have legal capacity to give consent; should be so situated as to be able to exercise free power of choice, without the intervention of any element of force, fraud, deceit, duress, overreaching, or other ulterior form of constraint or coercion; and should have sufficient knowledge and comprehension of the elements of the subject matter to enable him to make an understanding and enlightened decision. This latter element requires that before the acceptance of an affirmative decision by the experimental subject there should be made known to him the nature, duration and purpose of the experiment; the method and means by which it is to be conducted; all inconveniences and hazards reasonably to be expected; and the effects upon his health or person which may possibly come from his participation in the experiment.
    The duty and responsibility for ascertaining the quality of the consent rests upon each individual who initiates, directs or engages in the experiment. It is a personal duty and responsibility which may not be delegated to another with impunity.
2. The experiment should be such as to yield fruitful results for the good of society, unprocurable by other methods or means of study, and not random and unnecessary in nature.
3. The experiment should be designed and based on the results of animal experimentation and a knowledge of the natural history of the disease or other problem under study that the anticipated results will justify the performance of the experiment.

4. The experiment should be so conducted as to avoid all unnecessary physical and mental suffering and injury.
5. No experiment should be conducted where there is an *a priori* reason to believe that death or disabling injury will occur except, perhaps, in those experiments where the experimental physicians also serve as subject.
6. The degree of risk to be taken should never exceed that determined by the humanitarian importance of the problem to be solved by the experiment.
7. Proper preparations should be made and adequate facilities provided to protect the experimental subject against even remote possibilities of injury, disability, or death.
8. The experiment should be conducted only by scientifically qualified persons. The highest degree of skill and care should be required throughout all stages of the experiment of those who conduct or engage in the experiment.
9. During the course of the experiment the human subject should be at liberty to bring the experiment to an end if he has reached the physical or mental state where continuation of the experiment seems to him to be impossible.
10. During the course of the experiment the scientist in change must be prepared to terminate the experiment at any stage, if he has probable cause to believe, in the exercise of the good faith, superior skill and careful judgement required of him that continuation of the experiment is likely to result in injury, disability or death to the experimental subject.

Code of ethics of the Royal Australian Chemical Institute
(By-laws 1994, no. 26)

All Corporate and Associate members of the Institute shall observe and be bound by the following Code of Ethics.

26.1 A member shall endeavour to advance the profession of chemistry. However, notwithstanding this or any other By-law, the responsibility for the welfare, health and safety of the community shall at all times take precedence.
26.2 A member shall not except in circumstances establishing privileges at law make disparaging remarks or unwarranted comments about other members, nor shall s/he make any public statement purporting to be the policy of the Institute when such is not the case.
26.3 Reasonable criticism of a member's conduct or views at any meeting of the Institute, or at a council Meeting or at a Committee of the Institute shall be privileged.
26.4 A member may advertise her/his professional services but must include her/his grade of membership.
26.5 A member shall not use any unfair, improper or questionable method of securing professional work or advancement.
26.6 A member shall issue or publish only such reports or statements as are an accurate record of soundly based observation and experiment and of logical deductions therefrom.
26.7 A member shall not allow her/his name to be associated with a misleading advertisement nor with a statement which makes an unfair comparison between one product and another.
26.8 A member shall at all times avoid placing her/himself under any obligation to any person or firm in whose dealing with his/her employer or client s/he may be concerned.

26.9   A member shall inform her/his employer or client if circumstances arise in which her/his judgement or advice may be called in question by reason of business connections, personal relationships, interests or affiliations.

26.10   A member shall not receive, either directly or indirectly, any royalty, gratuity or commission in respect of any patented or protected article or process used in any work, with the design or supervision of which s/he may be connected, unless s/he shall have fully disclosed the fact, in writing, to her/his employer or client.

26.11   A member shall not use for her/his personal gain or advantage, nor shall s/he disclose, confidential information which s/he may acquire as a result of special opportunities arising out of work done for her/his client or employer.

26.12   A member shall inform her/his employer or client when, in her/his opinion the advice of a specialist or expert is desirable.

26.13   A member shall afford to those under her/his direction every reasonable opportunity to advance their knowledge and experience, and shall ensure that proper credit is given to each subordinate for work which has been performed by her/him.

26.14   A member whose certificate or report is published without her/his consent or is published with words omitted or is published in a form which makes it unethical should take steps to have the situation corrected.

26.15   A member shall not use in any estimate, report, testimony or other statement in connection with the promotion of a business enterprise any exaggerated, irrelevant or merely laudatory expression or any speculative opinion or forecast.

26.16   A member shall not be involved with harassment of another person in the course of professional activities, shall not condone such behaviour in a colleague or permit such behaviour by a subordinate.

26.17   A member shall not discriminate against another person by way of age, sex, race, religious belief, sexual preference, cultural or ethnic background in the course of professional activities, shall not condone such behaviour in a colleague or permit such behaviour in a subordinate.

CHAPTER 5

Controversies Regarding Science and Technology

Martin Bridgstock

Controversy is a normal and natural part of human existence, and also of science. If science is to advance at all, new theories and findings must be put forward, and older ones discarded. This often produces controversy, especially if the proponents of outdated findings and theories are still active. Therefore, how science handles controversies is an important aspect of how science actually works.

Conflict within science is inevitable, but so too is conflict in the larger community. Furthermore, an increasing number of these larger controversies involve science and technology. If an airport or freeway is to be built or expanded, questions arise about the science and technology involved: what construction techniques will be used, is there danger to anyone, is there pollution, and so on.

In this chapter, we shall review the different types of controversy, both within science and in the larger community, and also acquire some useful ideas which throw light on them. As part of this process, we shall look at two different controversies in some detail, examining the course they took, and the reasons why they worked out as they did. One of these controversies—continental drift—took place purely within science. The other—the New Zealand cervical cancer scandal—involved both science and medical technology, but took place primarily in the larger community.

Purely scientific controversies

The most straightforward type of controversy is the purely scientific one (Giere 1987). These are controversies in which only scientists take part, and the issues over which they disagree are completely scientific. Even so, there are several different types, and many factors influence how they turn out. McMullin (1987) argues that there are three main types of purely scientific controversy: they concern findings, theories, and principles.

The most basic controversy in science occurs over findings, or evidence. In this case, the results of scientific investigation are argued over. Did a certain scientist obtain a given result, or was she mistaken? Although the average scientific paper is referred to only once or twice (Hamilton 1991), important results receive concentrated attention. The reason for this is fairly obvious: surprising results may have implications that determine which theories are accepted, and so change the nature of knowledge in the field. Therefore, when important results are published by scientists, others often rush to replicate—to repeat—the original work.

A famous example of a controversy over findings in recent years was that over 'cold fusion'. Two scientists, Pons and Fleischmann, claimed that with relatively simple apparatus they had succeeded in fusing elements together in the laboratory without the enormous releases of energy predicted by theory (Close 1990). Scientists rushed to replicate their experiments. Results were mixed. A majority of scientists could not reproduce the claimed results, but a few reported that they had done so. After an untidy disagreement—much of it taking place over the Internet—the scientific consensus was that Fleischmann and Pons had not produced cold fusion. However, a minority of scientists continues to argue that they were successful (Close 1990).

It is reasonable to ask why replication is such a difficult and uncertain business. Why cannot the experiment simply be repeated exactly and everyone agree? Sociologist Harry Collins, well before the cold fusion uproar, studied a similar controversy in detail, and came up with some illuminating findings. Collins (1975; 1981) interviewed scientists who were involved in the 'gravity waves' controversy. Joseph Weber, a scientist at the University of Maryland, claimed to have detected, using fairly simple apparatus, the fundamental waves by which gravitational attraction is propagated. A number of other scientists set out to replicate this claim: according to current theory, the original apparatus should have been far too insensitive to make any such discovery.

Collins found that 'exact' replication is almost impossible to achieve. No scientific report can possibly encompass all the complexities and difficulties of doing an experiment. Inevitably, therefore, scientists differ on what counts as a relevant factor in doing an experiment. In addition it is natural for scientists to improve the apparatus, according to their own ideas, to make it more reliable and sensitive. In consequence, no two sets of apparatus were exactly the same. So, when replicating scientists did not find the same results as Weber, a controversy erupted over whether they had, in fact, replicated the work at all. Argument bogged down into details, with people disagreeing on what it all meant.

A useful picture of science

Sociologists of science have come up with several useful terms which help to understand how science works, and how controversies arise. One such idea is that of Stephen Cole (1992), who distinguished between 'core' and 'frontier' scientific knowledge. He defined the core—accepted scientific knowledge—like this:

> The core consists of a small set of theories, analytic techniques and facts which represent the given at any particular time. ... The core is the starting point, the knowledge which people take as a given from which new knowledge will be produced. Generally the core of a research area contains a relatively small number of theories, on which there is substantial consensus. [Cole 1992:15]

'Core' scientific knowledge is passed on to students in schools and universities. The other term Cole uses is 'frontier', and he describes it this way:

> [the frontier] consists of all the work currently being produced by all active researchers in a given discipline. The research frontier is where all new knowledge is produced. Most observers of science agree that the crucial variable differentiating core and frontier knowledge is the presence or absence of consensus. [Cole 1992:15]

For knowledge to get from the frontier to the core, there must be a consensus among scientists that it is true, and it must also be accepted as important. To Cole's description, this author suggests that one more term should be added: the scientific scrap-heap. Some theories in science—flat Earth, alchemy, astrology and others—were once accepted, but are now rejected by virtually all scientists. A new theory, therefore, originates in the frontier, and may either succeed and go into the core, or fail and be relegated to the scrap-heap. We should note, though, that the scientific scrap-heap resembles other scrap-heaps: occasionally something useful is found there.

If controversies over evidence are complicated, then the second type, those over theories, are doubly so. Resolution of theoretical disputes is very hard indeed. Theories are the essence of science; they are general statements, based upon evidence, which are used to predict further findings, and also, when well established, may be used in practical ways in the world. For example, Pasteur's theory of germs

(Vallery-Radot 1960) enabled him to prescribe conditions for preventing infections in hospitals, and also to vaccinate humans and animals against disease. A controversy over theory arises when two—or more— different theories are held by scientists, each purporting to explain the evidence. Theories go well beyond evidence, however: they often lead to predictions.

Perhaps the archetypal theoretical battle—though it was more than that—was the historic confrontation between Galileo and the Catholic Church over whether the Sun went round the Earth, or the Earth round the Sun. This came to a head in 1633 when Galileo was forced to renounce the view that the Earth moved. More recently, after much argument, Darwin's theory of evolution was accepted over theories about creation, and the Big Bang theory was accepted in preference to the 'steady-state' theory of how the universe began.

Arguments over theory are complex because they go beyond the question of which theory best fits an agreed body of evidence. Typically, in controversies of this kind, scientists do not merely argue whether the theories fit the evidence. They also work hard at producing new evidence, and attack the evidence, both new and old, produced by people with whom they disagree. As a consequence, a debate over scientific theories may well have all the complications of a debate over evidence, and will also have a different level entirely, as the merits of the rival theories are argued out. We shall look at one of the most famous controversies over scientific theories shortly.

The third, and most difficult, type of controversy in science is when a disagreement arises over methods and principles. In a sense, controversies over evidence and theory are simply the normal way that science operates. However, if scientists are disagreeing over the very way that science operates, then it is a sign that a crisis is occurring. For instance, an important disagreement over principle occurred when Isaac Newton put forward perhaps the greatest scientific work of all time—the *Principia*, or *Mathematical Principles of Natural Philosophy*, to give the full title in English. Opponents in the scientific community argued that Newton's law of gravitational attraction was unacceptable, because it posited action at a distance (McMullin 1987). We are so used to Newton's law now that it takes a few moments' thought to see just how powerful this objection is. How can the Sun, say, exert such a powerful pull upon the Earth when there is absolutely nothing connecting them? For many years this was advanced as an objection to Newton's laws, and the matter was not fully resolved until Einstein's work appeared.

In the twentieth century, Einstein was opposed to one of the central ideas of quantum physics, namely, that the basic patterns in nature are founded upon probability and can never be known with certainty. This seems to leave our understanding in an 'incomplete' state. He was never able to accept this, despite the powerful predictions of the theory. To Einstein, the very principle of a probabilistic universe was abhorrent, and he exclaimed 'God does not play dice!'

In terms of the core-and-frontier model of science, we may regard controversies over theories as arguments over which theories are promoted into the core of science. Controversies over scientific principles are arguments about the location of the boundaries of science—frontier and core. It seems true to say that the social sciences—sociology, politics and psychology, for example—have more crises of principle than do the 'harder', natural sciences. There are many different ideas about exactly what human beings are, and what affects the way they act, and this affects the range of theories which are put forward.

Resolving scientific controversies

As well as outlining the three types of scientific controversy, McMullin has suggested that there are three ways in which scientific controversies can be closed. The most common method of closure—and the healthiest—is by the process of resolution. When this occurs, scientists come to a consensus over the status of evidence or theories, and proceed to further study. In terms of Cole's view, we can say that, if it is a theoretical controversy, then one theory will probably enter the realm of core science, while another will be cast out onto the scrap-heap. Of course, there is nothing permanent about these decisions. As we shall see, the theory of continental drift came close to being cast on the scientific scrap-heap, only to return in a different form and enter the scientific core.

McMullin's second form of 'closure' is not well named. It happens through some form of force or pressure. Scientists are not left to work out an issue for themselves, but are subject to political interference by outside forces. Perhaps the best-known case of this happening is the infamous Lysenko affair in the Soviet Union. A plant biologist named Lysenko disputed, among other things, the existence of genes and the process of evolution. His work was not highly regarded among Soviet scientists—let alone those in the rest of the world—but he had one key supporter, the dictator Stalin. Through political pressure, the scientific 'dispute' was resolved in Lysenko's favour, and Soviet agricultural science was badly damaged for many years (Medvedev 1978).

It is worth pointing out that the effects of political interference were absolutely disastrous, but did not last. In general, when political dictators become involved in science, the result is damage to scientific knowledge in the short term. Once science is allowed to resume its

normal activity, the damage is repaired. It was slow in the case of the
Soviet Union, but eventually the advantages of normal scientific theories
were accepted.

Finally, in some cases, a dispute may simply be abandoned by scientists. The controversy mentioned above over 'action at a distance' as
involved in Newton's laws simmered for many years. However, there
seemed no point in pursuing it. Newton's laws were gradually accepted
as being valuable in explaining the movement of physical bodies, and
there seemed no advantage to be gained in arguing on and on about
action at a distance. As an illustration of a purely scientific controversy,
we now examine in detail one of the famous developments of the
twentieth century, the question of the acceptability of continental drift
theory.

Continental drift: a purely scientific controversy

In several ways, the debate over continental drift was most unusual
among scientific controversies. First, continental drift concerned the
basic features of the Earth. How exactly did the continents get to their
present positions, and why are they there? What forces mould the
Earth's features, and what is likely to happen in the future? These are
important questions, with implications far beyond the opinions of a
group of scientists.

Second, the arguments over continental drift took a long time to
settle. They began with an article written by Alfred Wegener in 1912,
and the issue was not settled until about 1966, when the modern theory
of plate tectonics won near-universal assent. Surprisingly, despite the
obvious importance of the question, the continental drift debate was
purely a scientific one. There were no commercial or political interests
involved. Scientists put forward the theories, did the research, and
argued about the results until a conclusion was reached. Their goal was
not to make money, to launch new products or to push a particular
political view. The aim was to explain how the Earth came to be as it is.

In this section, we shall examine the debate over the question of
whether continents move about the Earth. We shall briefly review the
arguments, theories and evidence and see what clues they give about
how science itself works.

Wegener and his theory

Alfred Wegener (1880–1930) was both a scientist and an adventurer.
He was, mostly, a meteorologist and spent much time in Greenland
making weather observations. He also crossed the Arctic ice cap.

Wegener packed much accomplishment into his short life—he died in Greenland when he was only fifty. However, he is best remembered for his idea of continental drift. This idea, for years after his death, seemed doomed to the scientific scrap-heap.

By his own account, Wegener was first alerted to the possibility that the continents might have moved by a simple observation, one that many of us have made. He looked at a map of the world, and noticed that South America and Africa seem to fit together, almost like pieces of a jigsaw puzzle. This suggested to him, not only that the continents had moved, but that at some stage they had all been united in one super-continent, which he called Pangaea.

Wegener's idea was not original. Several scientists and scholars had mentioned this possibility before him. However, Wegener was the first to carry the idea to the next step. He collected a mass of evidence supporting his theory, and published it, first in an article in 1912 and then in a book, *The Origin of the Continents and Oceans*, published in 1915. Wegener's breadth of experience stood him in good stead in his work. He was able to collect a mass of material from different scientific fields, all pointing to the idea that the continents, over hundreds of millions of years, had moved. From geography came the simplest and most obvious evidence: the continents can be made to fit into each other reasonably well. Wegener also pointed out that most of the large mountain ranges are on the edge of continents (look at the Andes and Rockies in South and North America, the Great Dividing Range in Australia, or the Atlas mountains in Africa). These, Wegener argued, were piled up on the leading edges of continents, as they ploughed through the ocean floors (Frankel 1987).

There is a problem with the mountain ranges, though. The largest mountain range of all, the Himalayas, is not near the coast of a continent. It is cut off from the sea by the sub-continent of India. Wegener turned this to his advantage. He argued that originally India had been separate from Asia. However, moving north at the rate of several centimetres per year, it had crashed into Asia. The greatest mountain range on Earth, he argued, was the result of a continent-sized collision.

Wegener pointed to geological layers in different continents, which fit together as nicely as the continents. He argued that mountain ranges in South America would be continuations of African ones if the con-tinents were side by side. He also used biology to support his arguments. He drew attention to biological species which exist on corresponding parts of separated continents. For instance the primitive fern *glossopteris* exists in many scattered places in both Africa and Brazil, and these line up when the continents are fitted together.

A big question remains with all this. If we grant that there is evidence that the continents do move, what moves them? Wegener portrayed the continents as being like boats, forging through the 'sea' of the Earth's mantle, but this idea, more than any other, brought him criticism from other scientists. Wegener thought that two forces might contribute to the movement of the continents. One was the effect of tidal forces—the pull of the sun and moon. The other, which he called *pohlfluct* (pole-flight), consisted of centrifugal forces caused by the Earth's rotation.

This is not very convincing. The total effect of the two forces would be to position the continents around the Earth's equator, moving slowly in an easterly direction. Instead, only two continents straddle the equator, Africa and South America, with the others well north or south of it. Further, one continent, Antarctica, is as far from the equator as it is possible to be. Another problem, equally difficult, stems from geology. Compared to the rocks in the Earth's mantle, continental rocks are light and soft. Therefore, even if we accept that there is some motive power, how is it possible for the lighter, softer continental rocks to forge through the others?

A complicated series of debates ensued in different fields—geology, climatology and biology—between the 'drifters' and the 'fixists' as the supporters of the two points of view came to be known. In general, these debates favoured the fixists. In addition, the fixists had the advantage that theirs was the established theory. One scientist was quoted as saying, if Wegener were right, 'we must forget everything which has been learned in the last seventy years and start over again' (Weiner 1986:16).

This is not a blinkered or contemptible view. Scientists know that an established paradigm (see below) helps them to explain and understand a great deal of what they see. A great deal of effort has been invested in building the paradigm and establishing its credentials. Quite understandably, scientists are cautious about rejecting such a paradigm, especially if the proposed replacement seems to have marked weaknesses.

In 1943 George Gaylord Simpson, a distinguished palaeontologist, made a powerful onslaught upon the idea of drift. He pointed to errors made by drifters in their anxiety to show that similar biological forms existed on different continents. He also developed ideas about the mechanisms by which living things could have migrated from one continent to another. The case of Australia, with its marsupials, posed an especial problem for fixists. Simpson offered solutions based upon land bridges at different times (Frankel 1987:217–19). Despite replies by some drifters, Simpson—a towering authority in the field of palaeontology—seemed to have permanently closed the case for continental drift. And so it remained for about fifteen years, until results from quite different fields of research reopened the entire debate.

What can we say about science in this field, up to the time of Simpson's important work? Clearly, the theory of continental drift had not made its way into the core of scientific knowledge. Although its supporters, starting with Wegener himself, produced much evidence to support continental drift, the objections were too strong for it to be incorporated as a core theory. On the other hand, it was never completely rejected. It remained in the realm of frontier science, part-way between acceptance and rejection.

Simpson's powerful intervention came close to achieving closure in the field. This eminent scientist demonstrated unexpected weaknesses in the evidence and arguments produced by the drifters, and greatly strengthened the fixist case. As a result, continental drift was forced from its position in the scientific frontier, almost out onto the scientific scrap-heap. However, we should not fall into the trap of regarding the fixist scientists as either short-sighted or narrow-minded. With the knowledge of the time, it was perfectly rational to regard the continental drift theory as unproved, and even as being too flawed to merit serious attention. Scientific knowledge can only be as strong as the evidence currently available. As we shall see, new evidence transformed the position with remarkable speed.

Palaeomagnetism and marine geology: new evidence

The break-through for continental drift came quite unexpectedly. Two scientific fields having, apparently, nothing to do with Wegener's ideas produced results which brought the theory right into the core of scientific knowledge. One, marine geology, arose as a result of World War II. This great war prompted expansions in many fields of science. For example, the development of radar led to the field of radio astronomy, which has transformed our view of the universe. In the same way, the development of underwater detection devices such as sonar enabled scientists, after the war, to begin the exploration of the ocean bed.

The scientists were astounded at what they found. First, running down the centre of the Atlantic, and winding its way through tens of thousand of kilometres of ocean, is a range of mountains. This is perhaps the largest geological feature in the world, far larger than any land-based mountain range. Second, contrary to expectations, the researchers found that the sea-bed was not composed of old, settled rocks, but of relatively new ones, in a state of constant upheaval. Harry Hess, the best-known scientist in this new field, wondered if the mountain ridge was composed of new rocks, welling up from the ocean floor. The rocks on either side, he suggested, were spreading away from the swelling ridge in the middle. The implications of this were clear: if the ocean floor was spreading in this way, might this not provide a force to move the continents?

However, the case was not proved until a second field of science provided more powerful evidence. This was the field of palaeo-magnetism, the study of the history of the Earth's magnetic field. The two leaders in the field were S. K. Runcorn at Cambridge University, and P. M. S. Blackett at Imperial College, London. The logic of this field is fairly simple. Imagine lava from a volcano as it is expelled, and begins to harden. If the lava is cooling in a magnetic field, then particles in the lava will line up with that field, and eventually be fixed in that direction. If a geological column of such rock can be obtained, then the strength and direction of the Earth's magnetic field can be measured over hundreds of millions of years.

Neither Runcorn nor Blackett was initially interested in continental drift, but a student of Runcorn's, Irving, saw the connection at once. He had samples of rock from India obtained in 1961. India, as we have seen, is important geologically, since it is believed by drifters to have moved north and collided with Asia. Sure enough, having analysed the Indian rocks, Irving concluded that India must have moved, for the apparent position of the magnetic poles varied over the millions of years. Runcorn, his supervisor, did not agree. He argued that polar wandering could account for the differences in the magnetic field. As evidence accumulated, however, Runcorn changed his view and became a drifter.

Throughout the 1950s, ancient rock samples were collected from the continents of the world. All told of the changing direction of the magnetic field. More important, the direction in which the pole seemed to move varied from continent to continent. This point is vital. The evidence from India of a moving magnetic pole could be explained either by the continent moving, or the pole moving, or perhaps both. However, if several different continents give contradictory results about the pole's position, then there is no alternative: the continents themselves must have moved.

Of course, things were never this simple. Some rocks gave contra-dictory results, and a whole new set of statistical techniques had to be developed for analysing the data. And there were practical problems as well: how did one break off a rock sample for analysis without hitting it with a hammer, and so destroying its magnetic orientation (Frankel 1987:223)? For many years, the complexity, uncertainty and novelty of palaeomagnetism left fixists unconvinced.

It was the conjunction of the two new fields—marine geology and palaeomagnetism—which created a convincing case for continental drift. Geologists had known for many years that the Earth's magnetic field occasionally reverses itself, with the north pole becoming south and vice versa. Three geologists, Vine, Matthews and Morley, considered Harry Hess's hypothesis that the sea floor is spreading and made a suggestion. If lava was spreading out from the ocean ridges, they argued, then on each side of the ridge, one would expect to find stripes of ancient lava, polarised in one direction and then in the other alternately. Strong evidence was found to support this: magnetically, the floors of the oceans resemble a zebra's stripes.

Once it was accepted that the sea floor was spreading, most of the resistance to continental drift faded away, and by about 1966, closure had been achieved in favour of it. The most illustrious exponent of fixism, George Gaylord Simpson, wrote this in 1971:

> I now believe that continental drift did occur ... but direct fossil evidence is still curiously scanty or equivocal. ... the whole subject of plate tectonics is very exciting and has revivified geology. I think it is great. [Frankel 1987:231–2]

It is fair to say that closure is now complete, and the new version of continental drift, plate tectonics, is now part of the scientific core. It is accepted by virtually all scientists, and taught in schools and universities. On the other hand, it should be noted that plate tectonics is by no means the same as Wegener's original theory. In plate tectonics the prime movers are not the continents, but huge plates on the Earth's surface. The continents do not forge through the Earth's mantle, but are carried along passively on top of the plates. The plates, in their turn, are moved about by massive convection currents in the Earth's mantle. The theory of plate tectonics has also proved useful in explaining earthquakes and volcanoes. These tend to occur where plates are grinding into each other, causing shocks, stresses and breaks in the Earth's crust.

Conclusions about the continental drift controversy

The remarkable things about the continental drift controversy are its length, about sixty years from beginning to end, and the way that the theory recovered from rejection, largely because of unexpected developments in apparently unrelated fields. No outside interests were involved in the controversy—such as political or commercial interests —but it was still complicated. As we have seen, Simpson was able to show flaws in the methods and findings of the drift advocates, and the palaeomagnetists ran into trouble because of the complexity of their findings. Scientific controversies are often conducted in this way.

Different groupings of scientists produce evidence which tends to support their cause. They also criticise the evidence and methods produced by other scientists.

This behaviour is at odds with the normal idea of scientists being completely open-minded. However, many scientists are also amenable to a good, logical argument or to a convincing piece of evidence. Simpson, as we have seen, attacked continental drift, but enthusiastically accepted it when the evidence became stronger.

In McMullin's terms, we can say that closure was achieved by resolution: new evidence made the new theory tenable, and the older theories much less so. In addition, we can say that continental drift wandered about in the frontier area of science for more than sixty years, before it was accepted as part of the core of science.

We might note one further point, as we move into the area of broader controversies. At no time was there ever any consideration of compromise between the fixists and the drifters. Compromises are not normally possible in controversies over scientific theory. This is not because scientists are especially unyielding, but because of the nature of research. The overall goal of science is to discover the truth about the universe, and compromising is clearly not the best way to do this. In larger human affairs, by contrast, compromise is often the order of the day.

Technical controversies

Controversies of the continental drift type, involving purely scientific considerations, and only scientists, are very much the minority. For every argument that occurs within science, many occur about the effects of science and technology in the larger community. We will term these 'technical controversies', and in this section we shall look at the types of technical controversy which can occur, and examine some examples of each. Then we shall look at one in some detail.

The community at large is, of course, quite different from the scientific community, and so the types of controversy differ as well. The distinguished historian Dorothy Nelkin has listed four main types of technical controversy which can occur in the larger community (Nelkin 1984). These are not by any means exhaustive, but probably are the most common ones.

Efficiency versus equity

Nelkin's first type of controversy concerns the balance between efficiency and equity. In this kind of argument, a certain use of technology presents considerable benefits to the community as a whole—at least in the opinion of decision-makers. However, to use the technology requires that the burden of disadvantages will fall unduly heavily on one particular group in the community. Examples are easy to find. The extra runway at Sydney airport undoubtedly was convenient for air travellers to and from Sydney, but it greatly disadvantaged residents in certain suburbs, who suffered from increased aircraft noise.

Clearly, controversies about efficiency versus equity activate a small section of the population to protest against a measure which they believe will be unfair to them. The campaigners may attempt to stop the project altogether, or may simply try to ensure that they receive fair compensation for their suffering. The main target is likely to be the government, which wishes to proceed with the project. If the campaigners try to stop the project, they may bring in scientific experts to attest to the terrible problems they will suffer, and also either scientists or technologists who will produce alternative plans for coping with the larger problem.

Sometimes a vigorous campaign can prevent a project going ahead. Both the third runway in Sydney and the freight rail line in Brisbane were carried through, despite the opposition. However, in the United Kingdom, a strong campaign against an airport in the village of Cublington was completely successful: in the face of strong pressure, the government backed down and decided to expand the existing airport at Heathrow instead.

Benefits versus risks

A second type of controversy described by Nelkin covers situations in which benefits must be balanced against risks. Nuclear power, of course, falls into this category: is it too dangerous to use, bearing in mind the benefits that can follow? In general, the world seems to be moving against nuclear power. The Chernobyl disaster has apparently swung public opinion against nuclear technology.

Nelkin does not mention it, but the general argument over the safety of medicines can also be seen as a major argument of benefits versus risks. The world has been horrified by a series of scandals involving prescribed drugs which have had appalling side-effects. Thalidomide is the most famous, but there are others, such as chloramphenicol, a powerful antibiotic which destroys the bone marrow and causes anaemia.

The pharmaceutical industry was bitterly attacked because of repeated scandals regarding drug safety. As a reaction, the US government introduced requirements for drug testing to ensure maximum safety. To get a drug onto the market, a pharmaceutical company must spend about $US200 million, and work at developing the drug for about ten years (Reuben and Witcoff 1989). In this area, the argument has swung right away from the view that drugs are a benefit to the view that they have considerable risks, and these must be guarded against. This story has an unclear ending. It is now becoming known that bacteria—previously controllable by antibiotic drugs—are evolving to be immune to those drugs. As a result, diseases such as tuberculosis are reappearing in the world. At least in part, this seems to be due to the decreased production of new drugs by the pharmaceutical industry because of the new controls.

Risks versus freedoms

Nelkin's third type of controversy occurs when some part of the population wishes to indulge in behaviour which is generally believed to be dangerous—to themselves, in particular. The question is, what should the rest of the community do? Should we permit those people to endanger themselves, or should we act to preserve their safety? Looking at these issues in general, it is hard to see a general answer emerging. Some addictive drugs are banned in Western societies, and there are usually harsh penalties for owning, using or selling such drugs. In the same way, most developed countries now require that people wear seat-belts, at least in the front seats of cars. On the other hand, smoking is known to be dangerous to health, and yet it is still perfectly legal for people to smoke, although they are not usually allowed to do it in public places.

People in favour of further regulation often argue that, by endangering their own lives, people are not just exercising their freedom. They are also endangering the welfare of their families, and, by needing large amounts of health care, costing the society money. On the other hand, it can be asked, very seriously, how far such controls should go. Many of us do not always maintain our ideal weight, and we eat foods which are bad for our health. How far, in the name of the larger society, is the government entitled to go in regulating our conduct for our own good?

It is clear that there is no simple answer to this, and the result is likely to be an uneasy—and temporary—set of compromises which may not make much sense when compared to each other. Thus, at present, using marijuana is illegal and can lead to a prison sentence in many Australian states. However, alcohol and tobacco, both dangerous drugs, are freely available. At the same time, there are movements to reduce the penalties for marijuana use, and to discourage both smoking and drinking. It is not clear what the final outcome will be.

Science versus faith

Nelkin's final category is that of science when it threatens traditional beliefs. Perhaps the most lurid recent example of this was the notorious 'creation science' debate, when biblical Christians tried to have their beliefs taught in schools alongside the scientific theory of evolution (Numbers 1992). The fierce and ongoing debate over abortion can be regarded in a similar way. Abortion is now, medically, a simple operation, and advancing technology has made it easy to detect a pregnancy at an early stage, and also to detect an increasing range of illnesses and defects in the unborn child. This has brought the whole question of abortion to the fore in modern societies, and their responses have varied widely. In the Republic of Ireland, for example, abortion is illegal. In the United States, on the other hand, there are few legal restrictions on abortion early in pregnancy, though the 'pro-life' lobby is working hard to reverse this situation.

Some useful ideas in thinking about technical controversies

A few ideas may help in thinking about controversies. One is the concept of 'interest groups'. These are groupings of people who have got together in order to press for the interests of a particular section of society. Some groups have perfectly clear interests. For example, the National Union of Students can be relied upon to support better conditions for students, including free education. The Cattlemen's Association and the Small Shopkeepers' Association also represent clearly the interests of particular groups in society.

Others are less clear. The writer of this chapter belonged for years to a Queensland organisation called Citizens for Democracy. This organisation did not represent an occupational or economic interest, but consisted of people who wanted to change the Queensland electoral system. Its main aim was to ensure that all elected MPs should represent the same number of people. Citizens for Democracy thus comprised people, diverse in other ways, who believed strongly in one particular cause. They came together to argue for—and eventually achieve—their particular goal. Other such groupings include environmentalists, the Society for the Protection of the Unborn Child, and Amnesty International. In each case, the people involved usually have no direct financial stake in the organisation's cause, but believe in it strongly.

We should notice that interest groups often do not expect to get everything they want. They make ambit claims, and settle for less than their demands. As a result, compromises are common in non-scientific disputes. A common example of this is industrial disputes. A trade union wants more money and better conditions for its members. A firm is reluctant to grant these, but wants more productivity. After extended bargaining, and perhaps a strike, they typically compromise upon more pay and more productivity. Sometimes, there is another outcome: an arbitrator or Royal Commission may be appointed to look into the matter. This cannot happen in science, where fresh information is often vital; but it can settle technical disputes, as we shall see.

One other point is worth noting. The language of scientific and public disputes is very different. In print, scientists communicate in a very abstract way. By contrast, the statements of public disputants are often punchy and hard-hitting. As we shall see, this difference caused some bewilderment in the next case study, as non-scientists found it hard to puzzle out exactly what was being said.

The Auckland cervical cancer controversy

We have already looked in Chapter 4 at the case of the treatment of cervical cancer at the National Women's Hospital in Auckland, New Zealand. The basic facts of the issue are these. Cervical cancer is a fatal disease, killing large numbers of women throughout the world. The medical profession is aware of the dangers of cervical cancer and has instituted screening procedures, in which a few cells are scraped from a woman's cervix—where the womb joins the vagina—and examined beneath a microscope.

Often, instead of finding cervical cancer, doctors find that the surface of the cervix has cells showing an abnormality. This is called *carcinoma in situ*, or CIS. Throughout the world, CIS is accepted as being a distinct danger sign: a woman with CIS has a much higher chance of developing cervical cancer. Therefore, if a woman's smear test shows CIS, doctors throughout the world would take action to head off the impending disease.

Throughout the 1960s and 1970s, this view was not shared by Associate Professor Herbert Green, at the National Women's Hospital. Green was horrified by the amount of surgery carried out on women, in his view largely unnecessary. He therefore began a course of 'conservative treatment' for women referred to him. Women with CIS were monitored, but received none of the more drastic treatments, surgery and radiotherapy, because Green regarded CIS as a harmless, symptomless disease. However, the women were not told that Green's treatment—or rather, non-treatment—was controversial.

Naturally, strong arguments raged among the doctors at the National Women's Hospital over Green's course of treatment. However, Green was a towering, strong-willed man, and his project was permitted to continue. The angry disputes were contained within the walls of the hospital. The first public attack upon Green's methods came in a paper with a harmless-sounding title: 'The Invasive Potential of *Carcinoma in Situ* of the Cervix' (McIndoe *et al.* 1984). In this paper, two of Green's long-time opponents within the hospital compared the fate of 817 women who had normal cells, and 131 women who had CIS. The paper showed that while only 1.5 per cent of the women with normal cells had developed cancer, 22 per cent (a total of twenty-nine women) of those with CIS had done so, and eight had died.

If Green's opponents had expected an outcry, they were disappointed for over a year. There was almost no comment upon their paper, even though it seemed to demonstrate that something was gravely wrong with Green's treatment. One possible reason for the lack of reaction has already been mentioned: it was written in typical dry research language. Green was not mentioned in the paper, and the deadly implications were not spelled out until two feminists had puzzled out what it meant.

Things changed when people outside the medical community became involved. Sandra Coney and Phillida Bunkle, two active feminists, were tipped off by a friend that the paper was 'dynamite' and they studied it closely. Then they began to ask questions about the treatment. The results of their research appeared in the glossy Auckland magazine *Metro* in June 1987. The article was hard-hitting, but it was also well-informed and well-researched. The article began:

> In October 1985 Ruth (not her real name, for legal reasons which will become clear later in this story) returned from National Women's Hospital and told her workmates she felt she'd just been to Auschwitz. 'I feel as if they've been experimenting on me' she said. [Coney and Bunkle 1987:47]

The article went on to explain the history of the National Women's Hospital, the controversy over cervical cancer and CIS, and the terrible outcomes of the conservative method of treatment. The article went on to point out that medicine is a self-regulating profession, and is largely beyond the control of patients or the general public. In a powerful conclusion to their article, Coney and Bunkle wrote:

> The right of the doctor to treat his patient as he wishes is absolute. For over 20 years no-one interfered with Professor Green's treatment of patients. Eventually, new cases were not referred to him but no-one intervened on behalf of the women he was already handling. In the medical system, there is no voice for the public interest ... To preserve this autonomy, the public must learn as little as possible about medical bungles. Left to them the story of the 'unfortunate experiment' would have been buried with the victims. [Coney and Bunkle 1987:65]

The article created an immense controversy, with doctors—and patients of Green—fiercely defending his actions, and others attacking the hospital. After about a week, the Minister for Health decided to hold an inquiry and appointed Judge Silvia Cartwright to investigate the matter. Judge Cartwright's commission began hearing evidence in late 1987, and presented its report on 28 July 1988. The crucial exchanges took place early in the inquiry, when Sandra Coney gave evidence regarding the article she had co-authored.

Coney was cross-examined for four days. Lawyers for the hospital and Green attacked her article, and cross-questioned her mercilessly about its meaning. At the end of the cross-examination, both Coney and the lawyers were exhausted. In many ways, this was the key incident in the inquiry, for if the article by Coney and Bunkle could be shown to be mistaken, most of their concerns about treatment at the hospital could be shown to be baseless. The general opinion was that the cross-examination, if anything, strengthened Coney's case.

The formation of interest groups in the matter was fairly predictable. The New Zealand medical profession was on the defensive. Many doctors seem to have viewed the controversy as an attack upon their freedom, and upon their status. At first, many other groups were silent, perhaps intimidated by the prestige of the medical profession. After some hesitation, some feminist groups and the New Zealand Cancer Society began to press for an inquiry.

Judge Cartwright's report broadly vindicated the article by Coney and Bunkle. Regarding the article itself, apart from a few matters, she concluded that:

> ... the factual basis for the article and its emphasis have proved to be correct. It was an extensively researched and professionally written piece. It displayed an understanding of the condition of carcinoma in situ of the genital tract and invasive cancer that few laypeople could hope to achieve. [Cartwright 1988:95]

The commission's conclusions were comprehensive, and a few matters were of prime importance. It recommended improvement in some areas, including

> (i) The significance of carcinoma in situ, its invasive potential, its incidence and its treatment ...
> (iii) Teaching students the importance of informing women patients about smear tests as a preventive health measure.
> The Director-General of Health should ... continue to give urgent consideration to the improvement of ethical standards in National Women's Hospital ... ensure that lay representation on the ethical committee approximate one half of the membership. [Cartwright 1988:212–14]

Clearly, the commission had largely upheld the original allegations by Coney and Bunkle, and had made recommendations in line with their suggestions. In addition, the medical profession's ideas about autonomy had received a severe blow, and some additional restrictions had been placed upon the ethics of experimenting upon patients.

What was the controversy about?

Although the course of the controversy was fairly simple, it does not fit easily into any of the four categories which Nelkin proposed above. It could be argued that it is about regulation versus freedom of choice, but it is clearly not in the same category as, say, the seat-belt controversy. The freedom of choice involved is that of doctors, not the general public. Again, it might be that it is, to some extent, a question of efficiency versus equity, and a stronger case can be made here. It would be useful, both scientifically and medically, to know exactly what happened when CIS was allowed to develop without medical intervention. In that sense, efficiency would be served. However, the women who suffered in this way would pay with their lives, which is clearly against every precept of medicine. The doctors seem to have recognised this, and both Green and the director of the hospital, Bonham, made great efforts to avoid admitting that it was a controversy of this kind. Therefore, this is also an inadequate categorisation of the controversy.

It could also be suggested that the Auckland controversy could be regarded as a confrontation of science and religious belief. Traditionally, doctors have been regarded with great trust, as healers seeking only the best for their patients. The article by Coney and Bunkle—and the results of the Royal Commission—directly contradicted this, and implied that some doctors were pursuing other interests at their patients' expense. As with the other possibilities, the Auckland case did not fit easily into this category. There is a sense of strain; one feels that there is more to it than this.

Rather than trying to fit the Auckland case into Nelkin's categories, we can suggest a fifth category into which it fits neatly. This category can be roughly termed the place of science and technology in society. It involves questions about who actually regulates science and technology, and how transparent the activities of its practitioners are.

In the Auckland case, the crucial medical technology was completely under the control of the medical profession. Because of the unusual beliefs of some doctors, and the weak system of ethical control, women who expected high-quality treatment were in fact being treated as guinea-pigs, without being told about it. The medical profession of New Zealand seemed unwilling to act, or even talk, about the matter, and it was only when Coney and Bunkle made it public that anything was done.

Other cases of controversy over the place of science and technology in society

It is easy to find other cases which fit into this fifth category of scientific and technical controversy. This is a sign that Nelkin's description was not complete. The key questions involved in this approach concern control: who does actually control science or technology, and who should. The ethical status of science falls clearly into this category. For many years, following the perspectives of sociologist Robert Merton discussed in Chapter 2, science was regarded as a self-policing system, where fraud and unethical behaviour were controlled by scientists themselves. However, a recent massive eruption of cases of fraud and misrepresentation (e.g. Higgins 1994) has thrown this into doubt. If scientists are in fact policing themselves properly, it seems reasonable to ask, how can there be so many cases of fraud and misconduct?

Some cases of scientific misconduct have produced major controversies of their own. Perhaps the most bitter and long-running of these is known as the 'Baltimore affair', after Nobel Prize–winning scientist David Baltimore. In fact, Baltimore was never accused of misconduct. The case revolved around his laboratory chief, Thereza Imanishi-Kari.

A postdoctoral (i.e. fairly junior) researcher in Imanishi-Kari's laboratory at the Massachusetts Institute of Technology, Margot O'Toole, became concerned when she could not replicate some results in an important paper published by Baltimore, Imanishi-Kari and three others. She inspected the original notebooks, and concluded that they did not back up the claims made. Imanishi-Kari had made the notes, and the controversy concerned her actions. Baltimore backed Imanishi-Kari strongly, and also resisted attempts at investigation. O'Toole's concerns resulted in two investigations held by universities, which dismissed the problem. Finally, powerful US Congressman John Dingell also held an investigation, during which the secret service analysed the notebooks. At the root of this whole controversy was the question: can science be trusted to police its own conduct, or must there be some sort of external policing? Understandably, scientists have a strong interest in being left to control their own conduct. On the other hand, the government, which actually foots the bill for much scientific work, argues equally strongly that it is entitled to know what is going on. The controversy continues, uneasily, with no clear resolution in sight. However, it is clear that O'Toole has been a major sufferer, with her career derailed (Bell 1992:113).

As we have already seen in the previous chapter, an ongoing controversy exists over whether scientists should do experiments upon animals. Left to themselves, scientists would undoubtedly conclude that such experiments are essential. However, great pressure is coming from outside the scientific community for change (e.g. Blum 1994). Again, this—at least in part—concerns the rights of scientists to pursue their research, as opposed to the rights of concerned non-scientists to play a part in the decision.

A more sweeping questioning of the role of science and technology in society has come from feminist researchers and thinkers. The two broad claims made can, roughly, be classed as moderate and radical. The moderate claim is that both science and technology have been dominated by men, and are run along masculine lines. One implication is that women are often excluded from these areas, or their contributions are under-valued. Consider, for instance, the physicist Lise Meitner (1878–1968) and the geneticist Barbara McClintock (1902–92). Both made momentous discoveries in their fields. Meitner first identified nuclear fission and predicted the nuclear chain reaction which is the heart of the atomic bomb. McClintock discovered that genes can change their positions on chromosomes. Important discoveries, yet Meitner never received the Nobel Prize, and McClintock had to wait until 1983—when she was in her eighties —for hers. Related to this perspective is the view that technology is often designed by men, and so is insensitive to the needs and views of women (e.g. Hynes 1990). This is especially so in the area of reproductive technology, where women are the most directly affected, but the practitioners are mostly men (Hepburn 1992: Kirkup and Keller 1992).

The radical claim begins with the view that masculine—and therefore scientific and technological—ways of thinking are fundamentally different from those adopted by women. Therefore, they stand as buttresses of male dominance in our society, and must be balanced, if not replaced, by other, feminine ways of thinking that are equally valid but currently under-valued (e.g. Harding 1986, 1991). The work of Carol Gilligan (1993) is often quoted in this context, with her evidence that 'women's ways of knowing' are quite distinct.

It is clear that these issues are important for the whole of society, and merit a book to themselves. Some writers have already argued strongly against some of these views. Gross and Levitt (1994) and Levin (1988) have criticised feminist approaches to science, and Denfeld (1995) has criticised Gilligan's research as poorly constructed and unconvincing. Further, Farrell (1994), Goldberg (1977) and Thomas (1993) have contested the entire feminist approach from differing perspectives. A useful overview of gender and science issues is provided in Jasanoff *et al.* (1995), where several chapters address the issue.

The author of this chapter has a personal view. First, feminism is an important movement and merits more attention than it has received, especially from men. Some feminist arguments appear to be well justified. However, this does not mean that all allegations by all feminists should be accepted. This writer would like to see more open discussion on the various feminist perspectives, with men playing a far larger part on all sides.

Concluding remarks

Controversies and disagreements are an integral part of human life, both within science and in the larger community. Further, because science and technology are becoming ever more important in the world, it follows that controversies about them will become more, and not less, pronounced. Scientific controversies are much more complex—and more passionate—than one would guess from scientific textbooks or the papers in scholarly journals. The paper written by critics of Professor Green, as we saw, did not mention him and was phrased in typical, colourless scientific language (McIndoe *et al.* 1984). In addition, scientific controversies may exist on several different levels at the same time: they may, for example, comprise arguments over theory as well as disputes over the validity of some of the evidence.

In the debate which took place within the National Women's Hospital, of course, there were other dimensions as well. Drs McIndoe and McLean did not merely doubt Professor Green's theory about the harmlessness of CIS, and did not merely question his scientific data. They were also deeply distressed about the ethics of using the women as unknowing subjects in a possibly fatal experiment.

When science or technology becomes involved in complex controversies in the larger community, things are more complicated yet. Nelkin's four types of technical controversy are useful, but, as we have seen, do not encompass all the kinds of disagreement which may occur. However, when looking at any controversy involving science or technology, it is always worth asking if it fits into one of Nelkin's categories. Finally, in Western-style democratic societies, controversies are often marked by the formation of pressure groups, which exist to promote particular causes. As the Auckland incident clearly showed, a small number of clear-thinking, articulate people can accomplish very important things.

Further reading

To understand more about scientific and technical controversies, there are two paths to take. One is to look in more detail at particular controversies, understanding the issues and how the disagreements proceeded. The other is to examine broad theories, and see how major thinkers have accounted for matters. Perhaps the most exciting work in the latter category is that of Kuhn (1970). This caused a great stir when it was first published, and is still influential. It is a short book, and unclear on some points, but can transform the reader's view of science.

Kuhn's book deals with scientific controversies only. He argued that scientific research is organised around the idea of a 'paradigm'—a broad set of ideas about how things are in a field of science, and how it is appropriate to do research. Darwinian evolution might count as a paradigm, as might plate tectonics and the Big Bang theory of the universe. For most of the time, Kuhn argues, scientists work within these paradigms, solving puzzles in terms of the larger framework. For example a biologist might seek to explain how an animal came to have certain characteristics, using Darwinian and related ideas. This is termed by Kuhn 'puzzle-solving' and 'normal science'. However, paradigms can run into problems. Scientists may find that they can no longer solve problems in the terms the paradigm provides. They may begin looking for other ways to explain anomalous findings. Eventually, a fresh paradigm appears, and overthrows the older one. Kuhn terms this a 'scientific revolution'. The continental drift controversy is one example of such a revolution. So is the overthrow, by Galileo and others, of the idea that the Earth stands immobile at the centre of the universe. Kuhn's ideas are still controversial, but have created much interest.

On technical controversies, the three chapters by Frankel, Giere and McMullin in the Engelhardt and Caplan (1987) volume are useful, as is Nelkin (1984). Less academically, Sandra Coney's book (Coney 1988) certainly gives the 'feel' of involvement in a major controversy, although her book closes before things were resolved. A wonderful history of a continuing controversy is provided by Numbers (1992) with his understanding account of the creation scientists, and their efforts to force science to acknowledge their deeply held beliefs.

References

Bell, R. (1992), *Impure Science*. New York: John Wiley and Sons.
Blum, D. (1994), *The Monkey Wars*. New York: Oxford University Press.
Cartwright, S. (1988), *The Report of the Committee of Inquiry into Allegations concerning the Treatment of Cervical Cancer at National Women's Hospital and into other Related Matters*. Auckland: Government Printing Office.
Close, F. (1990), *Too Hot to Handle*. Harmondsworth: Penguin.
Cole, S. (1992), *Making Science. Between Nature and Society*. Cambridge, Mass.: Harvard University Press.
Collins, H. M. (1975), 'The Seven Sexes: A Study in the Sociology of a Phenomenon, or the Replication of Experiments in Physics', *Sociology*, 9:205–24.

Collins, H. M. (1981), 'Son of Seven Sexes: The Social Destruction of a Physical Phenomenon', *Social Studies of Science*, 11:33–62.

Coney, S. (1988), *The Unfortunate Experiment*. Harmondsworth: Penguin.

Coney, S., and Bunkle, P. (1987), 'An "Unfortunate Experiment" at National Women's', *Metro*, 7:47–65.

Denfeld, R. (1995), *The New Victorians*. New York: Warner Books.

Engelhardt, H. T., and Caplan, A. L. (1987), *Scientific Controversies: Case Studies in the Resolution and Closure of Disputes in Science and Technology*. Cambridge: Cambridge University Press.

Farrell, W. (1994), *The Myth of Male Power*. Milson's Point, NSW: Random House Australia.

Frankel, H. (1987), 'The Continental Drift Debate', in Engelhart and Caplan (1987): 203–48.

Giere, R. N. (1987), 'Controversies involving Science and Technology: A Theoretical Perspective', in Engelhardt and Caplan (1987): 125–50.

Gilligan, C. (1993), *In a Different Voice*. Cambridge, Mass.: Harvard University Press.

Goldberg, S. (1977), *The Inevitability of Patriarchy*. London: Temple Smith.

Gross, P. R., and Levitt N. (1994), *Higher Superstition*. Baltimore: Johns Hopkins University Press.

Hamilton D. P. (1991), 'Research Papers: Who's Uncited Now?', *Science*, January: 25.

Hamilton, D. P. (1991), 'Verdict in Sight in Baltimore Case', *Science*, 251: 1168–72.

Harding, S. (1986), *The Science Question in Feminism*. Ithaca, NY: Cornell University Press.

Harding, S. (1991), *Whose Science? Whose Knowledge?* Milton Keynes: Open University Press.

Hepburn, L. (1992), *Ova-Dose?* Sydney: Allen and Unwin.

Higgins, A. C. (1994), *Bibliography on Scientific Fraud*. Albany, NY: Exams Unlimited Inc.

Hynes, H. Patricia (ed.) (1990), *Reconstructing Babylon: Essays on Women and Technology*. London: Earthscan Publications.

Jasanoff, S., Markie, G. E., Peterson, J. C., and Pinch, T. (eds) (1995), *Handbook of Science and Technology Studies*. London: Sage.

Kirkup, G., and Keller, L. S. (1992), *Inventing Women*. Cambridge: Polity Press.

Kuhn T. S. (1970), *The Structure of Scientific Revolutions*. Chicago: University of Chicago Press.

Le Grand, H. E. (1990), *Drifting Continents and Shifting Theories*. Cambridge: Cambridge University Press.

Levin, M. (1988), 'Caring New World', *American Scholar*, 57, Winter: 100–6.

McIndoe, W. A., McLean, M. R., Jones, R. W., and Mullins P. (1984), 'The Invasive Potential of *Carcinoma in Situ* of the Cervix', *Obstetrics and Gynaecology*, 64:158–62.

McMullin, E. (1987), 'Scientific Controversy and its Termination', in Engelhardt and Caplan (1987): 49–91.

Medvedev, Z. A (1978), *Soviet Science*. New York: Norton.

Nelkin, D. E. (1984), *Controversy: Politics of Technical Decisions*. Beverly Hills and London: Sage.

Numbers, R. L. (1992), *The Creationists*. New York: Alfred A. Knopf.

Reuben B. G., and Witcoff, H. (1989), *Pharmaceutical Chemicals in Perspective*. New York: Wiley.

Schroeer, D. (1972), *Physics and its Fifth Dimension: Society*. Reading, Mass.: Addison-Wesley.

Thomas, D. (1993), *Not Guilty*. New York: W. Morrow.

Vallery-Radot, R. (1960), *The Life of Pasteur*. Trans. R. L. Devonshire. New York: Dover Publications.

Weiner, J. (1986), *Planet Earth*. Sydney: Bantam Books.

PART TWO

Scientists and Technologists in the Wider Society

CHAPTER 6

The Industrial Revolution in Great Britain

John Forge

> These improvements [in production] constitute the Industrial Revolution. They yielded an unprecedented increase in man's productivity and, with it, a substantial rise in income per head. Moreover, this rapid rise was self-sustaining. [Landes 1969:41]

> What distinguishes the world since the Industrial Revolution from the world before is the systematic, regular and progressive application of science and technology to the production of goods and services. [Rostow 1971:26]

In Chapter 1 we said that technology is the means we use to change and exploit our surroundings. This is done because it is believed that these changes are for the better: that it is better to have a city here, a coal mine there, and so forth. (We make no judgement here about whether it really is better to have the coal mine, etc.) While *Homo sapiens* has always had technology, use has not always been on a large scale and hence has not always produced economic growth. It seems that the condition for the large-scale use of technologies is that the society in question is, or has been, *industrial*. (The qualification is needed because some highly technological societies are now termed *post*-industrial: they are no longer properly called industrial, but they were industrial at some time.) Thus, the process by which a society becomes industrialised is relevant to our overall purposes because it has to do with the optimal conditions for the application of technology.

This chapter is about the Industrial Revolution, the sequence of momentous events that began at the end of the eighteenth century, which produced the first industrialised country, Britain. The view taken here is that the heart of this process was a series of *technical* changes,

I am very grateful to Ian Inkster for extraordinarily helpful comments on this chapter.

some of which were significant enough to count as *technological* change. The role of science has been a matter of some debate. The passage from Rostow quoted above states that science was an integral part of the process as well. If this were true, then the Industrial Revolution might be explained with reference to the fact that, for the first time, science came to underpin technologies that came to have large-scale applications. In fact, that might be why technology became large-scale. This thesis will be discussed in the last section of the chapter. The chapter also has more general relevance in that it offers definitions and explanations of key terms that are in use throughout the book—terms like *economic growth*, *technique*, and so on.

Technical change and economic growth

A country, or state as it is more commonly called these days, has an *economy* associated with it. An economy comprises the production and exchange of those things that are considered to be valuable in the sense that a monetary value can be assigned to them. Typically, then, an economy is concerned with the production of goods and services: cars, video recorders, restaurant meals, aeroplane flights, etc.—we might think of an economy as the *organisation* of such production. The *size* of an economy is determined by the total (monetary) value of all goods and services produced in a given year—this is the so-called national product. An economy *grows* (in absolute terms) if more is produced than in a previous period, and this is normally expressed as a percentage increase with respect to the previous year's output. We tend to believe that a growing economy is a healthy economy and that economic growth is a normal state of affairs. This belief is, however, of fairly recent origin: indeed, it seems to have been an outcome of the Industrial Revolution. As the respected economic historian David Landes points out in the passage quoted above, the 'unprecedented' rises in productivity were self-sustaining in the period of the Industrial Revolution. The suggestion is that industrialisation and economic growth are related.

The prospects for sustained growth, particularly for sustained growth per head, in an economy that is primarily based on agriculture seem slim. There is a limit to how much agricultural produce an individual can consume, although that observation neglects the possibility of growth through export of agricultural surplus. It appears, rather, that growth presupposes a substantial *industrial* manufacturing or service sector. The consumption of goods and services from those sectors of the economy is not limited by the size of the stomach! Thus we could infer that the Industrial Revolution is associated with the beginning of the rise to dominance of the (non-agricultural) industrial and service sectors.

Indeed this is the usual interpretation—the 'received view'—with industrialisation being understood as the transformation of an agrarian society to an industrial society. (One should be careful to distinguish between the terms 'agricultural' and 'agrarian'. The former refers to the practice of cultivating the land for food production, whereas the latter refers to a type of society in which the main economic relationships involve land.)

How, in very general terms, could this happen? It was certainly not true that 'industry' suddenly appeared on the scene and brought forth all kinds of new things. The industries most closely associated with the Industrial Revolution—as we will see, these included textiles, coal and iron, and transport—were in existence long before the middle of the eighteenth century. So it must have been the case that these industries themselves were transformed in some way.

One kind of change that can take place in industrial production retains the techniques of production—the way in which things are made or done—and increases the inputs. Instead of, say, five machines, one hundred workers and one workshop, an entrepreneur might decide to invest in five more machines, hire another hundred workers and rent an additional workshop. All things being equal, we would expect twice as much product. But this would not result in any increase in efficiency or productivity; and it is not, in Landes's terms, an 'improvement in production'.

Another kind of change is *technical change*, in which the product is made in a new way. In the example just mentioned, suppose a new kind of machine, bigger, faster, more productive and capable of being run by just four workers, is introduced; say five of these replaced the old ones and are housed now in a factory. This is clearly technical change. And granted that the new machines are at least as productive as the old ones, there will be at least a fivefold increase in productivity: twenty workers now make at least as much as one hundred did previously.

Finally, there could be some change in what is *known* about the techniques of production, such that the way things are made, and perhaps the product itself, undergoes some radical transformation. In our example, the new machines might not only be bigger and faster but might operate on a quite novel principle and might give a much improved product. This last kind of change is *technological change*. It would be surprising indeed if anything properly called an industrial revolution could result from the first kind of change alone: we would expect at least a degree of technical change.

It is generally accepted that Britain was the first country to industrialise. Some historians have also agreed that this was accompanied by a take-off into sustained economic growth, and we have argued that

that adds up to the fact that the Industrial Revolution took place in Britain. The figures in Table 6.1 provide evidence in favour of this position. The table shows the (average) annual growth rates for the years in question and the last column gives the contribution of manufacturing (non-agricultural) industry. (Note that we can infer that there was a substantial population increase in the latter part of the eighteenth century which was sustained in the nineteenth century.) But do these figures really support the usual interpretation that there was indeed an industrial revolution in Britain beginning about 1780?

In the first place, it must be said that we cannot be certain that these figures are accurate: since there is no complete and unambiguous set of economic data available for the eighteenth century, the figures must be estimates and not hard facts. But let us assume that they are more or less correct, for we really have no other choice, and ask how they should be viewed. There is evidently no sharp discontinuity in the economic growth curve, such as seems to be implied by the term *take-off.* It appears, on the contrary, that there was steady growth, especially per capita, in the first half of the eighteenth century. Nevertheless, it is possible that some sectors of the economy experienced vigorous growth, but it was swamped or masked by sluggish performance in other, more traditional, parts of the economy (see Tables 6.3 and 6.4, and compare Mokyr 1993:12). In accordance with our remarks about technical and technological change, it is possible that some such 'leading sectors' might have been growing vigorously, fuelled by technical change, but the gains of the economy as a whole look much more modest. Indeed, this view seems to fit the facts and figures well. While it is even harder to find unequivocal evidence of an increased rate of technical change, Table 6.2 on patent statistics provides some grounds in favour of this view. The intuition here is that the number of patents correlates with invention and innovation in industrial production. (These figures also provide some support for the theory which suggests that there are waves

Table 6.1. Economic growth in Great Britain, %

Year	National product	National product per head	Industry
1700–60	0.69	0.31	0.71
1761–80	0.70	0.01	1.51
1781–1800	1.32	0.35	2.11
1801–30	1.97	0.52	3.00

Source: Crafts 1985:32, 45.

Table 6.2. Numbers of patents granted in Great Britain

Year	Total patents	Patents per decade
1700–60	370	60
1761–80	536	255
1781–1830	4,479	900

Source: Inkster 1991:41.

of innovations that peak periodically, a theory which is discussed at length in Chapter 8.)

The Industrial Revolution must not, therefore, be understood as a sudden and discontinuous upward move in economic growth and productivity throughout the whole of British industry. It was, rather, a period of considerable change that was concentrated in certain sectors, and also in certain geographical regions: sectors that were amenable to, and ready for, technical and technological change, and regions that were able to accommodate and service the new forms of production. We can sum all this up by describing the process of industrialisation as one of structural reorganisation of the economy, and of the country, whereby certain sectors and regions became the locus of economic growth, and experienced a move away from the traditional forms of activity of the agrarian state. Does all this really deserve the title Industrial *Revolution*? Why not? The term has had wide currency for one hundred years, and, given the qualifications just made, it is unlikely to be misunderstood. There are, then, a number of particular questions to address: we want to know *why* economic growth began to rise in this 'unprecedented' way and why the British economy underwent some structural change at the same time. More particularly, we want to know which technologies were involved, what some of the social consequences were, and of course whether *science* was implicated.

The nature of industrial production

To answer our first two questions, we need to think about the form of industrial production and consider just what it takes to manufacture goods—either goods for direct consumption, such as cotton cloth or china plates, or capital goods designed to produce consumer goods, such as steam engines or machine tools. In the first place, it is obviously necessary to know how to change raw materials into finished product, that is to say, recalling what was said above, it is necessary to have the requisite *technology*. For instance, the white lint of raw cotton is combed, cleaned, spun, woven and dyed or printed in the production of cotton cloth. (In fact, it is customary to distinguish *four* stages of textile production—preparation, spinning, weaving and finishing—although some stages involve several distinct steps.) It is, therefore, not possible to make cotton cloth unless one knows how to accomplish these four stages. Production thus requires certain *techniques*, certain ways of doing tasks, and having knowledge of these techniques amounts to being in possession of the corresponding technologies. There are, in fact, many different ways of making textiles, and it is a commonplace among historians that technical change, change in the way tasks were performed, in the textile industry was a cause of the Industrial Revolution. We will come back to cotton.

Knowing how to produce something is not, of course, enough. One also needs the capital to rent or buy premises or factories, equip them with the necessary machines, buy the raw materials, and one needs labour. One needs, that is, the classical 'factors of production', *capital* and *labour*. Capital can be defined as capital goods, like machines and factories, together with raw materials, but in many ways it is easier to think of it as money that is invested, or is available for investment, in production. It is necessary, therefore, to have money available for investment: to buy raw cotton, to buy spinning machines, to rent factories, etc. And it is necessary to have labour—spinners, weavers, etc.—to actually perform the work. A supply of labour is not the same as a pool of people available to work: persons who have the required *skills* and the disposition to be organised in certain ways constitute a labour force. There is also the need for someone, or some group, to put all this together: to conceive of the enterprise, raise the money, hire the labour and sell the produce. It has been said that the Industrial Revolution marked the rise to dominance of the *capitalist* class, the class of persons who owned the 'means of production'. Certainly it was marked by the emergence of people who were willing to invest in manufacture and to take risks. Such persons are now referred to as *entrepreneurs*. As Chapter 8 shows, these entrepreneurs have, in the view of people like Schumpter, played a critical role in the process of technological change.

The matters we have discussed thus far are, so to speak, internal to the process of production: labour, capital and technique come together on the factory floor and bring forth goods. However, such enterprise would be shortlived were there no outside *demand* for the goods in question. If people do not want cotton cloth, or if they cannot pay for it, then the cotton manufacturer will get no return on his investment, he will be unable to meet his bills and he will go out of business. According to the theory of economics associated with Adam Smith (1776/1970), it is consumer demand that determines the quantity and the nature of goods produced in any economy. The consumer allocates her income in a certain fashion and hence indicates a willingness to pay a given price for particular goods. The producer observes this behaviour and organises his manufacture accordingly. So if it happens that cotton cloth is quickly sold at market at a high price while woollen cloth is slow to move, then the rational manufacturer of textiles will look to ways to convert his workshops from wool to cotton. Nowadays it seems that the producer conditions or 'educates' the consumer into wanting his products, by the stratagems of advertising and marketing, rather than waiting for price signals via the market mechanism. Whatever the truth of the matter, demand for goods produced, whether conditioned or not, is clearly necessary.

Demand mops up the output of production, but there must also be inputs. We have already mentioned labour and capital as inputs, as 'factors of production', but there must also be physical inputs, raw materials to be fashioned by technique into commodities. Thus the manufacture of cotton cloth requires the *supply* of cotton lint. If there is none available, or if it is in short supply, then the manufacture of cotton cloth cannot proceed. According to the theory of the market just mentioned, shortages on the supply side will be remedied by increases in prices for raw materials: consumer demand will reach through the productive process and make itself felt in the cotton-growing countries, where more land will be taken up for the cultivation of cotton crop. Again, the initiative could come from the producer himself who sees scope for the intensification of consumer demand, and so seeks more raw materials. Conceivably, the initiative could come from the primary producer, who thinks that more raw materials could be absorbed by industry and who acts accordingly.

Further prerequisites for industrialisation

It is evident that the factors mentioned in the previous section are all necessary for the type of sustained economic growth identified by Landes as characteristic of the Industrial Revolution. However, they are not jointly sufficient for industrialisation; there are, in addition, certain other prerequisites.

The first and most obvious is that *agriculture* must have developed to the degree that it can support a population where a significant proportion no longer works the land. An agrarian society is one in which agriculture is the main economic activity. It is possible for such a society to produce a surplus, as France did in the eighteenth century. But if this surplus simply supports a large aristocracy that likes to indulge itself, or if it is wasted on activities such as war, then it will not form any basis for industrialisation. But we should note, in passing, that

British industry was thriving in a period of sustained warfare (the Napoleonic Wars, 1792–1815), with France. The state in Britain did encourage industry—textiles for uniforms, iron for cannon—that contributed to the war effort (but see Mokyr 1993:56). Returning to agriculture, it is evident that there must be such a surplus and it must be used for the right purpose, which is to say that it must be available to the new industrial working class. It has been said that there was indeed an *agricultural revolution* in Britain in the seventeenth and eighteenth centuries (Deane 1979:37). The outcome was greatly increased productivity, which was precisely what was required. This was due to improvements in the techniques of agricultural production—the introduction of the seed drill, better ploughs, etc.—and also to changes in organisation, with large-scale units replacing the traditional strip farming (see Deane for more on the agricultural revolution). It would be interesting to investigate why all this took place—perhaps the entrepreneurial spirit evident in the Industrial Revolution was also manifest in 'capitalist' farmers of the preceding generations—but we cannot do so here.

We should also note some wider economic, political and social circumstances that provided the context and background for the transformation to industrial society. For instance, medieval and late-medieval societies were subject to a number of restrictions that would have made industrialisation impossible even if all the other conditions mentioned above could have been satisfied. For instance, there was little infrastructure in the form of serviceable roads, canals or port facilities in late-medieval society, for there was little need for large-scale movement of goods or population—it was only in time of war that this was important. There were formal restrictions on trade and the mobility of goods, with tariffs payable on goods transported across many internal borders; there were regulations on the manufacture of goods enforced by the craft guilds, and prices were fixed. Again, whatever one makes of reference to market forces as an overall scheme of explanation, where arbitrary constraints are imposed on prices, manufacturing techniques and the supply of labour which make these insensitive to demand, economic growth is stifled. But in Britain, from the fifteenth century onwards, such constraints were gradually lifted.

'King Cotton'

The most convincing evidence for the occurrence of the Industrial Revolution comes from data on the textile industry, especially *cotton manufacture.* The amount of cotton cloth produced, the amount of raw cotton imported, the values and prices of these commodities and factors, the number of persons involved in manufacture of cotton goods, and the technical changes in the industry, all exhibit unprecedented rates of growth from the last two decades of the eighteenth century to the middle of the nineteenth century. Demographic changes and the rise of the cotton towns are no less dramatic.

Table 6.3 gives some substance to these claims. In some eighty years cotton, having started way behind, overtook wool in overall consumption of raw material, although the wool industry had been well-established since medieval times. During the eighteenth century the population of Lancashire, a county whose cool damp climate proved to be ideal for the industry, grew sixfold, compared to the national growth rate of 40 per cent, while the population of the city of Manchester grew tenfold. Cotton was, therefore, one of the leading sectors whose existence was conjectured at the beginning of this chapter.

If we ask why cotton experienced such spectacular growth, we need to refer to our previous discussion of the nature of industrial production. If that was correct, then the conditions mentioned there must have been fulfilled for cotton. And they were. In particular, many historians have focused on a series of *technical changes* that began in the first half of the eighteenth century, with an innovation to the weaving stage. The traditional Dutch loom used in weaving throughout Europe was a device in which spun cotton thread, the warp, was stretched lengthways on a frame; this was fitted with reeds that could raise every other warp thread, so that the weft thread could be interlaced crosswise to produce cotton cloth. Many texts produce diagrams and descriptions on spinning and weaving; Cardwell's is among the more comprehensible (Cardwell 1972:77–9, 94–7). The weaver wound the weft thread onto a shuttle, which he threw from one side of the loom to the other, working the reeds with a foot treadle. The productivity of the Dutch loom was thus limited by the speed at which the weaver could catch and throw the

Table 6.3. A comparison of cotton and wool

Year	Cotton		Wool	
	Consumption million lbs	Growth rate %	Consumption million lbs	Growth rate %
1741	2.06	1.37	57.0	1.30
1772	4.2	6.20	85.0	–
1798	41.8	12.76	98.0	0.5
1805	63.1	4.49	105.0	1.64
1820	141.0	6.82	140.0	2.03

Source: Berg 1985:28, 32.

shuttle, and also by the spread of his arms, which meant that only relatively narrow bolts of cloth could be made. In 1733 John Kay, who worked for a clothier, succeeded in mechanising the shuttle. He invented the *flying shuttle*, which was thrown automatically from one side of the cloth to the other by means of two spring-loaded boxes operated by pulling a string. The shuttle flew between the warp threads and was caught in one of the shuttle boxes; the weaver changed the reeds, pulled the shuttle thread, and the process was repeated.

Paul Mantoux sums up the implications of Kay's shuttle:

> This invention had incalculable consequences. The various processes in an industry form one whole, and are comparable to a system of interdependent movements all responding to the same rhythm. The effect of a technical improvement accelerating only one of these operations is to break the common rhythm. [Mantoux 1961:208]

In fact, even in 1733 and thereabouts there was a relative shortage of spinners, with six spinners needed to keep one weaver supplied with cloth. When the flying shuttle caught on in the 1750s, the consequent increase in the productivity of the weaver rendered this shortage of spinners critical. And it did take about twenty years for the flying shuttle to catch on, because Kay met with opposition both from the weavers themselves, who accused him of trying to deprive them of their livelihood, and from the manufacturers, who were ready to use the invention but refused to pay the royalties. Sadly, Kay was eventually forced to flee to France.

A similar pattern was to be repeated when the first spinning machine was invented. This pattern included sporadic riots and machine-breaking. While it is understandable, and perhaps not always inappropriate, for those employed in traditional labour-intensive techniques of production to react in this way to technical change, it is by no means always the case that technical change leads to unemployment. Indeed, it is common for such change to lead to new job opportunities. But what must be stressed is that these new opportunities entail different sorts of work. For instance, a machine hand whose job it was to mend broken threads on a power loom was doing work very different from that of the weaver in pre-industrial Britain. Those sections of the labour force unwilling or unable to adapt to new tasks will fall by the wayside.

We have just seen that the flying shuttle had destroyed the precarious equilibrium between the spinning and weaving stages, and demanded expansion of thread production. What was needed was a machine that could make more than one thread at a time. For instance, a spinning machine that could make ten threads for the same effort that was formerly required to make one would result in a tenfold productivity increase. The first and most famous spinning machine was the *spinning jenny*, invented by James Hargreaves in 1765, which came into use in 1768. In so far as it is possible to describe how this machine worked, it is difficult to improve on Mantoux:

> It consisted of a rectangular frame on four legs. At one end was a row of vertical spindles. Across the frame were two parallel wooden rails, lying close together, which were mounted on a sort of carriage and slid backwards and forwards as desired. The cotton, which had previously been carded and roved [combed and twisted into strands], passed between the two rails and then was wound on the spindles. With one hand the spinner worked the carriage backwards and forwards, and with the other he turned the handle which worked the spindles. In this way the thread was drawn and twisted at the same time. [Mantoux 1961:217]

The first jennies had six spindles, but eventually versions were built that had eighty.

There were, as we will see in a moment, other important technical changes to textile manufacture in the early period of the Industrial Revolution. But it is worth pausing here for a moment to consider the organisation of textile production and how technical change affected, and was affected by, that organisation. Until the end of the eighteenth century, the textile industry was a *cottage industry*. As the name suggests, this form of organisation is based on the home, on the traditional peasant cottage. Spinning had always been women's work, but the more physically demanding weaving was usually done by the man of the house. The loom was set up in the cottage and the weaver would weave the yarn brought to him by a travelling merchant, to whom he would deliver the finished cloth and be paid by the piece. This process was known as *putting out*: it represented an advance on the early handicraft system, whereby all stages of production were carried out under one roof, with respect to the division of labour and (hence) with respect to productivity. As it happened, even quite large machines like the early jennies could be housed in the cottage; certainly a loom fitted with a flying shuttle could be easily accommodated. And, moreover, they could be accommodated, several at a time, in workshops. But when it came to very large machines, the water-frame spinning machine, the 'mule' and the power loom, human strength was not enough. And power-driven machinery needed special buildings, it needed *factories*.

There were, however, other reasons that have been adduced for the rise of the factory system. The weaver was not necessarily a full-time textile worker; he might also be an agricultural worker—he would certainly help at harvest time. The job-specialisation that we know today is itself a product of industrialisation. The weaver's habits of work often did not suit the merchant; complaints were often made about the weaver embezzling cloth, not working hard enough, taking Mondays off, and so forth (for instance, see Pollard 1968:46–7; Clausen 1980:44–7). It was difficult to get him to do more work: if the price of labour went up, the weaver usually reacted by doing less, doing no more than was needed to earn his usual wage. Again, the idea that one has an incentive to work harder when one is paid more is also of recent origin. The weaver had a fixed set of wants and needs, and once he had earned enough to satisfy those, his week's work was done. The vast array of goods and services presented to us today by the modern industrial system to mop up our extra earnings was not, of course, accessible to the eighteenth-century weaver. If the merchant tried the other tactic, reducing wages, the weaver might well react by embezzling more cloth.

A labour force that has to earn its keep in the factory is in a much weaker position than one whose members work from home. It can be disciplined by the demands of the machine and the clock, and, if need be, by physical means as well. Stories of corporal punishment, especially of children in the early factories and 'mills', are more part of the folklore than the fact of the Industrial Revolution. Nevertheless, the long hours of work, for child and adult alike, the poor food and accommodation, undoubtedly amounted to mistreatment. It was, however, dismissal and the threat of it that was the main instrument for enforcing discipline (Pollard 1963:259). Locking the factory gates for twelve or fourteen hours was an excellent way of keeping the workers on the job.

One might be tempted to tease out of the foregoing discussion some *general explanation* of the Industrial Revolution and its attendant features, such as the rise of the factory system. It is, for instance, evident that the technical changes we have documented were essential in the sense that, without them, the increases in productivity and efficiency that define the Industrial Revolution would not have taken place. It was also necessary for factories to become ubiquitous to maintain these gains after the middle of the nineteenth century, and hence it was necessary for much of the workforce to submit to factory discipline. However, the sequence of technical change cannot be said to be the *cause* of the Industrial Revolution in the sense that the latter *had* to come about once the former was in place, regardless of the context in which the changes were embedded. Indeed, it should be clear that technical change can come about only if the industry in question, and the economy as a whole, are ready for it—the spinning jenny would not have made an impact in, say, 1568! Once we acknowledge this, we must allow the relevant 'contextual factors' as ingredients in the explanation as well. Thus, a general explanation that seeks to select just one of the elements that contributes to industrial production will be guilty of misplaced emphasis.

Moreover, it may also be unwise to press for explanations of one aspect of the Industrial Revolution in terms of others. For example, while it was certainly true that large power-driven machinery required large buildings, it does not follow that the invention of the former caused, or otherwise explained, the existence of the latter. After all, human decisions were needed to make and use the machinery— innovation does not always follow invention. It has, in fact, been said that we should not neglect here the relation between boss and worker, between capital and labour. This relation, as Karl Marx pointed out, is *political*: the factory system symbolised the newfound power which the capitalist, the factory-owner, had over the worker. Indeed, the entrepreneur had much to gain from the 'rationalisation' of production represented by the factory system. Further division of labour and long regular hours of work meant much greater productivity, which, combined with wages close to subsistence level, added up to a handsome return on the capital which the entrepreneur had had the foresight to invest. But, again, it would be unwise to 'explain' the Industrial Revolution along these lines. After this excursion into theory, let us return to textiles.

No account of the Industrial Revolution would be complete without mention of one entrepreneur, who was also one the great characters of the period, Sir Richard Arkwright (1732–92). Sir Richard was inventor, factory-owner, partner in various ventures and staunch defender of his patent rights in the law courts of England. He was credited by law with the invention of the water-frame, a spinning machine, in 1767, just after the appearance of the jenny. However, it is generally agreed that his was an adaption of a machine invented much earlier, by men who were not able to raise the capital to put it into use. In spite of its name, the water-frame did not require a water wheel to drive it. Like the jenny it came in many sizes: the first were driven by horses, but then came larger versions that were power-driven and housed in factories (Cardwell 1972:95). Arkwright himself had trouble raising capital until he teamed up with (the marvellously named) Samuel Need of Nottingham and Jedediah Strutt of Derby in 1771. The partners set up a spinning factory, or *mill*, in Cromford near Derby, in which power was provided by a water wheel; it employed some three hundred workers on several thousand spindles.

Arkwright's patents gave him exclusive use of the water-frame, and throughout the 1770s he built more factories in Derbyshire and Lancashire, ploughing his earnings back into his business. He was, however, engaged in disputes with other 'inventors', whose machines differed from his in only the smallest details. By the time the patent for the water-frame was deemed to have lapsed, in 1785, Arkwright was the richest cotton spinner in England. He was knighted by the king, the first manufacturer to have this honour, was appointed to the office of Sheriff of Derby, and died leaving his heirs half a million pounds. This was the fate of a man who started out with nothing, but who was able to take advantage of the opportunities that presented themselves in the early days of the Industrial Revolution. As such he was representative of the new middle class, of merchants, financiers and industrialists, who were to dominate economic and political life by the end of the nineteenth century.

We must bring our discussion of King Cotton to a close with some brief remarks about the development of the industry in the nineteenth century. First, we should mention that one great advantage of cotton was that it was highly *price-elastic*; this means that, as prices for thread, cloth, etc. dropped, demand increased at a greater rate. (The demand for cotton was not exclusively domestic: one of the great advantages of cotton over wool was that there were large export markets for the former. The versatility and serviceability of cotton clothing, bedsheets and so forth was even more manifest in warmer climes, which became the main export markets for British cottons.) Price elasticity gives a continued incentive to increase productivity. And this was indeed manifest right up to the US Civil War, when the supply of raw cotton was severely disrupted. The power loom and the steam engine were the most significant technical changes that enabled the continuing expansion of production to take place. The latter meant that mills need no longer be located near reliable sources of running water. However, British industrialisation could not be sustained by textiles forever: a commodity cannot be price-elastic without limit! Moreover, Britain became a model for other countries to copy, and rival textile industries grew up in France and particularly the United States. The British economy had to diversify and, in the nineteenth century, it had a strong capital base from which to do so.

The age of iron and steam

It will be recalled that a capital good is one that is used to produce other goods—a machine tool, for instance. One can therefore infer that an economy which needs a high volume of such goods is healthy because its productive capacity is being augmented, presumably because of increased, or continuing high, demand. In the nineteenth century, the consumption of coal and the production of iron were indicators of the state of health of the newly industrialising nations. As before, we restrict our attention to Britain, with the statistics shown in Table 6.4. The increase in the production of pig iron was nearly exponential— the period beginning 1806 is anomalous—with a doubling every ten years, and that is prodigious growth. The growth in coal output was strong and steady. Coal was used primarily in the smelting of iron ore, or as fuel for steam engines. Steam engines were either fixed in place and used to drive machinery and pump water, or mobile and used to pull freight and passengers. Iron was the main construction material: it was used to build factories, bridges and, most importantly, rails and rolling stock.

The first railway line that used a locomotive was from Darlington to Stockton in the north-east of England, 40 kilometres in all, which was opened in 1825. It was intended to deliver coal from Darlington, which is inland, to Stockton on the river Tees for transport by barge and ship. The next line was opened in 1830, between the port of Liverpool and the cotton town of Manchester, a distance of 130 kilometres. Besides linking two important centres of economic activity, this line was important for three other reasons: it carried passengers as well as freight; all traction was mechanical; and it used the Rocket, the famous locomotive designed by Stephenson, which was faster than a horse. While the earlier line was something of a curiosity and of only local significance, the Liverpool–Manchester line proved the value of the railways.

By mid-century Britain had almost 10,000 kilometres of track, and this is estimated to have cost more than three hundred and twenty million pounds! This construction phase took place primarily in two great episodes of 'railway mania', in the mid-1830s and the mid-1840s. The main trunk lines radiating from London were constructed in the earlier period, while much of the rest of the country was 'blocked out' during the second period (Deane 1979:172). Deane also reports that during

Table 6.4. Pig iron production and coal output in Great Britain

Year	Pig iron production tonnes	Coal output million tonnes
1788	68,000	9.9
1796	125,000	10.1
1806	258,000	15.0
1825	581,000	20.4
1835	940,000	27.7

Source: Landes 1969:256.

the second of the railway manias, in 1847, the moneys invested amount to more than the value of total British exports and were roughly one-tenth of the total national income. This rail network was responsible also for demographic change. The town of Middlesborough in the north-east grew up as the site of a new port that was linked with the rest of the country by the railways, due in no small measure to the Quakers. New towns were created, like Wolverton, Crewe and Swindon in the Midlands, to service the railway workshops for construction and repair of rolling stock.

The railways were instrumental in the continued expansion of the British economy after 1825. Mathias sums up their significance as follows:

> The importance of the coming of the railways as a service for the economy as a whole lies in the fact that they enabled economic activity in all other sectors of the economy to expand. But the railways were also important as an industry in their own right, creating employment, using capital and de-manding economic resources. [Mathias 1969:281]

In other words, the railways did double duty: they provided an efficient means of moving people, freight and raw materials around the country—and hence expanded economic activity—and they themselves amounted to an industry, which needed capital and labour, made profits, contributed to annual growth rates and so forth.

Science, technology and the Industrial Revolution

From the passage by Rostow quoted at the beginning of this chapter, we might infer that science played a crucial role in the Industrial Revolution. Moreover, we might expect this role to be concerned with technology, with science being utilised as a 'basis' for technology, although we have to explain what this means. But there seem to be dissenting voices. In a well-known and authoritative work, Musson and Robinson write: 'In the early mechanisation of the cotton industry, applied science appears to have played a very minor role. Inventors such as Kay, Paul, Wyatt, Hargreaves, Arkwright, Cartwright and Compton appear to have had little or no scientific skill' (Musson and Robinson 1969:81). Cardwell agrees: 'It is true that the mechanical philosophy [science] may have had some very general and indirect influence on the process of invention in the textile field but to all intents and purposes these inventions belong to the category that we have designated empirical and non-science based' (Cardwell 1972:100). Perhaps there is really no conflict here: maybe Rostow understands by 'the application of science' something rather less specific than science giving rise directly to new techniques of production, or perhaps he wished to exempt the British textile industry of the eighteenth and early nineteenth centuries. We need to consider both these possibilities.

There is a straightforward explanation as to why science can stand as a basis for, or can underpin, technology, and it runs as follows. While science does not necessarily give us an absolutely correct description of the world, in many cases it gives us an approximation that is good enough for all practical purposes. Such description aims, essentially, to discover the basic laws and patterns of the natural world, to catalogue the kinds of things that exist and to determine their properties. A mundane example is the fact that phosphorus combined with calcium carbonate forms a slag that does not dissolve in molten iron. Thus, to be able to smelt iron with coke that contains phosphorous—an element that normally dissolves in iron to produce an inferior sample of the metal—one should add calcium carbonate.

Suppose one *knows* these facts and then designs a new method for smelting iron by explicitly taking them into account: this would be an example of science underpinning technology. Notice that on this view of the nature of science, science is about *discovering* the way things are. The idea is that the basic patterns of the world exist independently of us and our concerns and interests: it has, for instance, always been true that phosphorus reacts with calcium carbonate. Suppose such a technique were invented by trial and error: it would still be based on the same facts about phosphorus, iron, calcium carbonate, etc., but these would not have been explicitly taken into account. So when we say that science underpins technology we must stress that the relevant facts, etc., were *known* and explicitly made use of in the design process. (Compare the discussion of the Manhattan Project in Chapter 3.)

As it happened, there is some dispute as to whether the technology just described, which was invented by Sydney Gilchrist Thomas and his cousin in 1878 (Landes 1969:258), was underpinned by science. There was a long tradition of ironmasters adjusting the composition of the charge and inspecting the results to improve the smelting of ore. It is generally agreed that after Thomas the industrial chemists, the scientists, came into their own, and so Thomas may have been the last of the gifted amateurs. It should be clear that, in general, as technology becomes more complex, it is less likely to have been invented by trial and error. The suggestion that, for example, an electronic computer could have been invented by pure trial and error is hardly plausible. What we can say for sure is that the Industrial Revolution marks a watershed in the relations between science and technology: before 1780 technology owed relatively little to science, but a hundred years later they were intimately connected.

We have understood science underpinning technology to entail the design of a process of production, in which the technique used is explicitly based on scientific knowledge. As we shall see at the end of this section, this is not the only sense in which science can bear on technology. But just as no account of cotton would be complete without mention of Sir Richard Arkwright, no discussion of the relations of science to technology in the Industrial Revolution would be complete without mention of James Watt's steam engine.

The first workable steam engine was the atmospheric engine designed by Thomas Newcomen in the first decade of the eighteenth century in Cornwall, where it was put to work pumping water out of flooded tin mines. The operation was based on the idea discovered by Torricelli that the atmosphere has 'weight', and hence will press down on a piston connected to a cylinder that is at least partially evacuated—the better the vacuum, the greater the 'weight'. The vacuum is created by letting steam into the cylinder and then condensing it: since water has a very much smaller volume than air, a (partial) vacuum is thereby created.

The efficiency of an engine—the amount of work obtained per unit of energy input—is determined in part by how good the vacuum is and that in turn depends on the standard of metal-working. In fact, the early engines were extraordinarily inefficient. And they were very slow because each stroke required heating and cooling of a large cylinder. In 1769 Watt improved the engine by adding a small condensing chamber and valve connector. The principle was that the large working cylinder was never cooled down: steam was fed into the top, driving the piston down; when the valve was opened the steam rushed into the cold condensing chamber, condensed, and thereby induced a vacuum in the cylinder. Watt made several other important changes and improvements to the engine, but we will focus on this one and ask whether it was based on science or trial and error.

The principle could have been based on trial and error in the sense that the facts about steam, heat, etc., on which it is based are just facts about how things are. Watt could thus simply have tried a separate condenser to see what would happen. But that is not what actually took place, as is clear from Watt's own account of the matter (Cardwell 1972:84-90). Rather, the principle was the result of analysis based on scientific theory. For instance, Watt knew that the inefficiency of the Newcomen engine was due to the high heat capacity of the working cylinder, and hence that to heat up and cool down only the small condensing chamber would require much less fuel. He employed here certain basic concepts of thermodynamics. He also knew that lukewarm water will boil in a vacuum, and hence that keeping the cylinder itself cool will prevent condensation and so prevent the engine from working at all. This is another *scientific* generalisation, expressing the relation between pressure, temperature and the vapourisation of water. Thus, Watt *understood* the reasons for the high fuel consumption and slow work rate of the old engines, and he knew this could not be remedied by keeping the cylinder cool. The only way to keep the cylinder hot, and hence improve efficiency, was to condense the steam elsewhere.

We can let Cardwell sum up Watt's achievement:

> This innovation could only have been made by a man of unusual scientific as well as technological abilities. A man, that is, who was familiar with the then known laws of heat and with a deep understanding of the properties of steam. It is profoundly unlikely that a practical engineer of the period could have been led to make this invention. [Cardwell 1972:88]

The last sentence here accords with our comment above: the more complicated the technology, the less likely it is that it could have been invented by trial and error. Watt's principle is by no means obvious and, while it is conceivable that it could have come about by trial and error, it makes much more sense to suppose that the innovation came about by the chain of reasoning summarised above.

When science underpins technology, we can say that it has a *direct* impact on production. Science can also have *indirect* effects. To the extent that science undermines traditional beliefs and entrenched practices, it contributes to a climate in which change is more likely. There is no doubt that the Scientific Revolution of the seventeenth century did undermine traditional beliefs. And there is no doubt that science was, in this sense, a necessary part of the Industrial Revolution. Without a climate in which new ideas could flourish and in which traditional methods and practices could be challenged and improved, there could have been no Industrial Revolution. The social and political context of the time was thus not unaffected by the impact of scientific ideas, and there is no doubt that this had an indirect effect on the Industrial Revolution. Thus, we can judge that Rostow, Musson and Robinson, and Cardwell are all correct in their views on the role of science in the Industrial Revolution.

Conclusion

This examination of the Industrial Revolution is not of mere historical interest; it has lessons for the present. Some of the consequences of industrialisation seem universal: higher standards of living, fall in birth rates, expectation of continued economic growth and innovation, and the continued utilisation of science in production. Many economic historians have therefore advocated industrialisation as a panacea for the problems of developing countries. However, these lessons must be tempered by the realisation that growth that uses up resources cannot be sustained in a world that is finite and in which there are, therefore, insuperable limits to growth.

From the standpoint of studies of Science, Technology and Society, the Industrial Revolution demonstrates the impact of technical and technological change on the economy of a country, and it shows how this can lead to economic growth and changes in work practices. These things necessarily lead to changes in the way people live, where they live, and what controls their lives. The Industrial Revolution did in fact mark a turning point for the economies of all countries of the world, though the impact has still to be felt in a small number. Henceforth a healthy economy is believed to be one that grows and those who are in a position to deliver growth are those who hold power over others.

Further reading

Mantoux (1961), Landes (1969), Mathias (1969) and Deane (1979) are classic texts on the Industrial Revolution. The book by Mantoux is perhaps the easiest and most interesting to read, but it is also the oldest; it is particularly good on textiles and the various ways in which the industry was organised. Landes's emphasis is on technology. Clausen (1980) and Pollard (1980) provide a contrast to Landes: whereas he seems to want to take technological change as the explanation of the Industrial Revolution, Pollard and Clausen take a more political stance. The books by Inkster (1991) and Mokyr (1993) are more modern, both focusing on technology, as does the article by Gaski (1982). As for the role of science, Musson and Robinson (1969) and Cardwell (1972) are the classic texts, Cardwell being particularly good. Donovon (1979) focuses on Watt. Finally, it has been argued by some that there was really no such thing as an Industrial Revolution. These debates are for the specialist historian, but the interested reader could look at the paper by Fores (1986).

References

Berg, M. (1985), *The Age of Manufactures*. Totawa, NJ: Barnes and Noble.
Cardwell, D. (1972), *Technology, Science and History*. London: Heinemann.
Clausen, D. (1980), *Bureacracy and the Labor Process*. New York: Monthly Review Press.
Crafts, N. (1985), *British Economic Growth during the Industrial Revolution*. Oxford: Oxford University Press.
Deane, P. (1979), *The First Industrial Revolution*, 2nd edn. Cambridge: Cambridge University Press.

Donovon, A. (1979), 'Toward a Social History of Technological Ideas: Joseph Black, James Watt and the Separate Condenser', in G. Bugliarello and D. Dowe (eds), *History and Philosophy of Technology*. Urbana: University of Illinois Press: 19–30.

Fores, M. (1986), 'The Myth of the Industrial Revolution', *History*, 66:181–98.

Gaski, J. (1982), 'The Cause of the Industrial Revolution: A Brief "Single-Factor" Argument', *Journal of European Economic History*, 11.

Inkster, I. (1991), *Science and Technology in History*. London: Macmillan.

Landes, D. (1969), *The Unbound Prometheus*. Cambridge: Cambridge University Press.

Mantoux, P. (1961), *The Industial Revolution in the Eighteenth Century*. London: Methuen.

Mathias, P. (1969), *The First Industrial Nation*. London: Methuen.

Michell, B. (1984), *Economic Development of the British Coal Industry, 1880–1914*. Cambridge: Cambridge University Press.

Mokyr, J. (ed.) (1993), *The British Industrial Revolution*. Boulder: Westview Press.

Musson, A., and Robinson, E. (1969), *Science and Technology in the Industrial Revolution*. New York: Gordon and Breach.

Pollard, S. (1963), 'Factory Discipline in the Industrial Revolution', *Economic History Review*, 26:254–71.

Pollard, S. (1968), *The Genesis of Modern Management*. Harmondsworth: Penguin.

Pollard, S. (1980), 'A New Estimate of British Coal Production, 1750–1850', *Economic History Review*, 33:212–35.

Rostow, W. W. (1971), *Politics and the Stages of Economic Growth*. Cambridge: Cambridge University Press.

Smith, Adam (1776/1970), *The Wealth of Nations*. Harmondsworth: Penguin.

Smith, Merritt Roe, and Marx, Leo (eds) (1995), *Does Technology Drive History? The Dilemma of Technological Determinism*. Cambridge, Mass.: MIT Press.

CHAPTER 7

Science, Technology and the Economy

John Laurent

In this book so far, readers have been introduced to a range of issues involved in the interactions of science, technology and society, and it has been seen that science and technology have been steadily growing in importance throughout history, especially since the so-called Scientific Revolution of the sixteenth century, at about the time of Copernicus. Much of this importance has arisen from the employment of science and technology, from an early date in the economic sphere—as was seen, for example, in Newton's attempted experiments in alchemy (Westfall 1994) and, more recently and seriously, the vast expenditure on R&D in the drugs industry. But contrary to a commonly held view— that there exists some kind of inevitability in scientific and technological 'progress'—it can be shown that *conscious decision* by policy-makers can have a major bearing on the directions taken by science and technology, including the kinds of economic activity in which science and technology are employed. In this chapter, specific illustrations of this general principle will be given, beginning with a study of the British alkali industry of the eighteenth and nineteenth centuries, and following this with a comparison of the ways in which science and technology have been utilised in Australia and in two highly industrialised nations— Sweden and Japan.

The British alkali industry

In Chapter 6, it was explained that the Industrial Revolution of the late eighteenth and early nineteenth centuries in England and Continental Europe, at first based on textile manufacturing, largely took place without science. This was also the case with associated industries such as the alkali industry, which grew with the need for washing and bleaching of raw cotton and wool. But industrial development could proceed only so far without science. Sooner or later, for manufacturing industries to remain economically competitive, they needed to adopt more scientific methods, and decisions had to be made as to how this could best be achieved.

For raw cotton and wool to be turned into saleable textiles, large quantities of sodium carbonate, or washing soda, needed to be produced. This had earlier been obtained from burning seaweed, but such a method could not keep pace with the new demand, and science eventually became involved in the search for an *economic* method of producing the quantities necessary.

Thus, towards the end of the eighteenth century, the French government offered a prize of 100,000 francs to anyone who could find a method of converting common salt into washing soda. A process was submitted by Nicholas Leblanc in 1791, in which salt was heated with sulphuric acid, producing sodium sulphate and giving off hydrochloric acid gas. The sodium sulphate was then roasted with limestone and coke to produce what was called 'black ash', from which soda was leached out with water, leaving calcium sulphide and carbon dioxide as waste products.

The first part of the process is:

$$\text{salt} + \text{sulphuric acid} \rightarrow \text{sodium sulphate} + \text{hydrogen chloride}$$

Then, with heat:

$$\text{sodium sulphate} + \text{limestone} + \text{coke} \rightarrow \text{soda} + \text{calcium sulphide} + \text{carbon dioxide}$$

For various reasons, including the fact that Britain and France were at war from 1793 to 1815, the Leblanc process was not taken up in Britain until the 1820s. In any event, the process was eventually adopted, but major problems quickly developed. Principally, in one of the first examples of environmental concerns, the ejected fumes of hydrochloric acid laid waste whole areas of the English countryside: the first environmental lawsuit of which we have a record concerned householders in Liverpool in 1823, who said the acid was eating their washing. Improvements, then, were needed, and in 1836 a technique was devised in which the hydrochloric acid was funnelled into a tower and washed out. The Leblanc process remained a seriously polluting and inefficient method, however, and various people began to search for a better one. In principle, a better method had been known since 1811, in which salt was treated with ammonia, and carbon dioxide. This yielded soda, but wasted ammonia by producing it as ammonium chloride.

The problem was eventually solved by a Belgian, Ernest Solvay, in 1863. Solvay's method was to utilise a former waste product, quicklime (calcium oxide, CaO), to heat with the products of the first reaction to produce further ammonia for recycling. There were some problems in developing the process for large-scale production, but by the 1870s Solvay-produced alkalis were able to undersell Leblanc products by 20 per cent. The process involved the use of a carbonating tower in which an ammoniacal salt solution and carbon dioxide entered at pressure: the gas, by rising, forced the ammonia-salt solution to atomise through small holes in a series of trays. This facilitated the reaction, producing sodium bicarbonate which was left at the bottom of the tower and which, on heating, was reduced to sodium carbonate.

Yet Britain persisted with the Leblanc process. In 1882 the Solvay process accounted for 44 per cent of German soda production, compared with only 12 per cent in Britain; by 1900, whereas over 90 per cent of Germany's production was by the Solvay process, only 40 per cent of Britain's production was. This odd and seemingly unnecessary backwardness of the alkali industry in Britain had wide effects. For example, as late as 1904 only 18 per cent of Britain's production of chlorine came from the much more efficient electrolysis of salt solution, whereas by that time 65 per cent of Germany's chlorine was produced by electrolysis, and *100* per cent of US production used this method. In fact, the last British Leblanc plant did not close down until 1920, having survived a number of commercial manoeuvres, and benefiting when World War I forestalled foreign competition for a time (see Pavitt and Worboys 1977).

How was the British Leblanc industry able to survive and apparently prosper for so long? There were several reasons. Its efficiency steadily improved over the period, but more important was a merging of firms to form the United Alkali Company, thus enabling economies of scale. (This company ultimately merged with another company, Mond and Brunner, to form Imperial Chemical Industries, or ICI.) Also, price-fixing agreements with British Solvay producers were entered into. Since fortunes had been invested in chemical plants utilising the Leblanc process, it was able to be kept alive and economically viable into the twentieth century—notwithstanding the seemingly inexorable march of science and technology. One author (Inkster 1991) has even spoken of the 'advantage of backwardness' in this respect (in terms of savings on new investment in plant). This case study, then, illustrates the importance of economic considerations in the involvement of science and technology in industry: not only in terms of the eventual universal adoption of the most economic method, but also in helping to explain the persistence of the older method in Britain.

We shall now broaden our discussion of the economic context of science and technology by examining the growing internationalisation of the world's economies since the late nineteenth century, and how the very different national economic policies of countries like Australia, Japan and Sweden can be seen to have profoundly influenced the direction taken by science and technology in these countries.

Internationalisation of the world's economies from the late nineteenth century

The growing economic rivalry between Britain, Germany and other nations throughout the late nineteenth and early twentieth centuries, already alluded to, became entangled with imperialist and military ambitions which resulted in the establishment of world-wide colonial empires and also led to World War I (1914–18). Following Germany's defeat by the Allies, Britain's overseas possessions were expanded by the accession of former German territories as Mandates, as were those of Japan and the United States. The economic power of these nations was augmented accordingly as a result, and the centre of gravity of world economic activity tended to move away from the European mainland to the overseas territories, Asia and North and South America.

Certain developments just prior to the war assisted in this process. Notably, the Panama Canal, completed by the United States in 1914, greatly facilitated trade between the east coast of North America and the Asia–Pacific region, a development which, in turn, had been made possible by the replacement of sail by steam in the last decades of the nineteenth century. One writer (Fraser 1913) prophetically wrote of the Panama Canal as it was nearing completion: 'The trend of civilisation and commerce has ever been westwards, and what the Mediterranean Sea was and the Atlantic is, the Pacific will become. ... Half the human race dwell on lands washed by the waters of the Pacific.' Today, the Asia–Pacific region is the fastest-growing economic region in the world: the economies of this region expanded by 7.0 per cent in 1992, compared with an average growth for the nations of the Organisation for Economic Cooperation and Development (OECD) nations of 1.6 per cent.

Australia's place in this economic order

A political map of the world from the 1920s shows that by then the British Empire had reached its largest extent, which greatly assisted the continuing internationalisation of the world economic order. Each member country of the Empire had its role to play in this order. Essentially, the function of countries like Australia was to provide food and raw material for the 'mother country', and also markets for the latter's manufactured goods (Anon. 1949). In Australia's case, the chief raw material was wool for Britain's still very important woollen textile industry. As is explained in a book called *The Wonder Book of Empire*, printed in 1925, 'All the best quality woollen clothes worn by the people of the United Kingdom are made from Australia's golden fleeces' (Anon. 1925). That year 64.4 per cent of Australia's export earnings were from wool and wheat, most of which was shipped to Britain (Butlin 1987), as shown in Figure 7.1.

Millions of tons of wheat were being exported to Britain at the time. Other foodstuffs were also important, including frozen mutton and beef (made possible by the invention of refrigeration by an Australian, James Harrison, in the 1850s) and dried fruits, jam and sugar. In 1922–23 Australia exported 11.4 million kilograms of dried fruit, 1.1 million

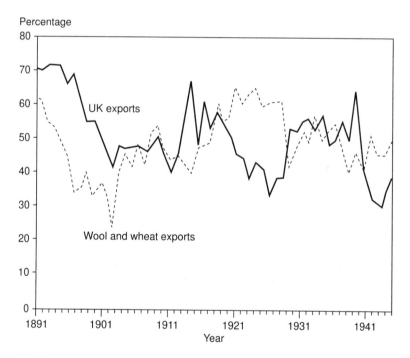

Figure 7.1 Australian exports, 1891–1945.
Source: Butlin (1987).

kilograms of jams and jellies, and in 1933–34, more than 200,000 tonnes of sugar (*Australian Encyclopaedia* 1926; *Commonwealth Yearbook* 1939).

Australia was also a major supplier of gold to Britain, which required considerable quantities to back its Gold Standard system of currency. (This had formed the basis of most international trade since the 1870s, and was readopted in 1925 after being temporarily abandoned during World War I.) By World War I, too, Australia was Britain's most important supplier of lead and zinc (from the rich Broken Hill lode). In all, by 1926, *96 per cent* of Australia's export earnings were from primary products (Page 1926a). As late as 1954, *The Australian Clear School Atlas*, which showed the produce of the various British Commonwealth countries, listed Australia's as 'wool, wheat, skins, butter, sheep, cattle, lead, gold, silver, cane sugar, fruit'. Manufacturing (the importance of which for a country's economic health will be shown below) did not rate a mention. Britain's products, on the other hand, are headed by 'textiles, coal, iron and steel, machinery' (see Figure 7.2).

The role of science and technology

Given this emphasis on commodity exports, it is not surprising that science and technology in a country like Australia tended to be concerned with primary production (Raby 1996). The invention of refrigeration has already been mentioned, and as might be expected, important innovations in gold extraction techniques were also developed in Australia (Todd 1995). Similarly, as in the United States and Canada, where labour shortages drove efforts to develop labour-saving agricultural machinery, so too in Australia technological innovation was a salient feature of economic activity. Notable inventions included the stump-jump plough, the stripper (mechanical wheat harvester) and the rotary hoe (Ingpen 1982).

Much of this inventiveness proceeded with minimal science, as did a considerable amount of innovation in crop improvement. Where science did become involved, it was overwhelmingly in the rural sector. The Commonwealth Scientific and Industrial Research Organisation (CSIRO) originated in a Commonwealth Advisory Council of Science and Industry established during World War I amid concerns that Germany's war effort was benefiting more from the applications of science and technology than was that of the Allies (Buckley-Moran 1987). With the defeat of Germany, such concerns virtually disappeared, and attention was diverted to what was seen as the needs of primary production. This is clear from the organisation's declared priorities. When the Advisory Council changed its name to the Council for Scientific and Industrial Research in 1926 (it became the CSIRO in

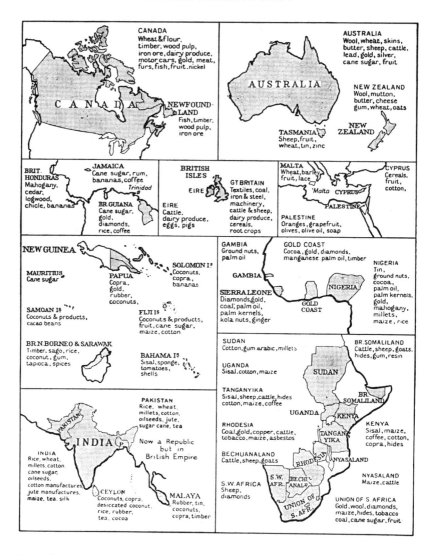

Figure 7.2   Produce of British Commonwealth countries, 1954.
Source: The Australian Clear School Atlas.

1949), the executive resolved at its first meeting that its research efforts would be directed to:

1. Animal Pests and Diseases;
2. Plant Pests and Diseases;
3. Fuel Problems, Especially Liquid Fuels;
4. Preservation of Foodstuffs, Especially Cold Storage; and
5. Forest Products. [Lamberton 1970; see also Minter 1941]

Interestingly, the CSIR's most acclaimed achievement during this early era was its *introduction* (not eradication), in conjunction with state Departments of Agriculture, of a plant pest. *Cactoblastus cactorum*, the larva of a South American moth, successfully destroyed large acreages of prickly pear (*Opuntia* spp.), an introduced cactus which had overrun much of the cultivable land of New South Wales and Queensland (Schedvin 1987). Previously, the only means of dealing with the plant was through burning or mechanical destruction (Wit 1992).

A not-so-successful attempt at biological control during this period was the introduction of the Hawaiian cane toad (*Bufo marinas*) into Queensland, in an attempt to control the larva of the cane beetle. The 1939 Queensland government's *Agricultural and Pastoral Handbook* says of this experiment: 'This toad has proved a very efficient agent in bringing about control of the white-grub pest of sugar cane in Puerto Rico, and [has been] introduced in the hope that it might prove of similar utility here.' All Queenslanders are today aware of the gross miscalculation this turned out to be: the cane toad, which has spread throughout the state and into New South Wales and even the Northern Territory, is itself one of the state's greatest pests.

Notwithstanding this heavy emphasis on rural-related research, some initiatives were devoted to manufacturing during the inter-war years (1918–39), and some of these came from the CSIR. The council's first chairman, George Julius, was an engineer by training, and one of his first moves was to ask John Madsen, professor of electrical engineering at the University of Sydney, to visit the National Physical Laboratory and National Bureau of Standards in the United States to find out what would be needed to set up a standards laboratory in Australia. The project was some years in getting started, but by 1936 the CSIR had established a Secondary Industries Testing and Research Committee with Madsen as chair. The Country Party (later National Party) leader and Commonwealth Treasurer at the time, Dr Earle Page, justified these initiatives on the basis of what he called 'the necessity for a national plan of development for Australia' (Page 1926b). The New South Wales and Victorian Chambers of Manufactures were invited to submit products for testing, but little was done, and with the outbreak of World War II in 1939 attention was almost totally diverted from the needs of civilian manufacturing.

Early Australian manufacturing

Manufacturing and such associated science and technology as existed in Australia up to World War II (1939–45) was, as might be expected, closely connected with the rural industry—specifically farming equipment (e.g. fencing wire, galvanised iron) and agricultural machinery.

Another focus was the motor vehicle industry, which partly grew out of the former. (This paralleled developments in North America, where the International Harvester Company, for instance, was producing a gasoline-powered 'auto buggy' in 1909.) In fact, considerable inventiveness and enterprise had been demonstrated by Australians in mechanical engineering from an early date. In 1836, to take as an illustration, Charles Darwin, during a visit to Tasmania, caught a steam ferry across the Derwent and noted in his diary: 'The machinery of one of these vessels was entirely manufactured in this colony, which, from its very foundation, numbered only three-and-thirty years!' (Laurent and Campbell 1987). This enterprise was usually on the part of private entrepreneurs, with little government support at first. For example, while it is generally agreed that the first commercially successful automobile was built by Karl Benz in Germany in 1885, that same year agricultural machinery engineers David and John Shearer of South Australia began work on a 'steam carriage' which was remarkably modern in conception, with a full differential and a complex steering mechanism, and capable of a speed of more than 25 kilometres per hour.

The employment of science and technology, or research and development, in these inventions was minimal, however, and further development of the automotive industry in Australia (with its tiny population) required foreign capital and government assistance. Both came with the establishment of branches of the Ford Motor Co. in Geelong, Victoria, and General Motors in Adelaide, South Australia, in the 1920s. General Motors reached an agreement with Holden's Motor Body Builders (which had started out as a family firm of saddlers in the 1850s) for that company to be the sole assembler of General Motors vehicles in Australia. (Holden was later—in 1931—taken over by General Motors, beginning a trend of foreign ownership which has persisted to this day.)

Government assistance in these developments took a number of forms. First, and most important, was tariff protection, which gave a strong incentive to overseas manufacturers to move in behind the tariff wall. Government support for the motor industry was also provided in the form of technical facilities and expertise originally established for defence needs. In the late 1920s and early 1930s, for example, the government Ordnance Factory at Maribyrnong in Victoria, in a joint venture with the Broken Hill Proprietary Co. (BHP), was producing motor axles from high-grade alloy steel for General Motors. With the resumption of munitions production at Maribyrnong with the approach of World War II, this technical know-how was passed on to the commercial sector (Buckley-Moran 1987).

The advent of World War II saw a further strengthening of ties between the motor vehicle and manufacturing industries generally in

Australia, and also much greater involvement of government planning and expertise. Soon after the establishment, in 1936, of a plant at Fisherman's Bend in Melbourne by General Motors, land adjacent to the plant was purchased by the Commonwealth for the building of an aircraft factory and also an aeronautical research laboratory, and as war approached, expertise flowed freely between these establishments and General Motors (Laurent 1994). During the war the Australian motor industry (which included a multitude of small motor-body builders besides Ford and General Motors—215 altogether in 1941) came into prominence as one of the country's major industrial activities, effectively organising the production of many types of essential transport equipment, as well as shell casings, torpedoes, landing vessels and diesel engines, and also aircraft. By the end of the war, some 3500 aircraft had been delivered to the Royal Australian Air Force. Many were from the Commonwealth Aircraft Corporation's works, which benefited from the production of engines at the General Motors plant (which had its own foundry), and also at the new Ford plant at Rocklea, Queensland. (Anon. 1946; A. Scurr, personal communication).

The Labor government in office at the end of the war, which had a strong ideological commitment to economic planning and to secondary industry, hoped to capitalise on this wartime infrastructure, as well as the skills developed in the workforce, to build up a strong post-war manufacturing sector. One major outcome of this policy was the production of the Holden car, American-owned but built and partly designed in Australia, which first came off the Fisherman's Bend assembly line in 1948. Other examples—in a much smaller way—of firms which got their start during or shortly after the war include Jeffres Bros engineers of Northgate, Queensland, whose co-founder, Lionel Jeffres, had trained as a fitter with the air force during the war (the firm's first lathes incorporated aircraft bearings); and Chief Kitchenware Pty Ltd of Salisbury, South Australia, which used aircraft aluminium in its early days and also presses which had made 25-pounder shell cases (L. Jeffres, interview; L. Heard, personal communication).

Australia and the world economy today

The internationalisation of the world economy in the years up to and following World War I increased in pace after World War II and has continued to do so ever since. Most world trade in the 1920s and 1930s was between advanced manufacturing nations and less developed countries, who provided raw materials and foodstuffs for the former. But increasingly over the past fifty years the bulk of trade has been in manufactured products, and this trend has been increasing in pace. As was pointed out in Chapter 6, consumption of such products is not limited by the size of the stomach. Australia, however, has not kept abreast of these developments. In 1985–86 for instance, while 65 per cent of the value of world trade was in manufactured products, 77 per cent of Australia's export earnings were from rural and mining products. An item in the National Australia Bank's *Monthly Summary* (December 1986) commented at the time: 'Given the unfavourable outlook for rural and mining commodities, a major improvement in exports will need to come from the manufacturing sector.'

This comment should be expanded upon. As has already been explained, Australia has traditionally been overwhelmingly an exporter of primary products (or commodities), a legacy of its membership of the British Empire. And it seems that trade negotiators in this country do not wish things otherwise. The Uruguay Round of trade talks concluded in December 1993 as part of the General Agreement on Tariffs and Trade (GATT) are said to be of major benefit to Australia, with additional export earnings per annum by 2000 likely to be about $240 million

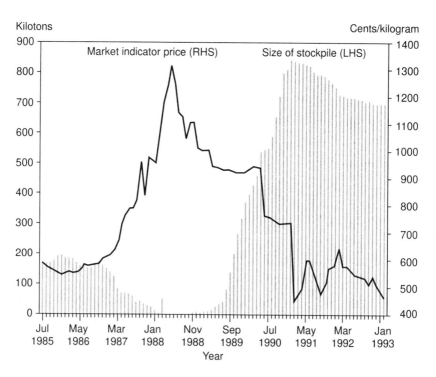

Figure 7.3 Australia's wool debacle.
Source: National Australia Bank, *Quarterly Summary*, March 1993, p. 18.

for beef, $250 million for wheat, $300 million for 'other farm products', and $500 million for coal at current prices. Significantly, wool was left out of these calculations, which presumably has something to do with the sad story concerning this commodity of late. Over the four years 1990–93, wool prices fell by 45 per cent, and in the first quarter of 1993 were at their lowest real levels since the 1920s. The problem has been over-production, resulting in huge stockpiles, as illustrated in Figure 7.3. In December 1993 the wool stockpile stood at 3.8 million bales and had been written down a further $708 million in value from earlier in the year, bringing to more than $2 billion the devaluation of the stockpile since the crash in prices in 1990 (as shown in the graph). By early 1996, wool prices had begun to improve, but only marginally, to around 583 cents per kilogram (*Australian Financial Review*, 23 February 1996).

Other major commodity exports have suffered similar price falls in Australia's trade history. Wheat, for example, Australia's second-largest export earner in the 1920s, steadily dropped in price throughout that decade due to world over-supply resulting from increased acreages and higher yields made possible by mechanisation and the application of fertilisers. Prices then plummeted with the onset of world-wide economic depression in the 1930s (Anon. ca 1930). The British writer J. H. Curle said at the time (1931): 'Owing to the invention of a machine— the tractor—wheat and other grains are ... being greatly over produced.' Curle was right: by the mid-1930s Australia was earning less from wheat than a decade before, even though it was producing and exporting more than twice as much (and wreaking terrible devastation on the land in the process—see Chapter 11, and also Flannery 1994).

Besides wool and wheat, prices for other commodities have periodically been depressed. Take coal and iron ore, for instance. In 1996 they were Australia's largest and fifth-largest commodity export earners respectively, and Japan has been Australia's biggest customer for them. Both have been subject to periodic price cuts: iron ore by 10 per cent and coking coal by 8–9.5 per cent in February 1994. In February 1996 exporters of steaming coal were also facing a price reduction. Constant price weakness also has been a feature of base metals—copper, lead, zinc, tin and aluminium. This situation was exacerbated by aggressive selling on world markets by the Commonwealth of Independent States (the former Soviet Union), which raised world stocks to record levels. Gold, too, recorded substantial price falls in the mid-1990s and there were fears for its future performance (*Australian Financial Review*, 19 February 1996).

What makes this situation particularly precarious for Australia is the country's large foreign debt, which tends to *worsen* at times of economic recovery, when greater volumes of manufactured goods are imported—

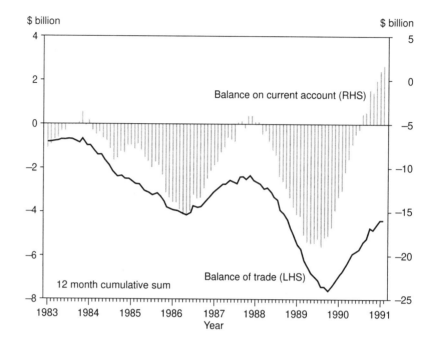

Figure 7.4 Australia's balance of trade and current account, 1983–91.
Source: National Australia Bank, *Quarterly Summary*, September 1991, p. 14.

for example, cars. The net foreign debt of a country is a cumulative figure, resulting from a series of current account deficits, which in turn reflect a negative total for the country's balance of payments. The balance of imports and exports—trade balance—is usually a major component of the latter (see Figure 7.4).

Despite an upturn in the trade balance from the late 1980s, Australia's current account was over $15 billion in deficit. More worrying for Australia was the net foreign debt position, which stood at $130 billion—with a *debt-service ratio* (interest payments on this debt as a proportion of export earnings) running at around 19.5 per cent. This figure has been exceeded in Australia's history only in the 1920s (a time of heavy borrowing from Britain for road and railway building) and the 1930s (during the Great Depression, when interest payments had to be met on previous borrowings while earnings from commodity exports slumped). By 1996 Australia's net foreign debt stood at some $180 billion, with a debt-service ratio of around 11.5 per cent: an improvement on earlier years, but still far from satisfactory.

Clearly, Australia *must* capture a greater share of its domestic market for manufactured goods and increase its exports of them if it is to avoid becoming a 'banana republic' as the then Treasurer, Paul Keating, warned a few years ago. As already explained, the most rapidly advancing economies are those trading in manufactures. Services—including financial services, shipping, tourism, education—have also been growing rapidly, and these may fill the gap for Australia (and other countries with balance of payments problems), though this is far from certain. It has been cogently argued (Cohen and Zysman 1989) that the relative economic decline of the United States compared with Japan is closely linked with the former's neglect of manufacturing. Similar concerns have been expressed about the UK economy. Certainly the underlying strength of the Japanese economy (see below) rests heavily on manufacturing. In Australia's case, while services currently make up around 70 per cent of GDP, they comprise only 17 per cent of exports, and in fact in 1988–89 ran a net deficit of $2.6 billion (AMC 1990).

Science, technology and the economy in Australia

There are, encouragingly, indications that the situation is beginning to change in Australia, in terms of the application of science and technology to economic needs. Just as these developments—as will be seen—are benefiting the economy, they are also beginning to affect the nature and practice of science and technology in this country.

Governments have paid particular attention to the automotive industry, especially under the former Commonwealth Minister for Industry, Technology and Commerce, John Button. He was largely responsible for the Labor government's car plan, instituted in 1985 and aimed at improving efficiency and product quality in the industry, and at increasing exports. At a business gathering at Ford's Geelong casting plant, Button praised the company's export performance, which at that stage was worth $400 million a year and included sales of complete Capri convertibles to the United States, as well as engine blocks to Japan under a $30 million contract with the Mazda Motor Corporation (*Ford News*, September 1992). The Capri program ended in 1994, but Ford Australia has recently (1996) announced plans to produce another small model to replace it, utilising a similar export credit arrangement under the car plan. Under the plan, the total value of motor vehicle and component exports rose by 282 per cent from 1984 to 1994, being worth $1.5 billion in 1994. This figure further increased to $1.8 billion in 1995 (Automotive Industry Authority 1990; *Bulletin*, 23–30 January 1996). It should be stressed, though, that Australia was still running an automotive trade deficit of $7.3 billion in 1994.

Changes in the applications of science and technology have been part of these developments. In response to the fact that manufacturing's share of GDP had fallen from nearly 30 per cent in the early 1960s to around 17 per cent in the early 1980s, the federal government took various initiatives aimed at stimulating manufacturing. A Division of Manufacturing Technology within the CSIRO was established in 1983, and the following year the government announced a 150-per-cent tax concession scheme for private-sector R&D. In 1987 the Department of Industry, Technology and Commerce assumed responsibility for all science and technology policy, including the running of the CSIRO; and in 1989 the Prime Minister's Science Council was formed, together with a program to set up Co-operative Research Centres and the extension of the R&D tax concession scheme to June 1993 (since cut back). The importance of manufacturing was recognised in a paper, *The Changing Role of Manufacturing Technology*, released by the Prime Minister's Science Council in May 1992, in which the second sentence reads: 'Manufacturing is the main wealth-creating sector in developed, economically vibrant economies.'

Of course, government support of R&D in industry is one thing; its effectiveness in promoting export-oriented growth in that sector is another. There is no *necessary* direct pay-off for the economy from government efforts at 'picking winners' in economic activity (see Joseph and Johnston 1985). Nevertheless, as history shows, there *can* be substantial benefits from an energetic, proactive industry policy.

It remains true, however, that Australian firms invest much less in R&D than their overseas counterparts in the same industry sectors. A 1989 study by the Australian Science and Technology Council (ASTEC), *The Contribution of Science and Technology to Australia's Balance of Payments to the Year 2000: The Manufacturing Sector* found that, given the bias of the Australian economy towards the primary sectors, Australia did not rank well against other nations of the Organisation for Economic Cooperation and Development (OECD) in private R&D expenditure. The study referred to work by the Department of Industry, Technology and Commerce which indicated that, based on the industry structure prevailing in Australia in 1984–85, business enterprise R&D spending needed to double to be in line with OECD countries with a comparable economic structure.

This general picture remained true in 1996. And the ASTEC study also went on to stress the need for economic *structural adjustment* if Australia was to effectively participate in the dynamic growth of the Asia–Pacific region. This will require further vigorous development of industries producing goods with a high value-added content—or elaborately transformed manufactured products—incorporating concomitantly more R&D. Australia still has a long way to go to reach the levels of research funding in highly successful manufacturing nations like Japan and Sweden, to which countries we shall now turn for comparison.

Science, technology and the Japanese economy

One could hardly find a starker contrast to the Australian economy in recent years than that of Japan. As against Australia's current account deficit of around $15 billion in June 1991, Japan was running a current account *surplus* of the order of $91 billion at about the same time. This has since further increased to $156 billion by 1996, despite a downturn in the economy since that time, in part reflecting a general world-wide economic slowdown. The Japanese economy is in fact still very strong—possibly the world's strongest—and soundly based, posting a trade surplus of $US146 billion for the year in 1994 (Roger Farrell, Embassy of Japan, Canberra, personal communication).

Recent years have seen spending policies amounting to a massive fiscal stimulus by the Japanese government, including $A100 billion approved in August 1992 for spending on public works and infrastructure, as well as on R&D facilities for universities and on government loans to small and medium-sized business. This exemplifies the strongly *interventionist* philosophy of that country's government, which contrasts with the *laissez-faire* policy which has been characteristic of English-speaking countries in recent times. The Japanese have long known the value of an interventionist industry policy, and arguably this has been a major factor in the country's remarkable economic success. Such a philosophy in fact can be traced back to the beginnings of the country's decision to 'Westernise' (industrialise) following the so-called Meiji Restoration (the abolition of the Shogunate and re-establishment of the Imperial throne) in 1868. This decision was taken after a perceived weakness of the country in the face of demands by the United States that it open its doors to trade. The Japanese government was then faced with the choice, as the 1911 *Encyclopaedia Britannica* put it, between 'entering the field as an instructor, and leaving the nation to struggle along an arduous and expensive way to tardy development,' or actively intervening in economic affairs; and so it was that the government became actively involved. It set up schools of applied science in universities; financed public works such as dockyards, shipbuilding facilities and railways; made low-interest loans available to business; and established an agency to familiarise overseas markets with Japanese products (much like the Ministry of International Trade and Industry—MITI—which was established after World War II).

At the beginning of the Meiji era, Japan had virtually no export-oriented manufacturing industries (and in fact in 1870 exported 'nil' manufactured goods). The result of all this government effort was that by 1906 the country possessed 9329 industrial and commercial companies with a paid-up capital of £107 million, with exports of manufactured products rising from £8 million in 1901 to over £20 million in 1906.

A commonly held myth about Japan is that its economic success is based less on technological innovation than on imitation. Certainly in the early days of the Meiji revolution this was substantially true. The country perceived that it had much catching up to do, and the government unashamedly borrowed ideas and employed British and German personnel. But this was quickly augmented by home-grown expertise and innovative practices. In fact, Western science had been known in Japan since almost the beginnings of the so-called Scientific Revolution in Europe. Indeed, even before that time—from at least the fourteenth century—Japanese artisans had been making swords, for example, from high-grade steel smelted from iron-bearing sand, a technique pioneered by the Japanese (see Pacey 1990). In shipbuilding, while it is true that the country's extraordinary naval and military victory over Russia in 1904–05 was achieved largely with vessels purchased from Britain, Japan built 27,000 tonnes of its own shipping during the war (using iron and steel from government foundries at Nagasaki and Wakamatsu), and by 1910 had built what was then possibly the world's most advanced battleship—the 19,370-ton *Satsuma*. In 1922 the Japanese built the world's first aircraft carrier, and by the 1930s had developed the Mitsubishi Type 96 Fighter, the world's first low-wing carrier-borne fighting monoplane (Mikesh 1981).

Let us turn to the motor vehicle industry, with which Japanese manufacturing and overseas-sales success have become so closely associated in the minds of many people. It may surprise the reader that here, too, the Japanese have been highly inventive and innovative from the beginnings of the industry—with this major difference from Australia: that the government has been closely involved from the start. The first commercially produced automobile, the Takuri Type 3 of 1907, was financed by the Imperial household, and more than likely drew on the iron and steel testing facilities of the government Industrial Experiment Laboratory established in Tokyo in 1900. By World War I the use of motor vehicles in warfare was being tested in the field, in the offensive in Tsingtao, China, by Japan against Germany in August–November 1914. In 1918 a considerable boost was given to the industry when the government announced subsidies for military vehicles, and by the 1920s commercial vehicles and, to a lesser extent, cars were being produced in their thousands by such companies as Mitsubishi (Ruiz 1986).

Government involvement in the economy increased throughout the 1930s, at a time of growing militarisation, and direct controls over the motor vehicle industry were established with such measures as a 1936 Motorcar Manufacturing Enterprise Law, which effectively ended any foreign ownership in the industry.

With the almost complete destruction of Japan's economic infrastructure towards the end of World War II, people again looked to the government for reconstruction. While the economy was in the hands of the Supreme Commander for the Allied Powers (General MacArthur), authorisation was given in 1947 for the recommencement of motor vehicle production. By 1949–50 production was up to 28,700 units per year. In 1952 MITI (whose origins can be traced to a Commerce and Industry Ministry established in 1937—see Nakamura, 1988) declared that it was 'vital for the national economy that a sound car manufacturing industry be developed', and introduced a series of measures which in practice ended motor vehicle imports into the country (Ruiz 1986).

The support that the Japanese government has provided for the motor vehicle industry has been most effective. By the early 1960s, companies such as Toyota were exporting to countries like Australia, and this growth has continued. Motor vehicles are still by far Japan's largest export earner, notwithstanding some recent cutbacks in production.

MITI has continued to nurture the automotive industry in a number of ways, not least through R&D support. It is true that innovation in the motor industry was heavily dependent on the import of foreign technology in the immediate post-war years (Kojima 1995), but home-grown R&D has become increasingly important. In ceramics research, for example, joint R&D by Toyota, Nissan and Honda, with backing from MITI, has given these companies a head start on the rest of the world. Ceramic materials able to withstand temperatures of up to 1500°C are already being used in engines; in the near future it is likely that, as a result of this MITI-supported research, materials producers and fabricators will become important manufacturers in joint ventures for development and production of cylinder liners, piston heads and rings, turbocharger rotors and other engine parts. The diesel-engine truck manufacturers Isuzu and Hino have already perfected engines with ceramic pistons, valves and other parts that eliminate the need for water cooling and reduce fuel consumption by half, with 30-per-cent higher output than conventional engines (ASTEC 1989).

Even further down the road in automotive technology, perhaps, are recent advances in electric and solar-powered cars in Japan. The Tokyo Electric Power Company has developed a vehicle capable of a speed of 130 kilometres an hour with a range of 250 kilometres between recharges (which can be done overnight from a conventional power supply). This project has also been backed by MITI, which agrees with the power company that some 200,000 electric cars will run on Japanese roads by the turn of the century. (For comparison, the estimated *total* number of vehicles on Japanese roads in 1948 was about 181,000.) In the more experimental area of solar power, Toyota, for example, has produced a solar-powered racing car capable of speeds of up to 120 kilometres an hour (*New Scientist*, 2 October 1993). Given our current profligate use of petroleum (see Chapter 11), this may point a way to the future.

MITI's overall budget in 1983–84 (the latest figures in ASTEC 1989) came to the huge sum of 224.4 billion yen (about $A2.9 billion), of which about 20 per cent was directed towards *basic* research at centres like the Institute of Solid State Physics at Tokyo University, the Institute of Mathematical Sciences at Kyoto, and the Protein Research Institute at Osaka University. Besides this spending in universities and other research centres, there is that by the Ministry for Education, Science and Culture (Monbush), the major funder of basic research in Japan, accounting for about 47 per cent of national science and technology spending. In 1993 the annual budget for basic research in universities from this source was around $A650 million (Lewis 1994).

This growing attention to basic research has been a feature of Japanese science and technology in recent years, reflecting a concern that exploitable areas of research have begun to show diminishing returns. As one recent commentator (Lewis 1994) put it: 'In the early 1990s [MITI] has shifted the emphasis ... away from applied industrial technology, while the number of cases of companies undertaking joint research with universities and Government research institutions has shown a steady increase.'

But likely economic benefits, even if they only materialise in the long term, are never lost sight of, and in fact in 1989, 42 per cent of MITI's funding went to supporting research in industrial laboratories and a further 21 per cent was spent on subsidising private-sector industrial research. A specific agency within MITI responsible for promoting industrial R&D, called the Agency of Industrial Science and Technology, had a budget of 119 billion yen in 1992. Significantly, in contrast with the kind of research usually supported by the private sector in Australia, MITI has become increasingly involved with industry in programs reflecting what have been described as 'national concerns to strengthen the research base for long term technological development' (ASTEC 1989).

Among these long-term programs is the Next Generation Base Technologies Development Program, which has been used to catalyse much of the private-sector R&D in new material such as the ceramics, composites and high-grade alloys already referred to. A specific program looking at developing so-called 'synergy' ceramics within this broader strategy was introduced in 1994 as a 'State project', despite the fact that demand for ceramics in major user industries in Japan, including in the automotive, electrical and electronics sectors, had been relatively static over the previous two or three years (Furumoto 1994). By and large, private industry has supported such initiatives, realising that co-operation with the government in these efforts can ultimately have significant pay-offs. In any case, the private sector is aware that government-funded research programs are generally less vulnerable than private ones to budget cuts in times of recession, so that, with a return to prosperity, co-operating firms can enjoy the benefits.

Science, technology and the Swedish economy

Sweden is another country which has successfully harnessed science and technology to economic needs. It, too, has pursued a strategy of producing manufactured goods for export, a strategy which has paid handsomely. As in Japan, this orientation of the country's economy has been a relatively recent phenomenon, dating only from the late nineteenth century. In fact, as late as 1913, Sweden's largest industry appears to have been forest products (timber and wood pulp—see Jörberg 1976). By that date, however, a transformation of the Swedish economy had already begun, and this change to export-oriented manufacturing has not been substantially altered since.

Again, the crucial importance of inventiveness and ingenuity on the one hand, and state support on the other, in the country's economic success is readily discernible. Remarkably successful companies like Volvo, Saab, Ericsson, Electrolux, Husqvarna and Borg-Warner were all started in the nineteenth or early twentieth century by entrepreneurs with a scientific and technical training in the country's universities and newly-established technical colleges. Gustaf de Laval, for example, who had trained at the Stockholm Institute of Technology, invented the cream separator (at a time when Sweden was still largely a farming and commodities-based economy). He founded a company—AB Separator —to manufacture and sell his invention in 1883; it produced more than 100,000 machines in the company's first fifteen years and exported four-fifths of them. The firm was later named Alfa-Laval, and in 1986 it was still the world leader in dairy equipment, with about 35 per cent of the market.

But Laval had quickly moved on to other areas of technology. By 1890 he had invented a steam-turbine engine capable of providing motive power for sea-going vessels and also of generating electricity: about 1400 of these had been manufactured by 1898, all except about 300 being exported. This invention was quite independent of that by the better-known Sir Charles Parsons in England, whose *Turbinia* first sailed under steam-turbine power in 1897 (Gustavson 1986).

Birger Ljungström (1872–1948) was another such inventor-entrepreneur. At the age of sixteen, Ljungström invented a bicycle with an adjustable gear shift, and for a time was making them with backing from

Alfred Nobel. By 1908, with his brother Fredrik, Ljungström had founded a company for manufacturing large turbines, one of the first big foreign sales being a 1000-kilowatt turbo-alternator with an efficiency of 77 per cent ordered by the London Street Car Company. It is worth noting that *steam* turbines were of limited use in Sweden, which had to import nearly all of its coal; so evidently from early on both Laval and Ljungström were aiming at the export market. By 1914 Ljungström was working on plans for a monoplane, on parts for automobiles and on apparatus for cellulose production (at that time important for the production of celluloid, a precursor of plastics, and used in aircraft windscreens during World War I).

The Husqvarna company was started by another enterprising individual, Per Froms (1856–1931), who had served an apprenticeship as an engineer with a company called Bolinders, and who also started out making bicycles. By 1900 around 5000 bicycles were being produced annually at Husqvarna, and by 1908 the company had started making motorcycles, which of course it is still doing.

Volvo, Saab and Scania also began at this time. As Sweden has next to no coal deposits, the country was forced to more or less by-pass the 'steam age' which had occupied nearly a century of British industrial history (as described in Chapter 6). Sweden does not have oil deposits of any consequence either, yet from an early date entrepreneurs like Alfred Nobel (1833–96), endower of the Nobel Prize, recognised the potential of this natural product and established some of the world's first refineries in Sweden, using crude oil from the Baku fields in Russia. The products of oil refining—kerosine, petrol, etc.—were quickly utilised as a power source by companies such as Bolinders for sawmilling equipment, and from there it was but a short step to automotive engineering. In 1897–98 a sawmill engineer, Gustaf Erikson, who had worked on Bolinders machines, made Sweden's first automobile, and eventually (in 1911) founded the Scania company. By 1914 Scania was producing 200 cars and trucks a year.

Volvo was originally the name of a ball-bearing company which had been founded in Gothenburg in the early 1900s. The company was joined in 1917 by Gustav Larson, who had worked for a British engineering firm in Coventry and who convinced Volvo that it could move into producing complete automobiles, which the company did from 1924 (Gustavson 1986; Berggren 1993). Volvo grew from strength to strength, being quick to see the commercial value of innovative safety features (such as the world's first safety-cage body and laminated windscreens, from 1944) as well as high-quality engineering. Saab, originally a military aircraft maker, expanded into motor vehicle production at the end of the 1940s (company data 1995).

As already indicated, the transformation of the Swedish economy had as much to do with government policy as with the ideas of a few enterprising individuals. As well as primary and higher education, the state provided a rail system from the 1870s, which greatly facilitated the movement of raw materials such as iron ore (with which Sweden, in contrast to coal and oil, is richly endowed). By the 1940s efforts were being made to strengthen government support for science and technology—a Technical Research Council was established in 1942, for example, and a National Science Council in 1946—and this momentum was maintained under Social Democrat Prime Minister T. F. Erlander (1946–69), a former Minister of Education. In 1960 Sweden spent 1.7 per cent of its GDP on R&D (compared with 1.1 per cent in Australia at the time), and this had grown to nearly 3.0 per cent in 1987—one of the highest figures among OECD nations—compared with a *decline* in Australia to 1.0 per cent (Lowe 1987; OECD 1989).

As in the past, there is close collaboration between business and government in Sweden. Co-operative research institutes, for instance, have tended to concentrate on research fields designated as priority areas by the government: over the last few years these areas have included electronics and computer technology, aeronautics, new materials, production engineering and energy technologies. Other government agencies concerned with R&D spending have included a National Board of Universities and Colleges (about a quarter of R&D in Sweden is carried out within the higher education sector), membership of which includes representatives of trade unions and other interested organisations, as well as the business community and the educational and research communities. A Council for Planning and Co-ordination of Research incorporates a Secretariat of Future Studies and, in stark contrast to Australia, overall responsibility for co-ordination of science and technology questions is vested in the Prime Minister as chair of a Research Advisory Board. According to a team of OECD examiners in 1987, the Research Advisory Board was 'an outstanding government structure which nurtures and actively promotes the interface of basic science with industry, with a co-ordinating overview of national benefit' (ASTEC 1989).

It should be said, though, that the so-called Swedish model, involving a large public sector (accounting for up to 70 per cent of GDP, compared with around 30 per cent in Australia) has come under strain of late. The country experienced an unprecedented deterioration in its current account in the late 1980s—though this was reversed after 1991, when the volume of imports fell more sharply than the volume of exports. In 1992, following volatility in European currency markets after attempts to bring the various currencies into line, the government was forced to adopt emergency economic measures to avert devaluation of the krona. Unemployment, which had not exceeded 3 per cent since the 1940s, soon rose to record levels, reaching 6 per cent (*Australian Financial Review*, 8 October 1992).

Sweden's resilience in the face of these difficulties has been remarkable, nevertheless, and the country continues to be an outstanding example of what an innovative, science-based, export-oriented manufacturing economy can achieve. In 1995 *Fortune* magazine ranked Volvo the world's tenth most rapidly expanding major company (*Volvo Journal*, Summer 1995–96). As an Australian Bureau of Industry Economics report (1987) emphasised, Sweden's success has undoubtedly been largely due to its early shift away from raw materials exports towards value-added manufacturing with a high technology content, as with transport equipment, and the country's industrial strength has continued to be dependent on its ability to apply new technologies and to adapt and develop them further. Also of considerable importance, it has been argued, is the country's long-standing social democratic ideology: it has encouraged a commitment to developing skills of a high order among the workforce, and has assisted in the implementation of such ideas as 'autonomous work groups', with flexible task allocation, which have been the practice of firms like Volvo for the past twenty years and are only now being adopted in Australia (*Ford News*, May 1994).

This combination of technological excellence and workforce commitment has enabled the production of highly marketable goods with an emphasis on quality (rather than mere price competitiveness) and innovative design. Safety, as mentioned, has also long been a concern of companies like Volvo, which until recently was Australia's highest-volume European car importer. Saab, too, has pursued similar philosophies as well as, more recently, showing a concern for fuel efficiency and stringent emission standards. The 1996 Saab model in the '9000 series', for example, recycles its exhaust gases and is said to be 13-per-cent more fuel-efficient. As with Toyota, Swedish car makers have also been showing much interest in recent years in electrification. The Swedish-British International Automotive Design and Clean Air Transport consortium has already won a contract from the Los Angeles council to design and build an electric vehicle specifically for use in that smog-bound city (*Sunday Mail*, Brisbane, 4 February 1996).

Conclusion

This chapter has examined the importance of economic considerations which must be taken into account in any attempt to understand the complex interactions of science, technology and society. We have looked at the subject from a historical perspective, beginning with a case study of the British alkali industry. The focus of attention then moved to Australia, where the country's place in the 'new world order' of the expanded British Empire following World War I was described, and it was seen that this position helped shape not only the Australian economy but also the direction of science and technology policy, oriented, as it was, almost entirely to the production of raw materials and foodstuffs. The recent decline of these sectors, and the implications of the same for Australia's serious foreign-debt situation, was discussed, and suggestions were made for the need for a reorientation of science and technology towards secondary production.

A comparison has also been made with the interactions of science, technology and the economy in Japan and Sweden, and it has been argued that deliberate decisions to industrialise towards the end of the nineteenth century in both countries, and government policies directed towards that end, have been important factors in the rapid development of these countries into highly successful export-oriented manufacturing economies. Australia, on the other hand, has been largely content to follow the patterns of the past: to continue to produce food and raw materials for the world's industrialised nations as it had once done for Britain, and, as in former times, science and technology in Australia have been predominantly directed towards this production of commodities. That is to say, in Australia the directions taken by science and technology have *not* followed some inexorable momentum. These human activities have been shaped by the economic contingencies of Australia's past as part of the British Empire—the decisions determining their orientation were largely made elsewhere, and they have not been substantially questioned since, only modified in line with changing patterns of world economic and political power. It is hoped that the case studies presented in this chapter demonstrate the importance of human decision-making in determining the *kinds* of science and technology that can be seen in different parts of the world at different times.

Further reading

There is a large literature upon this subject, some of it dealing with particular countries. Nakamura (1988) gives an important account of the rebirth of Japan after World War II, and its development into an economic superpower. Gustavson (1986) and Lowe (1987) are useful perspectives on Sweden, while ASTEC (1989) compares the policies of several countries regarding the use of science.

The book by Lamberton (1970) is rather old, but reviews important aspects of the organisation of science, technology and the economy in Australia, focusing upon aspects such as the legal, patent and tax systems. The papers by Buckley-

Moran (1987) and Laurent (1994) examine particular aspects of the Australian economy, while Todd (1995) examines Australia's early dependence upon other countries for its science and technology, and the changes which have occurred. Flannery (1994) outlines the history of life in Australia, pointing out how humans—especially in the last two hundred years—have been having impacts upon the Australian environment. Looking forward, AMC (1990) assesses problems and prospects for Australian manufacturing in this decade.

More generally, Inkster (1991) is mainly concerned with the changing relationships between science, technology and the economy from the eighteenth century to the present, while Pacey (1990) studies the processes of invention and technological change over the last thousand years. The paper by Cohen and Zysman (1990) argues that countries must not neglect their manufacturing industry in favour of a 'post-industrial' service economy. The short book by Pavitt and Worboys (1977) is a good approach to a range of issues in the area.

References

ABARE (1996), *Outlook 96, Conference Proceedings*, vol. 1: *Commodity Markets and Resource Management*. Canberra: Australian Government Publishing Service.

Anon. (1925), *The Wonder Book of Empire*. London and Melbourne: Ward, Lock & Co.

Anon. (ca 1930), *The Shell Manual for Power Farmers*. [New Zealand]: The Shell Company.

Anon. (1946), *This Is Australia*. Sydney: Oswald Ziegler.

Anon. (1949), *A Military Survey of the British Empire*. Melbourne: Australian Military Forces.

Australian Manufacturing Council (AMC) (1990), *The Global Challenge: Australian Manufacturing in the 1990s*. Melbourne: Australian Manufacturing Council.

Australian Science and Technology Council (ASTEC) (1989), *Public Policies for the Exploitable Areas of Science: A Comparison of the United Kingdom, Japan, the Netherlands and Sweden*. Occasional Paper No. 9. Canberra: Australian Government Publishing Service.

Automotive Industry Authority [Australia] (1990), *Report of the State of the Automotive Industry 1990*. Canberra: Australian Government Publishing Service.

Berggren, C. (1993), *The Volvo Experience: Alternatives to Lean Production in the Swedish Auto Industry*. London: Macmillan.

Buckley-Moran, J. (1987), 'Australian Science and Industry between the Wars', Prometheus. 5, 1:5–28.

Bureau of Industry Economics [Australia] (1987), *Studies in Industrial Development and Innovation Policy, No. 2: Sweden*. Canberra: Australian Government Publishing Service.

Butlin, N. J. (1987), 'Australian Wealth and Progress Since 1788: A Statistical Picture', in H. Gordon (ed.), *The Bicentennial Diary*. Brisbane: Sunshine Diaries, vol. 3:331–42.

Cohen, S., and Zysman, J. (1989), 'Manufacturing Matters: The Myth of the Post-industrial Economy', in T. Forester (ed.), *Computers in the Human Context*. Cambridge, Mass.: MIT Press.

Curle, J. H. (1931), *This World First*. London: Methuen.

Flannery, T. (1994), *The Future Eaters*. Sydney: Reed.

Fraser, J. F. (1913), *Panama and What It Means*. London: Cassell.

Free, R. (1992), *Science and Technology Statement, 1992–93* (Budget Related Paper No. 6). Canberra: Australian Government Publishing Service.

Furumoto, J. (1994), 'Japan's Fine Ceramics Industry Fulfilling International Obligations', *Japan 21st*, April: 53.

Gustavson, C. G. (1986), *The Small Giant: Sweden Enters the Industrial Era*. Athens, Ohio: Ohio University Press.

Ingpen, R. (1982), *Australian Inventions and Innovations*. Adelaide: Rigby.

Inkster, I. (1991), *Science and Technology in History: An Approach to Industrial Development*. New Brunswick: Rutgers University Press.

Jörberg, L. (1976), 'The Nordic Countries 1850–1914', in C. M. Cipolla (ed.), *The Emergence of Industrial Societies, Part Two (Fontana Economic History of Europe*, vol. 4). Hassocks, Sussex: Harvester Press/Barns & Noble by agreement with Fontana.

Jörberg, L., and Kranz, O. (1989), 'Economic and Social Policy in Sweden, 1850–1939', in P. Mathias and S. Pollard (eds), *The Industrial Economies: The Development of Economic and Social Policies (Cambridge Economic History of Europe*, vol. VIII). Cambridge: Cambridge University Press.

Joseph, R. A., and Johnston, R. (1985), 'Market Failure and Government Support for Science and Technology: Economic Theory versus Political Practice', *Prometheus*, 3, 1:138–55.

Kennedy, E. (ed.) (1989), *Ford in Australia, 1925–1989*. North Ryde, NSW: Universal Magazines.

Kirkwood, L., Gibson, G., Hermann, A., and Swiericzuk, J. (1983), *The Australian Economy: Problems and Issues*. Carlton, Vic.: Pitman.

Kojima, S. (1995), 'The Past and Future Patterns of Savings and Investment in Japan', *Asia–Pacific Economic Review*, 1, 1:64–78.

Lamberton, D. (1970), *Science, Technology and the Australian Economy*. Sydney: Tudor Press.

Laurent, J. (1994), 'Industry Policy and the Australian Motor Industry, 1920–1942', *Journal of the Royal Australian Historical Society*, 80, parts 1–2:91–115.

Laurent, J., and Campbell, M. (1987), *The Eye of Reason: Charles Darwin in Australasia*. Wollongong, NSW: University of Wollongong Press.

Lewis, J. (1994), 'Collision of Interests: The Role of the Ruling Party in Science and Technology Policy', *Japan Forum*, 6, 1:62–72.

Lowe, I. (1987), 'The Very Successful Swedes', *Australian Society*, 6, 1:17–19.

Mikesh, R. C. (1981), *Zero Fighter*. London: Jane's Publishing Co. Ltd.

Minter, R. D. (1941), *Textile Fibres and Wool Quality*. Sydney: D. S. Ford.

Nakamura, T. (1988), *The Postwar Japanese Economy: Its Development and Structure*. Tokyo: University of Tokyo Press.

OECD (1989), *Economic Surveys: Sweden*. Paris: Organisation for Economic Cooperation and Development.

Pacey, A. (1990), *Technology in World Civilization*. Cambridge, Mass.: MIT Press.

Page, E. (1926a), *Australian Industries: The Interdependence of 'Primary' and 'Secondary'*. Sydney: Simmons Limited.

Page E. (1926b), 'Address before the Victorian Chamber of Manufactures', in Victorian Chamber of Manufactures, *Minutes*, 22 February 1926.

Pavitt, K., and Worboys, M. (1977), *Science, Technology and the Modern Industrial State*. London: Butterworth.

Raby, G. (1996), *Making Rural Australia: An Economic History of Technical and Institutional Creativity*. Melbourne: Oxford University Press.

Ruiz, M. (1986), *The Complete History of the Japanese Car*. New York: Portland House.

Schedvin, C. B. (1987), *Shaping Science and Industry: A History of Australia's Council for Scientific and Industrial Research, 1926–49*. London: Allen and Unwin.

Slipper, P. (1996), *Industry and Commerce* (1996 Liberal Policy Statement). Alexandra Headland, Qld: D. Walker, Printer.

Stephenson, W. (1972), *The Ecological Development of Man*. Sydney: Angus and Robertson.

Stubbs, P. (1971), *The Australian Motor Industry: A Study in Protection and Growth*. Melbourne: Cheshire and Institute of Applied Economic and Social Research.

Todd, J. (1995), *Colonial Technology: Science and the Transfer of Innovation to Australia*. Cambridge: Cambridge University Press.

Westfall, R. N. (1994), *The Life of Isaac Newton*. Cambridge: Cambridge University Press.

Wit, K. (1992), *A History of Left-Hand Branch at Mt Sylvia*. Gatton, Qld: Lockyer Printing.

CHAPTER 8

Science, Technology and Economic Theory

Martin Bridgstock and David Burch

This chapter complements the last two by outlining some major ways in which economists have sought to understand the relationships between science, technology and the economic system. The economic impact of science and technology is probably the major reason why governments pay so much attention to these factors, as shown in Chapters 2, 6, 7 and 9. Equally, economists have expended much effort trying to understand how new knowledge, and new technology, fit into economics. Some surprising results have emerged: for one thing, the orthodox approach to economics has not proved very useful in understanding technological innovation and change, although it has continued to make major impacts in other areas (e.g. Becker 1976). For another thing, following one of the major themes of this book, it has become clear that where knowledge is produced in the economy, and how it is linked to business and industry, are crucial in determining the economic outcomes.

It is a characteristic of industrial societies that we tend to take for granted the flow of new products and processes, such as computers, drugs and food products, but this was not always so. As we saw in Chapters 6 and 7, science did not begin to influence industry directly until the middle of the nineteenth century. Technology has always been important to humanity, but in the past, change was much slower: entire generations might pass and experience little that was new or innovative (Clark 1985:27). It was suggested in the introduction to the book that, in a craft-based, pre-industrial society, knowledge of productive systems (for example in agriculture and building, and in the manufacture of implements) was passed down from one generation to the next virtually unchanged. When changes to productive systems were made, they were usually small and incremental, and departed from the *status quo* only a little. Even then, change was introduced only when some

159

external crisis (such as the depletion of raw materials or a change in climate) forced it. Then, and only then, would an adaptive change be introduced.

In an era in which craft-based production was dominant, science had a very limited role in the economy and the wider society. Of course, 'science' had a deep cultural significance before the nineteenth century, as a way of explaining and controlling physical phenomena and social events. Court astronomers were expected to predict the dates of eclipses—and sometimes their lives hung on their success! The findings of Galileo and Darwin had enormous effects upon our views of ourselves and the universe, and upon our religious views. However, they had almost no economic impact: no new industries were directly established as a consequence, and there were no new techniques developed for the manufacture of new products.

Some science still has this cultural importance today. Physicists such as Stephen Hawking (1988) and Paul Davies (1991) affect our view of the universe, where it has been and where it is going. This kind of impact is as important now as it has ever been. However, it is unlikely that billions of dollars would be spent if science related *only* to our views of the universe. If this were the case, it seems likely that science would be only a small part of academic life, rather like departments of classical studies and fine art. It is the link with technology, and through technology to industry, that has made science so important.

The concept of economic growth

Economic growth is measured by an increase in the gross domestic product (GDP) in a given period—usually over one year. This is not a simple matter. Critics such as Waring (1988) have argued that the concept of GDP itself is misleading. Further, as you read this text, you will come across differing views on the value, or otherwise, of economic growth. Chapter 7 shows how modern nations pursue economic growth as a desirable goal. On the other hand, Chapter 11 raises doubts about how far economic growth can continue, especially if the less-developed nations succeed in growing quickly. In the context of the different chapters, these different attitudes toward growth are not inconsistent. Virtually all the nations of the world, and probably most of the people in the less-developed nations, regard economic growth as desirable and necessary. On the other hand, environmentalists are quite legitimately questioning whether rapid economic growth can continue in a finite world with a fragile ecology.

Of course, these questions are bound up with matters of definition. What do we mean, for example, by economic growth? Often, growth is defined in terms of the use of natural resources. If this is so, then in the long run economic growth would appear to be unsustainable. On the other hand, a definition such as that of Norman Clark raises other possibilities: 'I shall define economic growth as the rate of change of the capacity of any economic system to produce goods and services for the consumption and investment requirements of its citizens' (Clark, 1985:23).

This coincides, of course, with John Forge's definition of growth in Chapter 6. Without doubt, even under this definition, some processes of growth are likely to be disastrous for the world in the long term. If we all wish to 'consume' large amounts of air-conditioning, larger cars and houses and endless kilometres of new roads, then growth will eventually lead to disasters as the world's resources run out or the world becomes polluted beyond tolerance. On the other hand, some aspects of growth are not open to criticism in this way. Our modern automobiles, for example, tend to be lighter and more fuel-efficient than they were in the 1950s. Therefore, while contributing to economic growth, they are also less disastrous for the world's ecological system. Even more dramatic has been the increase in computer capacity in the last decades of the twentieth century. For a few hundred dollars, we can now buy a computer with far more power than the greatest machine that existed before about 1960. What is more, the modern computer is smaller, uses far less material to build, and consumes far less electricity in its operation. Of course, as we use these machines more and more, the same problems may arise again, albeit at a higher standard of living.

These examples suggest that we cannot simply regard economic growth as an unmitigated good or a total disaster. We must accept that much of the world is going to pursue growth, and should therefore seek to understand how that growth can, as far as possible, be channelled away from the more disastrous areas. The economists, usually, have regarded growth as an unmitigated good, and we will encounter much of this perspective in this chapter.

Why do nations grow economically at different rates?

If you spend any time looking at the economic news, two points will strike you. One is that economic growth is regarded as vitally important by economists and by nations. The second is that national economies grow at widely differing rates. For example, some nations in Africa and some ex-communist nations, like Russia, appear to be growing at a negative rate: that is, their economies are actually producing less, year by year. On the other hand, some economies in Asia—notably China, Malaysia, Taiwan and Thailand—appear to be growing at spectacular rates. In one recent year, mainland China had a growth rate of 29 per cent, and had to take steps to reduce the growth rate to a more modest 12 per cent to avoid high levels of inflation.

Figure 8.1 shows a simple chart. For each of thirty nations, the amount of economic growth over the period 1980 to 1985 on the y-axis has been plotted against the GDP per head in 1980 on the x-axis. There is no inference that initial economic position determines the growth rate, but a couple of interesting facts emerge at once from the diagram.

First, as we have said, nations vary enormously in their growth rates. On the graph, the total growth over the five-year period varies from 69 per cent—for Singapore—to a negative growth rate (or contraction) of nearly 30 per cent for Chad and Liberia. These are huge differences, and continued expansion, or contraction, along these lines would probably permit some countries to join the group of developed nations, while others would regress to starvation.

Second, leaving aside the remarkable growth rate of Singapore, the overall shape of the graph is roughly triangular. Looking down the left-hand side of the graph, countries which were poor in 1980 showed a wide range of economic changes. Some, like Sri Lanka and Uganda, grew very fast, while others contracted. However, the group of nations on the right-hand side, which includes the United States, Japan and Australia, expanded at a much more uniform rate.

We should be cautious about reading too much into this observation, but it is an important one. It suggests that, for whatever reason, richer nations are more similar in their levels of progress than poorer ones. Perhaps the factors leading to the huge range in results from poorer countries are external: many of the poorer countries are subject to catastrophes like invasion, civil war, and famine. In other cases, though, it is possible to discern a whole range of factors from within the country which correlate strongly with economic growth.

Factors correlating with GDP growth rate

Economists have carried out much research on economic growth, and suggest that there are many factors which correlate positively with it. We will examine some of these factors, and discuss what they imply for national economies, and for science and technology. Some of these have been summarised by Grossman and Helpman (1993). We should note that these are statistical relationships, and some of them are not strong. As a result, it does not follow that in any particular case a country's growth rate can be predicted by these characteristics. With that in mind, the research results are as follows.

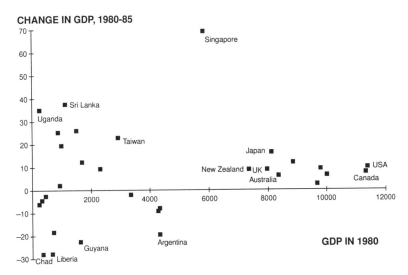

CHANGE IN GDP, 1980-85

Figure 8.1 Gross domestic product per head and economic growth rates for thirty countries: percentage change in GDP, 1980–85. (The horizontal axis is in 1980 international prices, rather than any specific currency.)
Source: Calculated from data in Summers and Heston 1988.

Investment to output ratios

In general, these are positively associated with the growth rate. The ratio is a measure of how much of the output of an economy is ploughed back to make more productive capacity. It is a basic theorem of economics that the amount of money invested must equal the amount of saving in an economy, but of course, this issue is more complex in reality, if we take foreign investment into account.

Qualities of the human capital stock

Economists refer to the education and increase in the skills of a work-force as an investment in the quality of the human capital, and indicators such as the literacy rate and the school enrolment rate also appear to correlate positively with the rate of economic growth.

Export as a large share of output

Countries which export a high percentage of their production appear to have faster growth rates. This is especially noticeable in the case of the 'tiger' economies of South-East Asia: Taiwan, Hong Kong, Singapore and South Korea. On the other hand, this finding seems to apply only to exports of sophisticated manufactured goods: many poor countries in the Third World export a great deal of their agricultural products, but find that their goods are declining in price over the long term. This explains why small, poor countries can export a great deal and still experience poor growth rates (Harrison 1991:307).

The number of scientists and engineers employed in research

This also seems to correlate with industrial growth, as does a *low rate of population growth* and a range of government policies, including a *low government consumption of GDP* and *low marginal tax rates*. However, with this and indeed with all of these correlations, it is important not to confuse cause and effect. As Ziman (1976) has pointed out, a high rate of industrial growth might lead to increased investment in the training of scientists and engineers. This may lead us to question the emphasis placed on low levels of government expenditure as a condition of economic growth. Does not a large education system tend to push up government expenditure? These sorts of conundrums have caused problems for governments all over the world, and in the next section we shall begin to analyse some of the theories about the relationships between science, technology and the economy, to see if they can shed any light on these issues.

Science, technology and economic theory

Since science and technology are important in the modern economy, it is logical that economists should try to understand them. Historically, economics has tried to do two things. It has tried to understand how economies work, often building ingenious models to do so; and it has tried to make suggestions about how the economy should be run, based upon these models. At best, though, economists have had only mixed success in terms of these two issues. Adam Smith (1723–90), was a Scottish philosopher who is usually regarded as the first person to analyse the workings of the free enterprise system. In his most famous work, *An Inquiry into the Nature and Causes of the Wealth of Nations* (1776), Smith advocated that a mass of rules and regulations should be swept away from the British economy, leaving people to pursue their own fortunes through the market (Heilbroner 1976). This, he argued, would lead to a great increase in wealth. As we might expect, though, many interest groups attempted to shield themselves from the effects of the market, as the full implications of Smith's ideas came to be understood. From the opposite perspective, Karl Marx was appalled by the poverty and squalor caused by the Industrial Revolution, and argued that eventually the working class would rise up, run the economy for themselves and sweep away all exploitation (Marx and Engels 1967). His ideas inspired the political movements that, at one time, governed the lives of one-third of the world's population. However, far from liberating the workers and the peasants, such governments often turned out to be dictatorial, inefficient and top-heavy with bureaucrats. More recently, John Maynard Keynes argued that governments should intervene at times of high unemployment, and ensure that the economy did not remain in a slump. His ideas were followed and, for several decades, higher levels of employment resulted (Stewart 1972; Donaldson 1976). In recent years, Keynes's approach has been abandoned and high levels of unemployment have now returned to most industrial countries.

In general, it seems, economics has at least two problems. First, it seeks to explain the actions of people, and people's ideas change— partly because their knowledge of economics changes. Second, econ- omies are constantly being transformed as a result of technological change. As a result, theories and ideas which might have been appro- priate in one decade may well be out of date in the next. Economists are aware of these problems, and have shown great ingenuity in adapting their ideas to the complex world of human activity.

In doing so, economists have utilised a number of key concepts, such as prices, labour, and wages, which are familiar to most of us. However, the concept of capital is less clear. To most of us, investment means saving money in an interest-bearing bank account. To an economist, investment means buying (or, in some cases renting) productive machinery and materials. Thus, if an entrepreneur starts up a new business, she might invest in a factory, machinery, raw materials, as well as hire labour to work the machinery and raw materials. The resulting products would, she hopes, be sold at a price which would enable her to make a profit.

Utilising concepts like these, economists have constructed sophis- ticated models and theories about the economy. They have produced theories of productive firms, and models of how markets work and at what price (the 'equilibrium price') demand and supply converge. They have also constructed complex models of entire economies. Science and technology do not often appear in these models, although they have not been totally neglected. Adam Smith, for example, anticipated that great increases in productive power could be achieved through the effects of the division of labour, by which a production process was broken down into a series of simple and repetitive tasks which could be easily per- formed by unskilled labour. Instead of one person working at all stages of production and applying diverse skills to produce a finished product (as was the case in the pre-industrial period when craft production was dominant), the Industrial Revolution saw the introduction of a system of production in which workers specialised in only one of the many tasks which were necessary to produce a finished article. Chapter 6 analysed the 'new' division of labour which emerged in the textile industry. Smith's own favourite example of the division of labour in the manufacture of a simple product, a pin, is famous:

> A workman not educated to this business ... nor acquainted with the use of the machinery employed could scarce, perhaps, with his utmost industry make one pin in a day, and certainly could not make twenty. But in the way in which this business is now carried on ... one man draws out the wire, another straightens it, a third cuts it, a fourth points it, a fifth grinds it ... the important business of making a pin is, in this manner, divided into about eighteen distinct operations. [Smith 1776/1970:109–10]

As Easlea (1973:97) notes, Smith suggested that ten workmen could make up to 48,000 pins per day on the basis of the division of labour. Without it, the same workmen could not have made more than 200 per day, and probably many fewer. In other words, the introduction of new machinery and new forms of industrial organisation led to massive increase in productivity for a given combination of capital with labour. In Smith's example, above, workmen were able to greatly increase the number of pins produced because they were working with new and more sophisticated technology which mechanised many operations and facilitated a division of labour. But without the use of new technology, the production of 48,000 pins per day would have required many more workers and would have made the price of pins very much higher.

Of course, this new system of industrial production would not have been possible without major changes in the organisation of production and the introduction of new technology in the factories. As we saw earlier, these were the key features of the Industrial Revolution. But to Marx and Engels, the Industrial Revolution and the technology it spawned was also a means of controlling labour and ensuring that it remained subordinate to the needs of the new capitalist class. Marx understood that technology need not only be used to improve the productivity of labour, but could also be used to *replace* workers. Technology made possible the production of large amounts of output with only a few workers, and to that extent, employers who developed new techniques of production could not only reduce their labour costs but also ensure compliance among workers who might otherwise create difficulties. As Marx stated:

> In England, strikes have regularly given rise to the invention and application of new machines. Machines were, it may be said, the weapon employed by the capitalists to quell the revolt of specialised labour. The self-acting mule, the

greatest invention of modern industry, put out of action the spinners who
were in revolt. [Marx, cited in Rosenberg 1976:118]

Whatever the validity of Marx's analysis, it seems clear that
there is a close relationship between technology and work. This raises
another important issue which needs to be addressed. In Chapter 6 we
saw that economists usually base their analysis on 'the factors of
production', which are the absolutely essential ingredients of any production process. The three factors usually referred to are labour, capital
and land (or natural resources), although for most purposes we refer
only to the factors of capital and labour. The key point is that capital can
be used to replace labour, as we saw in Chapter 6 when the new textile
machines (capital goods) greatly increased the productivity of labour.
This particular observation was taken up by another school of thought
which argued that it was the relative price of the factors of production
which determined the rate of technological change. In other words, if
the price of labour (i.e. wages) rose more quickly than the price of
capital (i.e. interest rates) then the businessperson had an incentive to
invest in labour-saving technology and increase their profit by saving on
the most expensive factor of production.

As Rosenberg (1976:109) has noted, however, this theory does not
fully explain the development of *new* technology, but only why businesspeople are likely to invest in labour-saving technology (which may be
innovative, but equally may not). Moreover, the focus on the relationship between capital and labour did little to explain what was the most
dynamic aspect of new technology—its effect on economic growth. As
Chapter 10 notes, it has been suggested that two-thirds of the economic
growth experienced by the United States between the 1870s and the
1960s was attributable to new technology and only one-third to the
increase in labour and capital. Even if this figure is only roughly correct,
it nevertheless indicates the power of new technology to generate
economic growth.

The role of technological innovation in generating economic growth
is clearly of major importance and, as we shall see in Chapter 9, this has
led some economists to refer to innovation, or to knowledge in general,
as a fourth factor of production. This idea originated with the work of
Burnham (1941), but its most persuasive advocate was the famous US
economist J. K. Galbraith (1975). However, his attempt to incorporate
science and technology into economic theory was not followed up by
other researchers. Instead, most economists went off in another
theoretical direction, and attempted to integrate science and technology into their area by analysing the boom-and-bust cycle that is
characteristic of advanced industrial systems.

Growth, decline and innovation

Whatever their affiliation, most economists agree that technological innovation is a major contributor to the growth of production and consumption. This does not imply that such growth is continuous and consistent. Indeed, many theorists have suggested that technological innovation is closely related to the boom-and-bust cycles which have long plagued industrialised societies.

The effects of such cycles are easy to observe. During a slump, economic activity is at a low level. Factories stand empty and idle, shops are boarded up. People are looking for work, and unable to find any. At other times, everything seems much better: jobs are easy to come by, firms are producing goods, and the economy is said to be in a boom. It has been observed that there is a short-term cycle, which normally lasts about seven years. There is also evidence of a more intense cycle of boom and slump, which appears to occur every forty or fifty years. It is this 'long' cycle which is of importance to our analysis, as it appears to be most closely related to the question of technological change and innovation.

Most of us are aware of the Great Depression of the 1920s and 1930s, when unemployment rose to over 30 per cent in many countries, including the United Kingdom, Australia and Germany. However, it is possible to point to similar events occurring in the 1840s and 1890s, when there were massive downturns in economic activity. In between these troughs of low economic activity there were peaks, when economic times were good.

One of the first economists to discuss these long cycles (or long waves, as they are also called) was van Gelderen. In 1913, he referred to the 'spring-tides' of rapid expansion, which were followed by the 'ebb-tides' of relative stagnation (Freeman 1981:239). However, it was the Marxist Nikolai Kondratiev who developed the concept, and after whom the phenomenon of long economic waves is named.

At the core of Kondratiev long-wave theory is the idea that innovations do not usually come along as individual occurrences (though this can happen), but as clusters of related changes introduced by a number of new, fast-growing industries organised around leading-edge technologies or basic innovations. During the upsurge period, new investment occurs as capital is invested in research and development facilities and in the establishment of new productive facilities organised around these leading technologies. During this period, employment rises and more rapid growth is generated. However, after a period of perhaps twenty or twenty-five years, these new sectors of the economy are firmly established and their role as generators of new jobs and rapid growth diminishes.

The first such cycle of innovation was the Industrial Revolution itself, in the latter part of the eighteenth century. Chapter 6 showed that this involved innovations in the wool and cotton industries in Britain, and consequent changes in such industries as coal, iron and mining. That chapter gives examples of clusters of innovations produced in weaving and in the advance of the steam engine. The second Kondratiev wave, (or 'K' as economists call them) began between about 1850 and 1870, and mostly concerned the huge boom in railways which swept across Europe and the United States. Norman Clark gives a good example of how this industry was necessarily based upon a cluster of innovations, rather than just one or two:

> The railway boom was not simply concerned with the building of steam engines and the laying of track. It involved also the development of signalling systems, the building of rolling stock, the manufacture of appropriate forging and machine-tool facilities, the establishment of stations and marshalling yards and the inculcation of the whole vast range of technical and managerial skills required to run a railways system. [Clark 1985:146]

In the same way, a third cluster of innovations appeared between about 1895 and 1914. These related to the growth of the automobile industry, the use of electricity and the radio industry. Finally, after World War II, from about 1950 to 1970, a series of innovations in chemistry, pharmaceuticals and electronics called forth another boom. In each of these four Kondratiev waves, there was an initial period of growth, followed by an eventual slump. Some researchers have argued that another Kondratiev wave is currently under way, powered by the cluster of changes and innovations taking place in the field of computing, semiconductors and telecommunications. Certainly, in the recent past, there was a substantial investment in research and productive capacity associated with the development of the personal computer and its application to a wide range of situations. It is likely that this boom period has peaked, and that a downturn in the economy is following as investment in R&D diminishes. Moreover, as the products of this earlier phase of research and development—computers—are applied to industry, they also reduce employment in a number of key areas such as banking, accountancy and printing.

Another important economist who analysed technological change in terms of waves (or 'swarms' as he termed them) of innovation was Schumpeter, who published his major book, *Capitalism, Socialism and Democracy*, in 1942. Schumpeter's approach focused upon a three-stage sequence underlying long waves of technological change. These were: invention; innovation; and imitation. To a significant extent, the first state, invention, tended to be treated as an exogenous (or external) factor, at least in Schumpeter's early work. The main focus, therefore, is on innovation and imitation. In terms of innovation, as we saw in Chapter 6, the figure of the entrepreneur is crucial. The entrepreneur is not simply a businessperson, but someone who has the capacity to make changes in business or any other area. As Clark (1985) says, the entrepreneur in Schumpeter's view is a comparable figure to a famous philosopher, knight or statesman. The entrepreneur is likely to use innovation in one of five ways:

1. The introduction of a new good or of a new quality of a good.
2. The introduction of a new production process (not necessarily one based upon scientific discovery).
3. The opening up of a new market.
4. The development of a new source of input supply.
5. Changes in industrial organisation. [Clark 1985:118]

Sir Richard Arkwright, whose contributions to industrial technology were described in Chapter 6, is a good example of an entrepreneur. It is worth noting that Arkwright had to defend his position against a large number of imitators, with devices only slightly different from his own. Important innovations, Schumpeter believed, sparked off booms in the economy, leading to new industries, investment and employment which were manifest in terms of 'swarms' of innovation. A key point is that, as innovations are used to their capacity, the rate of growth of production declines. The major reason for this is that imitators take over from entrepreneurs, and these imitators are less bold in their actions. Therefore, gradually, the dynamism of capitalism becomes exhausted. In one passage, Schumpeter described the change as follows:

> The new processes do not, and generally cannot, evolve out of the old firms, but place themselves side by side with them and attack them. Furthermore, for a firm of comparatively small size ... [this] is an extremely risky and difficult thing, requiring supernormal energy and courage to embark upon. But as soon as the success is before everyone's eyes, everything is made very much easier ... and a whole crowd invariably does copy it. [Schumpeter 1928:70]

In his later work, Schumpeter began to give greater significance to the process of invention in the development of innovations, as R&D capabilities were incorporated as regular features of the large manufacturing concern (Freeman *et al.* 1982). There were good reasons for this: large firms commanded more resources than small ones, and could absorb risks and losses more easily. For Schumpeter, this was not an entirely positive development.

The success of the capitalist mode of production makes capitalism itself redundant: capitalism undermines the social institutions which protect it ... The elimination of the socio-economic function of the entrepreneur, especially in large corporations where technical change is a matter of routine and management is bureaucratised, reinforced by the growing influence of the public sector, further undermines the bourgeoisie. [Heertje 1987:265]

Theories of innovation based on the concept of long waves have been very important in terms of integrating economics with science and technology, but they do not answer all our questions. In the rest of this chapter, a number of enduring issues relating to science, technology and economics will be considered. All of these questions are important in the modern world, and still generate much argument. The conclusions reached in each case are tentative, but the discussions give some idea of the issues involved. We shall start by returning to an issue touched upon earlier, namely the relationship between technological innovation and economic growth.

Recent perspectives on science, technology and the economy

We have already seen that Schumpeter's theory of economic growth focused on the actions of the entrepreneur. Schumpeter imagined a completely static economy, where all possibilities of improving profits have been explored and exhausted. Then:

Schumpeter ... introduces an innovation ... into this circular flow. The entrepreneurial response to this new profit prospect in turn generates a sequence of alterations in the behaviour of economic actors, beginning with an expansion of bank credit and including, eventually, a secondary wave of investment activity imposed on top of the primary wave as the expectations of the larger business community are affected by the evidence and by the consequence of business expansion. [Rosenberg 1976:412]

Of course, the innovation, as we have seen, need not be a technological improvement. It could be a new market, or some way of reorganising production to make it more efficient. It might even be a new piece of land to cultivate. However, as Schumpeter himself points out, there is a big difference between technology and some of these other types of innovation—technology does not seem to present diminishing returns. To illustrate this point, imagine that we are moving in to cultivate a large piece of land. If we want to maximise our profits, we naturally begin by cultivating the most suitable land, then proceed to less suitable land, Finally, there would only be land which it is not worth our while— economically speaking—to cultivate.

This example is old-fashioned, as not much unused land is available nowadays. However, the same point can be made regarding the exploitation of an oil field or a mineral deposit: the first people to begin extraction are likely to take the best sites, and latecomers will be relegated to inferior ones. By contrast, technology may—though we cannot guarantee this—continue to be as profitable in the future as it has been in the past. Unlike cultivating land, or trying to sell products to a given population, we do not begin with the most profitable and proceed to the least: we cannot predict the profitability of technology.

From a Schumpeterian viewpoint, the factors listed earlier as conducive to national growth—such as the investment-to-output ratio, and the quality and quantity of the human capital stock—appear to be highly relevant. If one has a better-trained, more literate population, then it is likely that more of them will make creative, technologically progressive innovations in the economy. By the same token, a country which saves a great deal has more money available to plough into these bold innovations. And, of course, a great many scientists and engineers employed in research increase the probability that creative, economically beneficial innovations will appear. From a government viewpoint, this suggests a whole range of measures which will help sponsor economic growth. For example, the Australian government's tax concessions for firms doing R&D was a logical step toward fostering creative entrepreneurship. So is making education available to a high proportion of the population, although in recent years, successive Australian governments have been less willing to invest in the growth of the higher education sector.

Do large firms innovate more?

Another important issue raised by Schumpeter, which still continues to be discussed and analysed, is the relationship between innovation and the size of the companies operating in the economy. A key point in Schumpeter's work was his view that, in the long run, entrepreneurs will be pushed out of the economic arena by large, bureaucratic organisations. Schumpeter saw several reasons for this: imitators and bureaucrats will displace entrepreneurs within firms, and large firms have built-in advantages because of their greater resources. They can, and do, devote much more of their resources to R&D.

There is a counter-argument to this, which suggests that larger firms, having introduced significant innovations which give them a larger market share, tend to 'rest on their monopolistic laurels'. Such firms are likely 'to stagnate and to become less innovative, thus providing continuous new opportunities for the small innovative firm to undermine the large monopolistic firm despite the scale of the latter's R&D and other technical resources' (Freeman *et al.* 1982:42).

There are a number of reasons why this is the case. First, there are often revolutionary advances in technology which enable small firms to compete in an area—to innovate as well as to invent—with limited resources. An obvious example is the computer industry. After decades of domination by IBM, the microchip enabled small firms to develop a market for microcomputers. Although IBM made a spectacular late entry into this area, it was eventually relegated to one competitor among many. Another way in which small firms can survive is in 'economic niches'. IBM dominates the manufacture of mainframe computers world-wide, but specialists can survive. For example, Cray Computers survives by making extremely large, high-powered machines.

Other studies have sought to throw light on the significance of the size of the firm by comparing successful and unsuccessful innovations. In these studies, the size of the innovating firm does not seem to be a vital factor in determining whether the innovation succeeds or not. Attributes such as the following are more important:

> The depth of understanding of the needs of potential users of the innovations and the steps taken to obtain this knowledge ... the research and development capacity to eliminate 'bugs' prior to the launch of the innovation; [and] internal communications adequate to ensure effective links between those responsible for R&D, marketing, and production within the firm. [Freeman 1987:859]

The argument is complicated, though, by factors such as the research intensity of the different economic sectors and the opportunities that this provides for innovation (Freeman *et al.* 1982). Clearly, some industries such as wood products and furniture, or paper and printing, are less research-intensive than others, and the question of firm size is relatively unimportant in determining R&D activity.

From another perspective, it seems clear that the situation also varies from one country to another, as a consequence of varying economic structures. In a resource-rich country such as Australia, economic activity tends to be concentrated in industries with low levels of R&D. In 1993–94, of the 447,000 employees working in large companies (i.e. with 100 or more employees), only 4.6 per cent were to be found in industries with high R&D, while 58.5 per cent were located in industries with low R&D (DIST 1996). In the Australian context, then, it appears that large firms are not the major source of innovation, since many of these companies are to be found in extractive industries, such as mining, which are not research-intensive.

Clearly, the size of the firm is only one of a number of factors which lead to successful innovation. Indeed, there are situations in which the size of a firm can be both a handicap at one point in time, and a distinct advantage at some other time. For example, as large companies become mature, they may lack the ability to discern what inventions can lead to major new innovations, and which innovations are likely to transform the industry. An example of this again is the giant computer firm IBM: its managers made error after error as they sought to cope with the rapidly changing computer market. However, it was also the huge size of IBM, and the great abilities of some of its employees, which prevented its complete destruction (Ferguson and Morris 1993). Interestingly, one of the recent successes of IBM occurred in one of its subsidiaries, which began to behave like an innovative small firm in its own right, and made a success of its new middle-range computers (Bauer *et al.* 1992).

Freeman (1987:859) summarises the complexities of the issue in this way: 'The debate continues but with increasingly general acceptance that both very large and new entrepreneurial firms enjoy advantages in distinct types of invention and at different stages of the evolution of new technologies.'

Perhaps another way of analysing the issue is to imagine new industries as constituting a 'fringe' around large, established industries. On the fringe, small firms may well have an advantage, in that their only chance for long-term survival is to innovate. However, once an innovation is established, as Schumpeter observed, large firms have great advantages. An obvious rejoinder is that large firms could split themselves into smaller sections, thus preserving some of the advantages of large firms while gaining the advantages of smaller firms as well. Clearly, there is much more to be said on this topic.

Science push versus demand pull: a major debate

A problem which has exercised economists a great deal—and still does —is the question of exactly what impels scientific findings to be transformed into economically important innovations. One theme—which makes a good deal of intellectual sense—is that scientific knowledge is produced by the scientific community irrespective of economic needs. Then industrial technologists pick up important ideas, and transform them into innovations. This idea squares with a good deal of the analysis we have presented so far. As we saw in Chapter 2, much basic science, carried out mostly in universities, is not primarily governed by any concern for social and economic needs. It is driven by the 'publish or perish' system, in which findings are sought and published because of their intrinsic interest. Therefore, it seems unlikely that new laws, theories and principles will be produced that automatically fit industries' needs. The work in atomic physics by scientists in the 1920s and 1930s was intellectually important but, as Robert Jungk (1960) has chronicled, was carried out with little consideration of the consequences.

From these examples, it seems plausible to regard science as pushing economic innovation. From this perspective, science produces a stream of new findings and theories, but many of these are not at all useful to business. Once in a while, though, a discovery is promising, and business uses applied research to turn it into a product or process. The science push view, then, accords with what we know of the role and behaviour of the scientific community. If this view is correct, it has clear implications for businesspeople. They cannot call forth important new products and processes merely by paying scientists to work on them. Instead, they must watch the development of pure science carefully, being ready to adapt and develop anything which looks promising.

This view implies that science is fundamentally deeply autonomous, and independent of the larger society. As Derek de Solla Price, the historian, commented:

> The structure of science at least, as one can analyse it from the connectivity of its papers, seems to show clearly that new knowledge grows out of old at a very steady rate without even very much sensitivity to what one would suppose that societies and [people] desire. ... Might it be that the cumulation of a technological art goes by the same sort of process and proves almost as intractable to the will of society and industry? [Price 1965:566]

However, things are not quite that simple. There seems to be no doubt at all that businesses can produce new products and processes. For example, Tracey Kidder (1982), in his powerful book *The Soul of a New Machine*, shows how a small computer company, Data General, set out to develop a new 32-bit processor for a computer, and how their young team of computer scientists managed this. The book gives a good idea of what mission-oriented industrial R&D can be like. It also shows that goal-directed research can produce new products. From this, it follows that business is more than just an adaptor of principles from academic science: it can be innovative and creative in its own right.

Another major example is to be found in modern biotechnology and the development of processes of genetic manipulation designed to alter the structure of living organisms. We can see in biotechnology the development of a whole new industry, with particular applications in agriculture, medicine, drug production and much more. All of this emerges from a purposeful analysis and manipulation of living organisms.

A major piece of work focusing on the 'demand-pull' relationship between science and industry was carried out by the American economist Jacob Schmookler (1966). Schmookler examined a whole range of American industries over 150 years, from railways to paper-making, and examined factors like investments and patents. His conclusions were important and surprising:

> Despite the idea that scientific discoveries and major inventions typically provide the stimulus for inventions, the historical record of important inventions in petroleum refining, paper making, railroading and farming revealed not a single unambiguous instance in which either discoveries or inventions played the role hypothesised. Instead, in hundreds of cases, the stimulus was the recognition of a costly problem to be solved or a potentially profitable opportunity to be seized. [Schmookler 1966:199]

Schmookler's formulation was moderate. He accepted that 'science push' was an important factor. His special contribution was the argument that 'demand pull' could bring about innovation too, through the promise of higher profits to the innovator. Other economists were less moderate, arguing that demand-led innovation should be regarded as the predominant factor in analysing the relationships between science and industry.

It is easy to find major examples of industrial need producing technological innovations. Ziman (1976) goes into considerable detail of the processes involved in the development of a new battery. Chapter 7 showed that an alternative to the Solvay process was much needed by the soda industry, and the Solvay process was an answer to industrial need. On the other hand, the economic historian Nathan Rosenberg has made a critical response to the extreme claims for demand pull. As he notes, there are some cases in which it seems quite inconceivable that industrial need can produce results:

> It is unlikely that any amount of money devoted to inventive activity in 1800 could have produced modern, wide-spectrum antibiotics, any more than vast sums of money at that time could have produced a satellite capable of orbiting the moon. [Rosenberg in Clark 1985:132]

Rosenberg, with colleagues, has also researched this question and concluded that both science push and demand pull play a part in industrial innovation. This conclusion has implications for industry, and it is worth enumerating some of these. First, if we accept that industry can call forth important innovations in response to need, then we can ask questions, like: What structure of firm is best for innovation? What sorts of innovation come from industry, and what sorts from scientific discovery? What balance should there be between firms undertaking their own R&D and firms making use of pure science advances for innovation?

Conclusions

This chapter has covered a lot of ground, and we have not always come to firm conclusions about the effectiveness or relevance of the theories discussed. The theory of long waves is a broad concept, exciting in its ability to predict broad sweeps in human affairs. However, one can raise a number of questions about it. For example, why do different innovations come in 'swarms' rather than singly? And to what extent does the evidence back up the theory of Kondratiev waves? Freeman *et al.* (1982) investigated the evidence for the waves, taking care not to be rigid or dogmatic about exactly when the waves appeared. They found that the waves varied in characteristics, but that broadly speaking they were a useful way of explaining long-term movements in the economy.

As Freeman *et al.* (1982) point out, if Kondratiev waves exist, then it is imperative for governments to be aware of them, and to know what can be done to shorten, or to eliminate, the costly slumps and recessions which lie between them. If governments can sponsor, or assist, the production of innovations, then there is a possibility that they can reduce the intensity and the costs of a major recession. On the other hand, there is a widely held view that governments should play only a limited role (if any) in the process of innovation, since this involves decisions about which industries to support and which to ignore. In the view of some researchers, governments are not very good at 'picking winners', and should leave such decisions to the private sector (Irvine and Martin 1984).

However, as Lowe points out in Chapter 9, there are strong arguments in favour of a role for government. Thus, the Australian government's tax concessions for firms doing R&D (see Chapter 2) appear a far-sighted measure. It is understandable that a good deal of protest went up at the decision by the government in 1996 to reduce the concession from 150 per cent of costs to 125 per cent. With changes in the tax rates, this actually amounted to doubling the costs of doing R&D for industry in Australia.

In attempting to understand the contemporary significance of long wave theory, it is also important to note that the first Kondratiev wave occurred in a world in which there was only a single country going through the Industrial Revolution. The fourth wave occurred in a world in which many countries had become industrialised, and other countries were beginning to move that way. Further waves will meet a quite different world again. Roughly speaking, about 750 million people live in developed countries. At the time of writing, about another 1500 million people in Asia are living in countries which are likely to be fully industrialised some time in the twenty-first century. Other countries—

notably China and India—are showing signs of moving in the same direction. Any future Kondratiev waves will clearly operate in a different sort of world. It is not clear whether their effects will be the same, or spectacularly different.

Economics is often regarded as one of the most prestigious of the social sciences. At the same time, other observers have described the discipline as being in a state of crisis (Ormerod 1994). Certainly, economists have found it difficult to accommodate scientific and technological change within their elaborate models. One reason for this is that technological change fundamentally alters the relationship between all the other variables. The theories we have considered in the chapter, though, place technology at the heart of economic analysis, and we believe that this is the correct approach. As we have argued consistently throughout this book, science and technology influence society more and more, and it is vital for all of us that the important discipline of economics applies itself to these issues and adds to our understanding.

Further reading

Even more than the topics of other chapters in this book, the area of science, technology and economics is vast. Rather than trying to understand it all, the reader is advised to focus upon particular topics of interest and to study those. If a general overview of economics is required, then the books by Lipsey and Chrystal (1994) and Samuelson (1992) are both good. However, Clark (1985) both gives the flavour of classical economics and summarises many important issues regarding science and technology: this is probably the best starting-point for study in this area.

The performance of economies has tremendous effects for the people who depend upon them for their livelihoods. Stewart (1972) gives a good idea of how the Great Depression affected people's lives (though his description of Keynes's ideas is not very clear). To understand the passions and concerns that drove Marxism, the *Communist Manifesto* (Marx and Engels 1967) is still good: it is fierce and clear.

An important economist, whom we have rather neglected in this chapter, is J. K. Galbraith. His major work (Galbraith 1975) provides a good—although controversial—overview of how modern economies work. Among modern researchers, we recommend almost anything by Chris Freeman, Keith Pavitt and Nathan Rosenberg. They specialise in different parts of this vast field, but all have important things to say, and say it in clear English. In addition, Paul Romer (1994) is an important economist whose less technical work is well worth reading.

References

Bauer, R. A., Collar, E., and Tang, V. (1992), *The Silverlake Project*. Oxford: Oxford University Press.

Becker, G. (1976), *The Economic Approach to Human Behavior*. Chicago: University of Chicago Press.

Bellamy, D. (1975), *Environmental Philosophy*. Oxford: Basil Blackwell.

Burnham, J. (1941), *The Managerial Revolution*. Westport: Greenham Press.

Clark, N. (1985), *The Political Economy of Science and Technology*. Oxford: Basil Blackwell.

Clemence, R. V. (ed.) (1989), *Essays on Entrepreneurs, Innovations, Business Cycles and the Evolution of Capitalism: Joseph A. Schumpeter*. New Brunswick: Transaction Publishers.

Davies P. (1991), *The Mind of God*. New York: Simon and Schuster.

Donaldson, P. (1976), *Economics of the Real World*. Harmondsworth: Penguin.

Department of Industry, Science and Technology (DIST) (1996), *Australian Business Innovation: A Strategic Analysis*. Canberra: Australian Government Publishing Service.

Easlea, B. (1973), *Liberation and the Aims of Science*. London: Chatto and Windus.

Eatwell, J., Milgate, M., and Newham P. (eds) (1987), *The New Palgrave*. London: Macmillan.

Ferguson, C. H., and Morris, C. R. (1993), *Computer Wars: How the West Can Win in a Post-IBM World*. New York: Times Books (Random House).

Freeman, C. (1987), 'Innovation', in Eatwell *et al.* (1987): 858–60.

Freeman, C. (ed.) (1981), 'Introduction' to Special Issue on Technical Innovation and Long Waves in World Economic Development, *Futures*, 13, 4:239–41.

Freeman, C., Clarke, J., and Soete, L. (1982), *Unemployment and Technical Innovation: A Study of Long Waves and Economic Development*. Westport: Greenwood Press.

Galbraith, J. K. (1975), *The New Industrial State*. Harmondsworth: Penguin.

Grossman, G. M., and Helpman E. (1993), *Innovation and Growth in the Global Economy*. Cambridge, Mass.: MIT Press.

Harrison, P. (1991), *The Third World Tomorrow*. London: Penguin.

Hawking, S. (1988), *A Brief History of Time*. London: Bantam.

Heertje, A. (1987), 'Schumpeter', in Eatwell *et al.* (1987): pp. 4, 263–7.

Heilbroner, R. (1976), 'Homage to Adam Smith', *Challenge*, 19, 1:6–11.

Irvine, J., and Martin, B. (1984), *Foresight in Science: Picking the Winners*. London: F. Pinter.

Jungk, R. (1960), *Brighter than a Thousand Suns*. Harmondsworth: Penguin.

Kidder, T. (1982), *The Soul of a New Machine*. London: Allen Lane.

Kondratiev, N. (1935), 'The Long Waves in Economic Life', *Review of Economic Statistics*, 17, 105–15.

Lipsey, R. G., and Chrystal, K. A. (1994), *An Introduction to Positive Economics*. Oxford: Oxford University Press.

Lowe, I. (1989), *Living in the Greenhouse*. Newham, Vic.: Scribe.

Marx, K., and Engels, F. (1967), *The Communist Manifesto*. Harmondsworth: Penguin.

Merton, R. K. (1968a), *Social Theory and Social Structure*. New York: Free Press.

Merton, R. K. (1968b), 'Science and Economy of Seventeenth Century England', in Merton (1968a): 661–81.

Ormerod, P. (1994), *The Death of Economics*. London: Faber and Faber.

Price, D. J. de S. (1965), 'Is Technology Historically Independent of Science?', *Technology and Culture*, 6:553–68.

Romer, P. (1994), 'Beyond Classical and Keynesian Macroeconomic Policy', *Policy Options*, July–August.

Rosenberg, N. (1976), 'On Technological Expectations', *Economic Journal*, 86:523–35.

Samuelson, P. A. (1992), *Economics*. Sydney: McGraw-Hill.

Schmookler, J. (1966), *Invention and Economic Growth*. Cambridge, Mass.: Harvard University Press.

Schumpeter, J. A. (1928), 'The Instability of Capitalism', *Economic Journal*, September: 361–86.

Schumpeter, J. A. (1976), *Capitalism, Socialism and Democracy*. London: Allen and Unwin.

Smith, A. (ed. A. Skinner) (1776/1970), *The Wealth of Nations*, Books I–III. Harmondsworth: Penguin.

Stewart, M. (1972), *Keynes and After*. Harmondsworth: Penguin.

Summers, R., and Heston, A. (1988), 'A New Set of International Comparisons of Real Product and Price Levels for 130 Countries in 1950–1985', *Review of Wealth and Income*, 1:1–25.

Waring, M. (1988), *Counting for Nothing*. Wellington: Allen and Unwin/Port Nicholson Press.

Ziman, J. (1976), *The Force of Knowledge*. Cambridge: Cambridge University Press.

CHAPTER 9

Science, Technology and Public Policy

Ian Lowe

This chapter begins by explaining why governments take an interest in science and technology. Some of the problems of determining the collective will of the community are then analysed, showing that it is often difficult to decide priorities for allocation of public resources. This leads into a general discussion of what constitutes public policy, including the process of policy development. Science and technology policy raises particular issues which are especially important for professional scientists and engineers, but are also of broad public interest. These issues are considered in general terms before the chapter concludes with a discussion of some specific problems affecting Australia and New Zealand in the 1990s. These problems illustrate once more that the way we treat science and technology affects what is produced.

Why public policy for science and technology?

Public policy for science is necessary because a significant fraction of all science is funded by government, so decisions must be made about the scale and direction of that funding. We are talking about large sums of money. In Australia in 1996 government spending on science and technology was running at about $4 billion per year, so on average each person in the community was supporting science with about $200 per year through taxes. Because choices about which technologies will be used and how they are used have significant social impact, governments intervene to try to keep those impacts acceptable to the community. This is public policy for technology. It has also been a traditional concern of governments to try to maintain some level of equity in access to the benefits and bearing the costs of technological change, though this concern has steadily been eroded in English-speaking countries as governments have scaled down their capacity to fulfil this function.

Various rationales have been advanced for the funding of scientific research from the public purse: an investment in the future, a sign of being civilised, a way of producing skilled people, even as a way of keeping the nation's best scientists in the country! Reports by the Australian Science and Technology Council are typical of those produced by science advisory bodies around the industrialised world in giving traditional views on the government's motivation (ASTEC 1990). While the range of reasons is still advanced from time to time, the broad trend of the 1980s and 1990s was to focus attention on the potential economic benefits of science.

In terms of the process of allocating research resources, it has been usual for scientists to argue that they should be given complete autonomy to decide appropriate directions. This ideal, it will be recalled from Chapter 3, has been described by Polanyi as 'the republic of science': scientists as a self-governing elite, free to decide the best use of the resources available to them (Polanyi 1968). There are two problems with this approach. First, it gives no guidance at all on the overall size of the cake to be divided between the competing research programs. It is always possible to argue that science deserves more money. The second problem relates to the argument whether the scientific community, left to itself, will fund the most deserving research. Chapter 2 discussed the social structure of the scientific community, showing clearly that no group of scientists can make completely objective decisions about the merits of research proposals.

When the research community is given freedom to allocate resources, the collective values of those making the decisions inevitably shape the direction of research. Studies of such bodies as the former Australian Research Grants Committee show that there is a striking similarity from year to year in the fraction of funds going to each discipline area! Success rates of new applications in a particular field like chemistry vary dramatically from year to year, but the share of the overall budget that goes to chemistry stays remarkably constant (Lowe 1987). This suggests that there is an implicit view of what fraction of the research budget should go into each field, so that judgements about the excellence of projects is shaped by that view.

The political problem with this approach is clear. Most governments now think that they cannot just give large sums of money to the scientific community and allow scientists to do with it as they wish. Governments inevitably wish to see effort focused on what are regarded as broad national objectives (McGauran 1996), although there is a fundamental problem in getting agreement to a broad set of objectives which is nevertheless specific enough to assist in setting priorities. In recent years there has been an increasing tendency for government to take a more directive role in the research area. Around the world, both government research bodies and universities are now getting more of their funds with strings attached, and more is allocated specifically to nominated areas of inquiry or specific research programs (ASTEC 1990; Slatyer 1993).

Problems also arise with the ownership of results obtained by research funded from the public purse. It is understandable that governments want the results to be in the public domain, but this can inhibit commercialisation. Many countries now seek to promote commercial use of the results of their local research. This commercial imperative is in conflict with the traditional scientific ethos of open sharing of the results of research with the scientific community. As we saw in Chapter 2, it leads to pressure on scientists to hold back from publishing their results until commercial avenues are explored (Lowe 1996).

Government is also expected to act as the keeper of society's conscience with respect to the ethics of applying research results. Thus in such areas as recombinant DNA research and genetic engineering, the government is expected to regulate research activities within what it perceives to be the limits of community acceptability. As society's collective values change, so do those limits; since they must face the electors from time to time, politicians are supposed to be aware of the prevailing community standards.

All of these specific issues show why there is a need for broad policy guidelines. Rather than making thousands of particular decisions about funding of particular laboratories or ownership of research results, politicians prefer to spell out the general principles and leave the details to their public servants. These general principles, such as more money for agricultural research or less support for universities, add up to the public policy. To understand science and technology policy properly, we need to look first at the general process of policy formation in a modern society. Be patient as you work through this general material; it is all needed to get a grip on the way government decisions influence science and technology.

Problems of collective choice

There are some general problems associated with determination of the collective will. The issue is discussed in detail in the literature of politics (Walker 1994). In principle, the task of government is to do what is best for the community. The problem is that most policies do not affect all members of the community equally. A change to the tax system usually leaves some people better off and others worse off. Sometimes a change leaves everyone better off in the short term, for example an all-round reduction in income tax rates, but even then some people will benefit more than others. In that case, there will be losers in the long term, as a government with less income will have to reduce the services it provides. So the goal of government might be to do the best it can overall, matching the losses to some people against the gains to others.

As you will recall from Chapter 4, the utilitarians, most notably Jeremy Bentham, argued that government should aim to produce the greatest good for the greatest number. He tried to define a 'felicific calculus', measuring the extra happiness produced by a policy as the algebraic sum of all the benefits and all the disadvantages to different individuals, to help decision-makers determine which policies would provide the greatest good for the greatest number. While that is now seen as a quaint notion, the general idea underpins the school of welfare economics, which seeks to maximise a 'welfare function' as the sum of individual benefits.

The famous paradox of voting, identified more than 200 years ago, is an extreme example of the difficulty of finding the option which provides the greatest overall benefit. Suppose that Aravinda, Betty and Chu have decided to share the cost of buying a large block of ice-cream, and have agreed to abide by the majority view on the choice of flavour. Each lists an order of preference between three flavours: chocolate, strawberry and vanilla. Imagine that they write down their preferences as follows.

- Aravinda: strawberry, chocolate, vanilla
- Betty: chocolate, vanilla, strawberry
- Chu: vanilla, strawberry, chocolate.

Each of the three has a different favourite flavour, so there is no clear decision from their first preference. So Aravinda suggests a way of deciding. 'Let's see what the choice would be between chocolate and vanilla', he says. Two (Aravinda and Betty) prefer chocolate to vanilla, while only one (Chu) prefers vanilla to chocolate. So the group preference is for chocolate over vanilla. Now compare strawberry with chocolate. Two of the group (Aravinda and Chu) prefer strawberry to chocolate, with only Betty liking chocolate more than strawberry. Since the group's collective choice prefers chocolate to vanilla and strawberry to chocolate, it seems clear that strawberry is the flavour preferred by the group. Or is it? How many prefer strawberry to vanilla?

Two of the three (Betty and Chu) prefer vanilla to strawberry. This is known as the *paradox of voting*: the summing of a set of rational choices can sometimes lead to the irrational position that the overall preference depends critically on the order in which the options are presented. If the group had compared strawberry with chocolate and then chocolate with vanilla, the overall preference would have been vanilla!

It is not inevitable that this sort of cyclical result will occur; for three options, the probability is less than 10 per cent. However, if there are ten options, the probability of there being no majority choice rises to almost 50 per cent. This is one reason why control of the agenda is so important: the choice of the preferred outcome can be determined by the order of presenting the options. The paradox poses an important qualification to attempts to determine a rational collective choice so that policy can be what provides the greatest good for the greatest number. Even if every individual had a known preference ordering for the options available and the government had all that information, it would still be impossible to determine a rational social ordering of choices from those individual preferences.

Another problem is that the collective impact of a set of decisions based on individual self-interest can be detrimental to the collective interest of the group. A classic example is Garrett Hardin's famous parable of 'the tragedy of the commons' (Hardin 1968). He told the story of a village with a common large enough for each of the thirty households to graze one cow. Each villager obtained milk and cream, while those with the energy could make butter. The common was just large enough to support thirty cows, so the overall arrangement was stable. Then one villager realised that there would be great benefit in smuggling a second cow onto the common late at night. The household would get twice as much milk and cream, double the benefit. At what cost? There would be a small increase in wear and tear on the common, but there isn't much difference between thirty cows and thirty-one, so it was possible nobody would even notice. Of course, sooner or later somebody does notice that there are now thirty-one cows on the common. That alert villager does the same calculation and concludes that the huge benefit from having the produce of two cows rather than one is worth the small extra load on the common. After all, there isn't much difference between thirty-one cows and thirty-two ... I am sure you can see where the tale is heading: many more cows and a degraded common that will no longer support any livestock at all!

The moral is that it is entirely possible for the overall sum of a set of perfectly rational individual decisions to lead to a very bad outcome for the group as a whole. This parable has been re-enacted in real life in many fisheries, such as the North Sea herring, the Peruvian anchovies, and the Southern Blue-Fin Tuna in waters around Australia and New Zealand. In each case, individual fishing boats pursued their self-interest until the stock was seriously depleted. The North Sea herring industry was completely wiped out, while the Peruvian anchovy catch is now a small fraction of its former level. As this book was being written, a rescue mission was being mounted to try to rebuild stocks of Southern Blue-Fin Tuna, but the whole exercise relies on an unusual level of international co-operation.

This example has implications at all levels, from the care of shared goods in a club to the use of shared environmental goods, such as clean air, the oceans, the Amazon rainforests and Antarctica. Interestingly, different values lead to different conclusions from this parable. Hardin's belief in the benefit of self-interest led him to conclude that there is a fundamental problem with shared ownership of a valuable resource. He argued that an individual who owns a resource will use it sustainably, so resources should be under private control. The counter-argument is that many farmers do not manage their land sustainably, so private ownership and the resulting self-interest does not guarantee sound management. Those who distrust self-interest argue that valuable resources should be communally owned to prevent misuse (Walker 1994). The counter to this counter-argument is that governments also sometimes fail to manage the common assets in a responsible way. So Hardin's parable warns us of the dangers of depleting shared resources by over-exploitation, but it does not provide a clear strategy to prevent the problem.

What is public policy?

Policy has been defined as a *deliberate* course of *action or inaction* taken by those *in office* under the influence of *values and pressures* about the way *resources* are to be used *in pursuit of objectives* or *in support of other policies*. This is a very academic definition, covering all contingencies, but it includes several important points. Policy is the sum of deliberate decisions. From time to time, the decisions of governments have side-effects that were not predicted, but these are usually not regarded as part of government policy. Second, policy includes both action and inaction. It can be a deliberate policy to do nothing about a particular issue; in one episode of the British television series *Yes, Minister*, Sir Humphrey Appleby urged the minister to adopt a course of 'masterly inaction'. As an example, one response to a problem of growing traffic congestion might be to allow the problem simply to get worse, in the hope of encouraging people to choose other transport options, such as trains or bicycles. Policy decisions are taken by those in office; Opposition politicians can make speeches, but they cannot make policy. When governments make policy decisions, they are always influenced by the pressures on them and their own values. Some politicians are driven

by their values to seek ways of resolving problems by government intervention, while others have values that lead them to seek market-based
solutions. Some try to find equitable solutions that take account of the
disadvantaged, while others are quite unabashed in pandering to
specific interest groups.

Policy is often directed toward the allocation of resources. Just as
the way you spend your own money is the most honest statement of
your priorities, so the way a government allocates its funds is the real
indication of its priorities. If a government cuts funding for universities
but spends money on cruise missiles, it is effectively saying that cruise
missiles are more important than universities. If the research budget for
nuclear science and technology is ten times the allocation for solar
energy, the government is effectively saying that it regards nuclear
research more highly than solar.

Finally, most government policy decisions are aimed at fulfilling some
broad objective, such as boosting the economy or solving a particular
social problem. It is important to note that policy is by no means
permanent, since a variety of different interest groups are always trying
to modify policies to suit their particular interests. Thus a decision about
a proposal for a new road may be attacked by local people and environment groups, trying to stop the road being built, alter the route or
otherwise modify its impact on natural areas. At the same time, the road
lobby of construction companies may be urging the government to
build a wider road or one with more intersections. What finally happens
is the result of this political struggle. You may think this sort of political
battle is a modern phenomenon, but the process was summed up by
the American political analyst Earl Latham more than forty years ago:
'What we may call public policy is actually the equilibrium reached in
the power struggle at any given moment; it represents a balance which
contending factions constantly seek to weight in their favour' (Latham
1952).

Who makes public policy?

The institutions and functions of government are analysed thoroughly
in general books about public policy. For example, Australian readers
would benefit from reading a standard public policy text (Davis *et al.*
1988: 16–19). Davis *et al.* define the state as 'an agency of control, social
order and cohesion, legitimacy, socialisation and economic intervention', and categorise its institutions as follows (Davis *et al.* 1988: 16,
17–19).

First, there are elected representatives meeting in parliament to form
the legislative arm of the state. In the system of government used in

countries such as Australia, New Zealand and the United Kingdom, ministers who form the Executive are chosen from the members of parliament. Other countries have different arrangements; for example, in the United States the President is elected separately and then chooses other members of the Executive, generally not from the ranks of elected politicians. Second, the government departments administer the business of government and provide advice to the Executive on policy questions. Thus the minister responsible for science is served by a department that provides advice on policy issues. The department is also responsible for putting the policy decisions into practice.

Laws are produced when a Bill passes through the parliament. Those laws are then interpreted by the judiciary (the courts) and regulatory bodies, such as specialist tribunals. In Australia, the High Court can be asked to decide if a new law is consistent with the national Constitution, as when the state government of Tasmania challenged the right of the federal government to prevent the damming of the Franklin River (Davis *et al.* 1988:134). In that case, the High Court decided that the new law was acceptable. That decision effectively widened the power of the federal government to over-rule states on environmental issues. There have been other instances in which the government of the day has been stopped by the High Court. For example, the 1950 attempt by the Menzies government to outlaw the Communist Party was ruled by the High Court to be outside the powers that the Constitution gives the government. The proposed law was therefore invalid. The issue of the rights to land in Australia of Aborigines and Islanders has been dramatically influenced by two High Court decisions: the Mabo decision ruled that indigenous people effectively owned the land before the establishment of British colonies, ending the previous legal fiction that the land had been empty, while the 1996 Wik decision stated that the granting of mining or pastoral leases did not extinguish native title. These are examples of court decisions that have effectively determined public policy.

Enforcement agencies, such as police and armed forces, ensure compliance with laws and government policies. This can be a crucial aspect of policy. If the official policy set down in the law is that the speed limit in urban areas is 60 kilometres per hour but the limit is not policed, the unofficial policy that results can be a licence to drive much faster. The introduction of random breath-testing has greatly increased the chances that a drunken driver will be caught and prosecuted, so it has effectively toughened the long-standing policy to ban drunks from driving. If the police are unable to prevent widespread use of a drug that is officially illegal, such as marijuana, the drug becomes unofficially tolerated. In general, a policy exists only if it can be enforced.

Some countries such as Australia, the United States, Canada and Germany are not unitary but are federations of states or provinces which retain a range of powers (and duplicate many functions of the national government). The result may be that there is no co-ordinated national policy for science, but a mixture of a broad overall policy at the national level with provincial variations. Local councils also have important powers over development of land, and sometimes over such services as transport, so they effectively make policy decisions about transport technology.

The list could be extended still further, but the general point should already be clear. The making of public policy is by no means confined to elected politicians. A variety of other people, such as public servants, judges and police officers, are effectively making policy decisions.

Governments have a wide range of functions in a modern industrialised state (Davis *et al.* 1988:33–4). They are active agents of economic development, providing infrastructure such as roads and electricity supply, subsidising industries ranging from farming to aluminium smelting, and using public resources in various ways to stimulate economic growth. Governments protect sectional groups from the forces of the market by such measures as tariffs and welfare provisions. They regulate various economic activities, such as shopping hours and fair trading, as well as setting limits on individual behaviour through legal restrictions on activities they believe to be harmful to society as a whole. The balance between these activities is a function of the political culture of the country concerned at a particular time. So is the enthusiasm with which any one activity is pursued. For example, Australia was seen in the 1980s as an activist state, though the public sector is very small by international standards. Australia is certainly not a nation of 'big government', but has one of the smallest government sectors in the developed world.

It is, however, a society in which the government does intervene frequently and heavily to promote its preferred pattern of economic development (Davis *et al.* 1988:35). As this book was being written, a report to the Australian government calculated the annual public subsidy to the principal resource industries (energy, water, forestry and fisheries) as a massive $14 billion (NIEIR 1996:11). That is nearly four times the total public support of science and technology, or about 3 per cent of the total economic output of the country! Recent trends in English-speaking countries have been for governments to withdraw from both regulation and production, putting more faith in the private sector and forces of the market. This is a reverse of the trend in earlier decades, when the broad pattern was for increasing regulation and government control of key services. As discussed earlier, a decision not to control electricity supply can be just as much a policy as a decision to control it; a decision not to regulate an industry can be just as much a policy as a decision to regulate it; and a failure to refurbish ageing research laboratories can be a policy just as much as a decision to spend millions on new facilities.

Formation of public policy: theory and practice

In countries which have derived their government system from English precedent, the formal process of policy formation is based on a written constitution, which can be changed by a prescribed process, and a set of conventions which are known as the Westminster system. For example, the Australian Constitution says that 'the legislative power of the Commonwealth shall be vested in a Federal Parliament, which shall consist of the Queen, a Senate and a House of Representatives'. There is no reference at all in the Constitution to the Prime Minister, Cabinet, political parties or their consequences, such as factions or other groupings. So the Constitution sets out a legalistic framework for policy formation, but says nothing about the real world of practical politics, dominated by political parties, factions and coalitions of interests.

Dean Jaensch summarises the Westminster conventions as follows, noting that they are not legally binding or enforceable, but rely on the willing compliance of all involved (Jaensch 1986:111). The government is formed from the group or groups which command a majority in the elected house of parliament, and the government remains in office while it commands a majority. Sometimes one political party has a majority, as the Labor Party in Australia and the National Party in New Zealand did before the 1996 elections in those countries. Sometimes political parties campaign as independent units with an explicit understanding that they will form a coalition after the election, as the Liberal Party and National Party usually do in Australia. In other instances, a coalition between separate parties needs to be assembled after the election when no party commands a majority. This process took months after the New Zealand election in 1996, with feverish speculation about which parties would combine to form a government.

Once formed, the government is supposed to speak with one voice in parliament and in public, having resolved its collective position behind closed doors; in practice, in modern politics, the differences between different ministers or coalition partners can be very public. It is not at all unusual, for example, for an environment minister to oppose a development which is supported by other members of the government. This is understandable, because a proposal that looks positive from the narrow economic perspective of a development agency may threaten serious environmental damage. In Australia, there are often conflicts between the Liberal Party, with its support mainly in the cities, and the National Party, mainly supported by rural areas. The conflicts can be over pragmatic political issues, such as gun control, since rural people are more likely than city-dwellers to own guns and to see gun ownership as acceptable. There are also conflicts that are ideological in nature—for example, the Liberal Party tends to be dogmatic in support of lower tariffs, while the National Party tends to favour tariff protection for local industries.

The Westminster conventions also hold ministers responsible to parliament for their own conduct and the conduct of their departments. The ritual of Question Time, allowing any member of parliament to ask a minister a question without warning, is intended to ensure this responsibility by forcing ministers to account for their actions and those of the departments they administer. In that way the government is collectively responsible to parliament, which is held under the Westminster system to be sovereign. Finally, the head of state, such as the Queen in the United Kingdom or the Governor-General as her representative in Australia or New Zealand, is supposed to act on the advice of the ministers. The celebrated instance of the dismissal of the Whitlam government by the then Governor-General was in clear breach of this principle; there has been a continuing debate in Australia about whether the action of Sir John Kerr was strictly legal, but there can be no doubt that he breached the Westminster conventions (Sawer 1948:23; Whitlam 1978).

To summarise, the theory of the Westminster conventions is that:

> Ministers are responsible for determining policy, for deciding what the executive will do. Non-partisan public servants implement policy and serve all elected governments with equal loyalty and dedication. An informed parliament authorises expenditure and legislates in response to executive proposals. Parliament may scrutinise government behaviour, but it does not directly govern. The notion of parliamentary sovereignty views the legislative body as the supreme authority in the land. Ministers can be held accountable, parliament can control the actions of the executive, and it can use control over granting funds to require the redress of grievances. The temporary and responsible ministers appointed by parliament provide direction because they have specific policies they wish to pursue and can direct the permanent and non-partisan public servants. [Davis *et al.* 1988:62–3]

There are substantial differences between the idealised world described by the Westminster system and the real world of practical politics. Some are common to all political systems. For example, ministers are not normally chosen for their knowledge of the subject matter of technical portfolios, so they are reliant on advice from public servants. As discussed below, this advice is rarely impartial—it usually reflects the culture of the government department concerned. Governments are elected on the basis of a broad platform put forward during an election campaign, but the choice of which particular policies to pursue on assuming office is a reflection of the priorities of the government or the individual minister. In the modern world, situations often arise in which the government does not have complete control of the parliament, and so must negotiate with other political parties for support for its proposals. The process of negotiation may lead to significant concessions. For example, a provision to subsidise production of power alcohol from plant material in Australia in the 1990s resulted from a deal the Labor government of the day made with a minor party, the Democrats, in return for support of legislation. After being lobbied by oil companies, the incoming coalition government scrapped the arrangement in 1996.

The policy-making process is rarely confined to those who strictly need to be involved, in terms of the idealised Westminster system; pressure groups often play a significant role in the process, and a variety of political forces use the technique of leaking information when they think that their ends are likely to be advanced as a result. For example, an environment department usually loses the bureaucratic battle with an industry department over an initiative that will cause environmental damage, because most governments put a higher priority on economic development than on environmental protection. If the public or green pressure groups hear about the proposal, however, the resulting outcry might cause the proposal to be abandoned. In those circumstances, you can well imagine that an officer in the environment department might be tempted to be careless with the information about the project. On the other hand, government sources sometimes let it be known that they are considering a proposal to test public reaction. If there is an outcry, the government can back down without losing face, claiming that the idea was never officially supported; if there is little public opposition to the proposal, the government can move forward confidently. Leaks are rarely accidental!

You should also note that parliament rarely exercises any great degree of formal power over the Executive, despite the theoretical position that the government must answer to parliament. A particular political party forms a government because it has a majority in the parliament, so that government can usually expect to get its way in parliament. Members of a government party rarely vote against their own leaders: it is not a way to become identified as a suitable candidate for higher office. An unqualified statement of the realities of modern political parties comes from one Australian analyst:

> The major political parties are run by self-perpetuating executive oligarchies and tiny memberships; and the people they choose, when in Parliament, consider that their main duty is to keep in office as Ministers, irrespective of their performance, a collection of party hacks who behave as yet another oligarchy in relation to the parliamentary members, but are actually the serfs of the bureaucracy. [Sawer 1973:173]

Public servants play a key role in determining policy through the advice they give to government ministers. They also administer policy, and the effects of a policy can be determined by the way it is administered. Some places have strict environmental laws, but such weak enforcement that the laws might as well not exist. Since the policy that is decided and the way it is administered are both heavily influenced by the responsible public servants, the backgrounds and values of the leading members of the public service have come under scrutiny. Michael Pusey studied the senior levels of the Australian government's public service and found it to be dominated by people with formal qualifications in economics. He also found, perhaps not surprisingly, that these officers have generally conservative views about the role of government, the distribution of wealth and the power relations in society. For example, they were much more likely than the overall population to think that the reward structure favours workers rather than owners, that the industrial relations system favours trade unions rather than employers, and that government intervenes too much in the economy. These views inevitably colour the advice public servants give ministers, and the way they administer policy (Pusey 1991).

Pusey's observations are general, but more specific conclusions can be drawn about particular areas of government. A department of mines is likely to be staffed by people with a background in the mining industry and a generally positive view of the industry, while many of those working in the department of health will have a medical background and be favourably disposed toward the medical profession. Thus each department has its internal culture which inevitably attracts and promotes those who are comfortable with that culture. Members of Greenpeace would be unlikely to apply for a job in a department of mines, would be unlikely to be appointed if they did apply, and would be even less likely to feel comfortable in the department if they were appointed. This idea of a departmental culture supporting sectional interests is now so well entrenched that the head of the Department of Mines and Energy in the Northern Territory recently told a Senate committee that there is no conflict of interest between promoting the mining industry and regulating it (Plummer 1996).

Any significant policy decision affects more than one portfolio: for example, a decision to increase funding for environmental research into

sustainable management of forests would influence departments responsible for science, for environmental issues, for finance and for
forestry, and possibly other areas such as the wood and paper industries,
transport and local government. So a policy initiative from one area
often results in the formation of an inter-departmental committee to
look at the implications for the government as a whole. In theory, the
idea is to identify unexpected consequences and fine-tune the proposal to get the best result overall. Studies of the workings of inter-
departmental committees show that these bodies often become the
arena for resolving the ideological and territorial disputes between
departments (Painter and Carey 1979:11). Members of the committee
are seen as departmental delegates and judged in career terms by their
success in imposing the departmental view. Thus a finance department
representative is usually expected to promote the view that extra government spending is undesirable, and she is judged by her department
according to her success in imposing its view on other departments
(Painter and Carey 1979:67–9). This is one reason for the bizarre concentration of economists in the senior ranks of government departments. With government increasingly dominated by economic issues,
much of the discussion in inter-departmental committees is in the
language of economics, so those who speak that dialect are most likely
to shine and be promoted.

In a complex modern society, collective decisions are made through
the political process. Lindblom has identified two models, the *rational
comprehensive* approach (which is not common!) and the *incremental*
approach (Lindblom 1959). He argues that the rational comprehensive
approach to a policy decision involves clarifying goals, identifying a
range of means to achieve those goals, then identifying the most appropriate means after a comprehensive analysis of every relevant factor.
This can be a long and difficult process. It also requires a clarity of
thought not always found in political circles! Much more common,
Lindblom argued, is the incremental approach, starting from what was
done last time and making small adjustments. As an example, most
governments draw up this year's budget by starting with last year's and
making the changes they want—a bit less in this area, a bit more in that.
In the incremental approach, goals may not be distinct, since making
policy does not require agreement on goals. Two pragmatic politicians
could each agree that a railway should be built, one because of a desire
to see a better public transport system and the other because of a
wish to provide work for the local steel industry. In the real world of
politics, ends and means are often confused. Facilities such as roads,
power stations or hospitals should not be seen as ends in themselves,
but as means of allowing transport, energy supply and good health

respectively. If good health is the overall goal, rather than building another hospital, it might make more sense to fund medical research into better treatment, or to run a campaign to encourage healthier lifestyles. In the incremental approach, the worst problem is fixed first and analysis is usually limited to finding the first solution that works, rather than looking for the *best* solution.

The incremental approach is common, but it works only if the general policy is broadly acceptable, the problems remain broadly the same, and the solutions available are unchanged. The political theorist Etzioni has suggested a refinement of the incremental approach. He called it 'mixed scanning', with most decision-making of the incremental type, but occasional upheavals that set the broad context for incremental choices (Etzioni 1968:23). For example, astronomy has mainly relied on optical telescopes, and the history of the twentieth century has been one of gradual refinement of telescopes, making them larger and siting them in clearer air. The discovery that radio waves were reaching the Earth opened up the whole new sphere of radio astronomy. Within that new framework, we have seen steady refinement of the techniques for gathering the tiny amounts of energy concerned and turning it into useful information about the skies. Etzioni suggests that different styles of decision-making are suited to different political systems; incrementalism is most likely to occur in pluralistic democracies, while some forms of dictatorship are more likely to lead to the rational comprehensive approach. It can be argued that pluralistic democracies are not able to respond effectively to major new threats or problems; democracy is usually abandoned in wartime, for example. This is a troubling conclusion if you believe that the world faces serious problems requiring structural change or a new shared vision: there may be a fundamental conflict between having a pluralistic democracy and being able to respond flexibly to changing circumstances.

Science and technology policy: economic dimensions

One key element of science and technology policy, as discussed earlier, is its impact on the economy. The factor inputs to production were recognised over 200 years ago to be capital, labour and land or natural resources (Smith 1776/1970:104–6). In those terms, research and development in the productive sectors of the economy can be aimed at improving the economics of production of goods or services, or it may be aimed at putting new goods or services on the market. While traditional economics assumes we will always find more resources and usable land if the economic conditions are right, there is now evidence that this is not a valid assumption, as discussed in Chapter 11. It is reasonable to argue that there is now a fourth input to the production of marketable goods and services: technical innovation. There are particular problems in being innovative in relatively small economies such as those of Australia or New Zealand. As Walsh has pointed out:

> Firms in a country with a small domestic market will have to export to gain the benefits of economies of scale and to recoup the money spent on R&D. As technology increases the sophistication of products and processes, so the scientific, technological and industrial resources and skills for development and production become more costly and complex. The increasing trend towards long production runs, economies of scale and greater standard-isation increases the need for larger markets than the domestic economies of most small countries. The smaller the country, the greater is the pressure, so the need to turn to the international market is felt sooner ... And the proportion of the country's industries which are required to export is larger. [Walsh 1989:37–8]

Because they need to achieve economies of scale which can recoup research expenditure, small countries therefore are more dependent on trade than large ones. While there are exceptions, including Australia, in general there is an inverse relationship between the size of an indus-trialised economy and its dependence on trade, as shown by Table 9.1.

It has been argued that the successful small countries are those which have a successful export strategy, often based on a flexibility to respond

Table 9.1. Imports and exports as a percentage of gross domestic product, OECD countries, 1983

Country	Exports	Imports
USA	5.4	8.7
Japan	13.3	9.9
Greece	13.9	31.2
Australia	14.6	15.2
Spain	14.7	18.2
Turkey	15.0	21.5
France	19.0	21.0
Italy	21.9	25.2
UK	22.6	24.2
Canada	25.2	22.2
New Zealand	25.4	27.3
Switzerland	29.3	32.8
Sweden	30.3	28.4
Netherlands	54.8	52.3
Eire	56.9	55.1
Belgium/Luxembourg	64.9	67.8

Source: Walsh, 1989:39.

rapidly to changing requirements. Small countries have several dis-advantages, however. The risks and uncertainties of innovation are greater when the market is an international one than when local demand is large enough to ensure profitability, with exports a bonus. Small countries have less influence over international markets than large ones, and the increased distance between the innovator and the user makes it less likely the innovation will meet the user's needs, especially as radical innovations are likely to require education and training for users, as well as technical back-up which it is difficult to supply from a distance. A cruel dilemma now faces small industrialised countries.

The world markets for comparatively simple products based on mature technologies are increasingly dominated by the so-called newly industrialised countries, such as Singapore and South Korea, which have clear cost advantages because of low wage rates. The world markets for products which are complex or based on newly emerging technologies are dominated by the industrial superpowers, because only they can afford the massive investments required in capital equipment and research. The intermediate domain, the natural territory of small econ-omies, is being squeezed from both sides. The newly industrialised countries are expanding their capability to use new technology and consequently move beyond their traditional industries. From the other end of the economic spectrum, flexible manufacturing is allowing the superpowers like Japan to adapt products to local markets (Walsh 1989:48-50).

A number of broad economic strategies are open to countries with relatively small economies, such as Australia or New Zealand. One option is to try to find market niches, gaps in the market where large firms do not compete, either because they are too inflexible or because the size of the market does not interest them. This requires a sophis-ticated capacity to identify trends and direct R&D resources toward emerging opportunities.

A second option is to encourage development of multi-national corporations. It has been suggested that the small countries which have been successful in developing high-technology industry are those with their own multi-national corporations; this has been argued to be the basis for the success of Switzerland, Sweden and the Netherlands, for example. Even though small firms appear to be more innovative than large ones in some industries, large companies have crucial advantages in terms of marketing expertise and availability of capital. Australia's only significant multi-national corporation, BHP, is in the resource area rather than value-added production, so such a strategy does not appear viable there in the short term. A similar argument applies to New

Zealand. A refinement of this strategy is to encourage existing multi-nationals to invest locally. While this has been argued as a possible strategy for small countries, there is little in the experience of small European countries to give grounds for believing that the approach is likely to bring widespread benefits to a nation.

It is sometimes suggested that small countries could have greater impact if they were to pool their R&D efforts and make co-operative attacks on particular areas. To date, there is limited evidence of the success of the strategy; most of the co-operative research ventures which have been established are instances of co-operation between large countries, making it more difficult for small economies to compete.

Finally, it has been argued that a country with limited resources can compete only if it concentrates its limited resources, both human and financial, in a limited number of areas. The Australian National Technology Strategy, for example, suggested that a country should focus on areas which were:

- fundamental to a new generation of technologies
- applicable to a range of economic sectors
- particularly important for small domestic markets
- able to reinforce and extend areas of comparative advantage
- able to develop value-added goods for export markets
- offering prospects of developing whole new industries. [Department of Science, 1985:47]

This is a specific form of a general argument that small economies should not try to compete with the large countries in the high-technology sectors, but should put their efforts into improved competitiveness in medium-technology areas, preferably based on particular local attributes such as resources, labour skills or design traditions. This is a more sophisticated case than the traditional economic interpretation, which sees what economists call comparative advantage only in costs of labour or capital. This argument also recognises a need to involve those likely to be affected in decision-making. It recognises that research is now a crucial input in the production of goods and services.

As argued by Dosi *et al.* (1988), the most fundamental problem in much of the policy debate is the assumption that mainstream neo-classical economics is a valid analytical framework. It is more helpful to recognise that technical change is a fundamental economic force, involving mechanisms of dynamic adjustment quite different from traditional economic theory. These mechanisms are related both to technical change and to institutional change (or the barriers to such change). These changes are in turn affected by social and institutional forces in a way that is much more fundamental than can be explained by such economic ideas as market imperfections, requiring a recognition that our social and political institutions strongly influence the way markets work.

To take a particular example, there is no rational basis for believing that market forces will lead to an optimal level of investment in R&D. A range of factors tend to produce under-investment. Most obviously, the difficulty of protecting technical advances and thus harvesting the full commercial potential of innovations arises from problems of patenting and from the mobility of technical expertise. On the other hand, market competition can also produce over-investment in particular areas, as when an attractive field engenders a clustering of effort that amounts to duplication. This concentration of effort can also lead to the neglect of promising alternatives, the exploration of which would be in the long-term interests of society as a whole. These arguments are strong enough for most countries to see a government role in the funding and the direction of R&D (Johnston 1990).

The problem is, however, broader than just the direction of R&D. Innovation and the development of new industrial processes are complex social questions, rather than being driven simply by economic forces. That means that policy analysis needs to address these wider issues, ranging from the availability of skilled workers to the culture of innovation, from the research effort to purchasing policies, from venture capital to industrial relations. There is little doubt that this is a major challenge for government. Technological innovation needs to be stimulated for a variety of reasons, and there is a growing concern that a *laissez-faire* approach is not adequate. Not only do market forces not guarantee the sort of innovation which is needed, but they also pose the possibility of the sorts of innovation which are detrimental; there is an increasing tendency for public opinion to want some form of regulation of advances in technology (Collingridge 1984).

In the mid-1980s the Australian Minister for Science and Technology, Barry Jones, attempted the sort of comprehensive overview which seems to be needed. The National Technology Strategy contained an integrated package of policy measures for education and training, skills development, R&D, protection of intellectual property, provision of venture capital, development of management skills, purchasing of high-technology equipment by government, social assessment of new technology, and support of export industries (Department of Science 1983). Such an integrated strategy offers a better prospect of meeting future needs than a series of band-aid measures directed at urgent short-term problems. The National Technology Strategy was too radical an approach for a public service which was growing increasingly hostile to government intervention in the economy, as discussed earlier in this chapter, and the whole plan was effectively scuttled by the bureaucracy. The treatment of the Jones proposal illustrates the political difficulty of such a rational comprehensive approach.

The priorities for public-sector support of research in any country should be closely linked, or at least broadly related, to social and economic priorities. The rapid changes in both technology and the world economic order pose particular problems for small economies. The growing public concern for a pattern of development which can be genuinely sustained adds an additional dimension to the difficult task of determining priorities for research and development.

As discussed earlier in this section, research is now an important input in the production of goods and services. Johnston (1990) has pointed out that the R&D investment of major Japanese manufacturing companies is now running ahead of their capital investment. The difference is clear in the area of information technology; in companies such as Fujitsu and Hitachi, R&D spending was about double capital expenditure. Those fields which offer the greatest prospects for economic development are precisely those in which research is most expensive. A small economy faces the dilemma between abandoning whole areas of endeavour, thus being resigned to not competing, or trying to match the spending of the large economies (Walsh 1989:61).

A corporation sets the level and direction of its R&D according to its business plan, which balances such goals as corporate survival, short-term earnings and long-term development. The Australian Science and Technology Council suggested that the same principle holds true for each nation: it should have a strategic plan which balances aims such as survival as an industrially developed country and improvement in the level of production of goods and services with developing new capabilities and opportunities. These goals should dictate a balanced portfolio of research (ASTEC 1992).

Johnston went on to suggest that this 'investment model' of research has the following consequences for science policy:

1. a need to direct research to areas of high potential—hence forecast and foresight;
2. a need to concentrate resources to increase the probability of an effective outcome—hence priority setting;
3. a need to manage the research process to ensure greater productivity and efficiency—hence new management methods;
4. a need to determine if research is being conducted effectively and improve productivity—hence research evaluation and performance indicators;

5. a need to ensure the products of research are protected—hence intellectual property protection and surveillance; and

6. a need to ensure effective exploitation of research—hence linkages of knowledge, production and application. [Johnston 1990]

A second Australian attempt at this sort of rational comprehensive approach was the 1990 ASTEC consultative exercise 'Setting Directions for Australian Research', based on these principles. A draft Issues Paper was drawn up and was considered at a national conference. The avowed aim was to produce a White Paper which would shape government policy (including budget decisions) for a four-year cycle before the next review of priorities. Once again, that laudable aim was a casualty of bureaucratic in-fighting. The White Paper which finally emerged was little more than an apologia for the 1992–93 budget allocations. The same advisory body made a further attempt at strategic planning with a major foresight exercise during 1995–96, culminating in an impressive report on the problem of matching science and technology to Australia's future needs (ASTEC 1996). When this book was being written, there had been no government response to this report.

Australia is an interesting case study of the problems of developing a coherent overall policy for science and technology. For about twenty years, the rhetoric of successive governments has emphasised the need for integration of science policy with economic and social policies, as well as exhorting the private sector to devote more resources to the development of value-added goods and services. Despite that trend in government pronouncements and ministerial statements, it remains true, as the OECD noted, that 'the overall R&D effort in Australia is weak whether measured in volume or as a proportion of GDP. Furthermore, the distribution of this effort, by source of funding or by sector of execution, is unique among countries of comparable size' (OECD 1986).

Although Australian overall expenditure on R&D is relatively small as a proportion of GDP, the level of government funding is high, while the level of business expenditure is very low (see Chapter 2). As a result of the concentration of research effort in the public sector, there is a strong orientation toward basic research rather than applied research or product development. Nearly a quarter of all publicly funded research is aimed at the advancement of knowledge. There is also a strong emphasis on agriculture, partly for historical reasons and partly due to the fact that about 75 per cent of all state government funding of R&D is in the area of agriculture and forestry. The business effort is much more diverse (McGauran 1996).

Australia's unusual research profile can be expressed in comparative terms. The level of spending on basic research, as a fraction of GDP, exceeds that of Japan, the United States and Switzerland, is more than double the figure for Italy and about four times the figure for Ireland. Expenditure on applied research is, on the same basis, less than half the figure for Switzerland, about two-thirds the value for Japan and the United States, about the same as Italy and well above the figure for Ireland. In terms of spending on experimental development, turning the results of research into marketable goods and services, Australia's proportional effort is about one-eighth that of the United States, one-sixth that of Japan, one-quarter of the figure for Switzerland, half of Italy's and two-thirds of the value for Ireland (Slatyer 1986). Among the OECD countries listed in a recent report, only Iceland and Spain spent less on experimental development (as a fraction of their national wealth). Australia and New Zealand are the only two OECD countries in which the government spends more on R&D than the private sector (McGauran 1996:45). The reforms of public-sector science in New Zealand in the early 1990s were specifically aimed at aligning public-sector research more closely to commercial goals (Hammond and Devine 1993), while the establishment in Australia of Co-operative Research Centres had a similar aim (Slatyer 1993). These particular examples illustrate a general trend to try to establish mechanisms to direct science more strongly toward commercial ends.

Science and technology policy: broader issues

The discussion above concerns the economic role of science. A significant fraction of basic research is conducted without any aim of economic return. Astronomy aims at a better understanding of our place in the cosmos, while much of such sciences as botany and zoology is aimed at achieving better knowledge of the local biota. There is contention about the appropriate level of funding for this sort of basic research, aiming only to extend knowledge. In Australia, about a quarter of publicly funded research is in this category, accounting for about a billion dollars a year (McGauran 1996:3, 13). In an era of contracting government, that sort of expenditure has been under attack. As one bureaucrat recently put it, 'increasingly it is necessary to demonstrate the social utility of taxpayer-funded expenditure' (Gallagher 1993:158). During 1996, the Australian government decided not to proceed with a proposal for participation in an international project to build a large optical telescope in Chile. This was seen as a blow to basic research. The Australian Academy of Science has criticised the level of funding for taxonomy, pointing out that it will take another thousand years to document all the species in the country at the current rate of progress.

Governments are also increasingly involved in difficult and divisive questions about the sorts of science and technology which are acceptable. Probably the most complex policy questions are in emerging areas of biology, such as reproductive technology, organ transplantation and genetic modification of species. The capacity of humans to change the web of life raises serious ethical issues for policy-makers as well as scientists. Some scientists clearly believe that governments should put few restrictions on research, while others argue for a more cautious approach to these areas of biology (Haynes 1991).

There is also questioning of the broad emphasis of technology policy from at least three directions. Social analysts are critical of the way social impacts are down-played in a welter of technical enthusiasm for big projects (Collingridge 1984; Scott 1992). Feminists are critical of the dominance of men and masculine values in decision-making groups (Wajcman 1991). Ecologists criticise the failure to include an understanding of ecological impacts in decisions about technological change (Trainer 1985; SoEAC 1996). So government policies about technology are likely to receive increasing scrutiny and more detailed criticism. All these features are visible in the debates about such major issues as urban transport. If you live in a city large enough to have a university, there is likely to be such a debate raging near you at this time. Think about the way the values of individuals and groups influence their views on the options being discussed.

Conclusion

As argued above, science and technology do not exist in a political vacuum. A nation's policy for science and technology should be integrated with more general goals. Ideally, we should have a vision of the sort of world we want to live in and choose research activities to form an integral part of the program for achieving that vision. A problem arises from the tendency for government-funded R&D to concentrate on basic science rather than the sort of product development which is normally conducted by the private sector. Government policy can easily affect the pace and direction of pure science, but has much less impact on technological innovation, which usually comes from the business sector.

This chapter has outlined the problems of developing coherent public policy in general. All of the problems apply with particular strength to science, since there is often a long lead-time between investment in research and the development of new goods and services. It is often not clear where effort can most profitably be applied; for example, a new health problem such as HIV/AIDS can be tackled either by trying to find treatments, or by trying to prevent exposure in the short term, or by a program of basic research that tries to improve our overall knowledge of the immune system. Even with hindsight, it is not always clear what was the right balance between different approaches.

Further reading

Barry Jones's book *Sleepers, Wake!* was first published in 1982 and has become an international best-seller, translated into several languages. It addresses the broad sweep of technological change, with its associated social and economic impacts. The revised and updated 1995 edition gives an excellent general extension of the issues discussed in this chapter. The title of David Collingridge's book *The Social Control of Technology* accurately describes its content; it is an excellent analysis of the problems in exercising social choices about which technologies will be used and how they will be used. Roslyn Haynes's edited collection *High Tech, High Co$t?* is a series of interesting case studies of the social relevance of current research and development. The collection by Wood and Meek, *Research Grants Management and Funding*, contains chapters which analyse the problem of managing research to produce desired outcomes. The Australian Science and Technology Council's 1996 report, *Matching Science and Technology to Australia's Future Needs*, is a comprehensive analysis of the way the future can be shaped by choices in the broad area of science and technology.

References

Australian Science and Technology Council (ASTEC) (1990), *Setting Directions for Australian Research*. Canberra: Australian Government Publishing Service.

Australian Science and Technology Council (ASTEC) (1996), *Matching Science and Technology to Australia's Future Needs*. Canberra: Australian Government Publishing Service.

Collingridge, D. (1984), *The Social Control of Technology*. London: Frances Pinter.

Davis, G., Wanna, J., Warhurst, P., and Weller, P. (1988), *Public Policy in Australia*. Sydney: Allen and Unwin.

Department of Science (1985), *National Technology Strategy: Revised Discussion Draft*. Canberra: Australian Government Publishing Service.

Dosi, G. *et al.* (1988), *Technical Change and Economic Theory*. London: Frances Pinter.

Etzioni, A. (1968), *The Active Society*. New York: Free Press (Macmillan).

Gallagher, M. (1993), 'Getting Value for Money from University Research', in F. Q. Wood and V. Meek (eds), *Research Grants Management and Funding*. Canberra: ANUTECH: 157–68.

Hammond, L. S., and Devine, S. D. (1993), 'The New Zealand Experience of a Comprehensive Fully-costed Science Funding System', in Wood and Meek (1993): 105–11.

Hardin, G. (1968), 'The Tragedy of the Commons', *Science*, 162:1243–8.

Haynes, R. (ed.) (1991), *High Tech: High Co$t?* Chippendale: Pan Macmillan.

Jaensch, D. (1986), *Putting our Houses in Order*. Sydney: Penguin.

Johnston, R. (1990), 'Strategic Policy for Science', *Australian Universities Review*, 33:2–7.

Jones, B. O. (1982), *Sleepers, Wake!* Melbourne: Oxford University Press.

Latham, E. (1952), *The Group Basis of Politics.* Ithaca, NY: Cornell University Press.

Lindblom, C. E. (1959), 'The Science of Muddling Through', *Journal of Public Administration*, 19:79–99.

Lowe, I. (1987), 'University Research Funding: The Wheel Still is Spinnin'', *Australian Universities Review*, 30:2–11.

Lowe, I. (1991), 'Science Policy for the Future', in R. Haynes (ed.), *High Tech: High Co$t?* Chippendale: Pan Macmillan.

Lowe, I. (1996), 'Censoring Science', *Australia Nature*, 25, 7:80.

McGauran, P. (1996), *Science and Technology Budget Statement 1996–97.* Canberra: Australian Government Publishing Service.

Martin, B. R., and Irvine, J. (1989), *Research Foresight: Priority Setting in Science.* London: Frances Pinter.

National Institute of Economic and Industry Research (NIEIR) (1996), *Subsidies to the use of Natural Resources.* Canberra: Department of Environment, Sport and Territories.

Organisation for Economic Cooperation and Development (1986), *National Reviews of Science and Technology Policy: Australia.* Paris: OECD.

Painter, M., and Carey, B. (1979), *Politics between Departments.* St Lucia, Qld: University of Queensland Press.

Plummer, P. (1996), *Submission to Select Committee on Uranium Mining and Milling.* Canberra: Australian Parliament.

Polanyi, M. (1968), *Knowing and Being.* London: Routledge & Kegan Paul.

Pusey, M. (1991), *Economic Rationalism in Canberra.* Cambridge: Cambridge University Press.

Sawer, G. (1948), *Australian Government Today.* Melbourne: Melbourne University Press.

Sawer, G. (1973), 'Parliament: Progress in Small Steps Only', in H. Mayer and H. Nelson (eds), *Australian Politics: A Third Reader.* Melbourne: Longman Cheshire.

Scott, P. (ed.) (1992), *A Herd of White Elephants.* Sydney: Hale and Iremonger.

Slatyer, R. O. (1986), 'Balance of National Research Effort, in Policies and Directions for Science and Research', *Conference Proceedings.* Canberra: Department of Science.

Slatyer, R. (1993), 'Co-operative Research Centres: The Concept and Its Implementation', in Wood and Meek (1993): 121–30.

Smith, A. (ed. A. Skinner) (1776/1970), *The Wealth of Nations.* Harmondsworth: Penguin.

State of the Environment Advisory Council (SoEAC) (1996), *State of the Environment Australia 1996.* Melbourne: CSIRO Publishing.

Trainer, E. (1985), *Abandon Affluence!* London: Zed Books.

Wajcman, J. (1991), *Feminism Confronts Technology.* Sydney: Allen and Unwin.

Walker, K. J. (1994), *The Political Economy of Environmental Policy.* Kensington, NSW: University of New South Wales Press.

Walsh, V. (1989), 'The Problems of Small Countries', in C. Freeman and G. Dosi (eds), *Technological Change and the Competitiveness of Small Countries.* London: Frances Pinter.

Whitlam, E. G. (1978), *The Truth of the Matter.* Melbourne: Penguin.

Wood, F. Q., and Meek, V. (eds) (1993), *Research Grants Management and Funding.* Canberra: ANUTECH.

CHAPTER 10

Science, Technology and the Less-developed Countries

David Burch

Much of the content of any textbook on science, technology and society inevitably concerns the richer countries of the world, where most of the technological change associated with industrialisation has occurred, and where most of the world's research and development are carried out. But the world's wealthier countries contain only about one-third of the population of the globe. The remaining two-thirds live in the poorer countries, sometimes referred to as the Third World.

Despite their low levels of industrialisation, these poorer countries still have a major interest in science and technology, especially in terms of the contribution that they can make to solving some of the problems of poverty, malnutrition and low levels of output of goods and services. Equally, though, the nature of the relationships between science, technology and society are very different from those which occur in the rich industrialised countries. In the Third World, for example, some 70–80 per cent of the people usually still live in the rural areas and are involved in agricultural production as a way of life. This compares with a figure of 5 per cent or less for most of the industrialised countries. Differences such as these dramatically illustrate the need to think carefully about the role of Western science and technology in the less-developed countries. Before going on to consider this in more detail though, it is important to discuss a little further what is meant by the Third World.

Where is the Third World?

The *Third World* is a term used to identify the poorer countries of the world, which are found in parts of Asia, Africa and Latin America. Several methods can be used to distinguish how rich or poor a country is. One of the most common measures is *per capita income*, a figure (usually expressed in terms of US dollars) that indicates how much income a person would receive if the value of all goods and services produced within a country in one year (its gross domestic product, or GDP) were equally shared. Using this measure, we can see that the per capita income in Ethiopia in 1994 was about $100 and in Indonesia it was $880. While there is a considerable difference between these two countries, they are both far behind the very rich countries, such as Japan, with a per capita income of $34,630, the United States ($25,880) or Australia ($18,000) (World Bank 1996). Both Ethiopia and Indonesia therefore are classified as less-developed.

Another method for comparing the rich and the poor countries uses social indicators, which measure factors such as birth and death rates, life expectancy, health care, education, food and nutritional intakes, and many aspects of social life. One of the health indicators we use, for example, tells us that in 1988–92 there were 2.29 doctors for every 1000 people in Australia, compared to a figure of 0.14 doctor for every 1000 people in Sri Lanka (formerly Ceylon) (World Bank 1993). On this measure, Australia obviously performs better than Sri Lanka, because the wealthier country has more resources to allocate to health services.

Some criticism has been levelled at the use of such social indicators because they do not take into account non-statistical measures of 'development', such as respect for human rights, the existence of democratic institutions, access to a free press and so on. There are other criticisms of these ways of measuring the status of the less-developed countries. Most importantly, all the above measures are averages or generalised aggregations of data, which ignore the significant variations that can occur in reality, as a consequence of class, ethnic, gender, cultural or other differences. For example, while the average (or per capita income) in Bangladesh appears to be very low (at $220 in 1993), this does not mean that everyone in Bangladesh is uniformly poor. Societies everywhere have rich and poor people, and Bangladesh is no different. The richest 10 per cent of households in Bangladesh receive some 23.7 per cent of national income, while the poorest 10 per cent of households share only 4.4 per cent of national income (World Bank 1996). In other words, there are a number of very wealthy people receiving well above the average income, and many very poor people well below the average.

In cultural terms also, the official statistics do not always paint a full picture of what it means to live and survive in the Third World. For example, statistics regarding measures of health-care delivery are often ethnocentric in their approach and exhibit a cultural bias which, probably unconsciously, reflects official assumptions about the superiority of Western medicine. As noted earlier, the official statistics show that Australia has 2.29 doctors for every 1000 people, compared to 0.14 doctor for every 1000 people in Sri Lanka. But these statistics refer to doctors as defined by a Western model or standard—that is, a six-year trained medical practitioner whose education is oriented towards Western practices and assumptions about the causes of particular ailments and how they might be treated. But such an accounting system leaves out the many thousands of Third World medical practitioners trained in traditional health-care systems, such as the Ayurvedic medicine of South Asia and acupuncture in China, which have been in existence for many hundreds, if not thousands, of years, and which still represent the first point of medical reference for millions of poor people living in the rural areas of the Third World. Such indigenous health-care systems are not, as their detractors like to suggest, un-scientific mumbo-jumbo, but are usually well-grounded in empirical, psychological and cultural terms, and represent an important part of the total picture of the delivery of health care in most of the less-developed countries (Harrison 1983:223–55). But this total picture is distorted when traditional medical practitioners are excluded from the official statistics.

Such issues not only indicate the complexities which emerge when attempting to define the less-developed countries, but also suggest that the concept of 'development' is a many-faceted phenomenon which defies simple definition. While many observers suggest that 'development' can be equated with economic growth, or simply becoming more like the industrialised countries, many researchers reject such simple formulations. Economic growth is not necessarily of benefit to the poorest people in a country with high levels of income inequality, where the benefits of economic expansion have been captured by the richest 10 or 20 per cent of the population. And to become more like the industrialised nations may also mean experiencing not only the benefits of industrialisation, but its costs as well, including problems of environmental degradation, increasing urbanisation, social alienation, and rampant consumerism. Many observers in the Third World question the benefits of such 'development' and believe instead that an emphasis on sustainability in production and consumption, combined with some of the residual characteristics of pre-industrial societies (decentralisation, social integration, resource conservation and so on) provide a more effective definition of 'development' (see for example, Harrison 1983: 11–22).

Clearly, conceptions of what is, and what is not, 'development' are not neutral scientific definitions, but judgements that reflect the interests and values of whoever is offering a particular definition. The same is true of those theories which are offered as *explanations* of Third World poverty. Some observers suggest that poor countries have always been that way and are simply 'late starters' which have only recently begun to 'develop'. Such countries can become more advanced if they look to the examples provided by other 'successful' countries and pursue similar policies. However, other researchers have suggested that Third World countries have been made 'underdeveloped' by the colonial experience most of them underwent, and which made them dependent upon the advanced countries. Under these circumstances, the less-developed countries cannot simply emulate the experience of the industrialised world, but must find some alternative path to improving their standards of living (Hettne 1990).

Despite a lack of agreement over the meaning of development, it must be noted that definition and analysis are always more than just an expression of a personal opinion or an ideological dogma. Any attempt to debate issues in development must be supported by plausible assumptions, accurate data and logical argument. As long as these ingredients are present, it does not matter that there is disagreement over definitions; at least a reasoned debate will be possible, which may facilitate the emergence of some common ground as we seek solutions to the pressing problems of the less-developed countries.

In the search for such solutions, many observers have turned to science and technology, and to Western science and technology in particular. There is an assumption that these factors played an important role in the industrialisation of the developed countries, and that it is therefore inconceivable that science and technology would be any less significant for the eventual transformation of the poor countries. However, as we shall see in the course of this discussion, such assumptions have not always been justified. As with the concept of 'development' itself, the role of science and technology in this process has been the subject of intense debate and much disagreement. There has seldom, if ever, been any consensus on what Western science and technology could, and should, offer to the less-developed countries. The divisions which exist amongst social analysts will inevitably suggest a range of prospects and possibilities. What this chapter seeks to do is to outline the major schools of thought regarding science and technology in the less-developed countries, and to evaluate the strengths and weaknesses of each approach. In this way, it will at least be possible to make some judgements about the likely impacts of different policy choices and to evaluate the costs and benefits to different social groups.

Post-colonial optimism: 'science and technology for development'

After the end of World War II, there was growing pressure on the colonial powers such as Britain and France to grant independence to their colonial territories in Africa and Asia. As the post-war process of decolonisation gathered pace during the 1940s and 1950s, increasing attention was devoted to the ways in which the many problems of these relatively poor countries could be solved. To many of the emerging Third World leaders, prosperity was inevitably linked to industrialisation, and it was generally assumed that the rapid transformation of 'backward' economies, hitherto based on agriculture, would lead to a more dynamic and rapidly expanding system of production. Moreover, orthodox economic theory taught that technological innovation was the most significant factor in generating increased output. One researcher estimated that more than two-thirds of the increased national income generated in the United States in the period from the 1870s to the 1960s was attributable to technological innovation, and only one-third to increases in labour and capital (Wellisz 1966:234).

Of course, most of the newly independent countries did not have the capacity to produce for themselves the technological innovations that were thought to be necessary for 'development', and they looked to the industrialised countries for sources of technology. India was a case in point. Although the Gandhian rhetoric of the independence movement emphasised economic regeneration on the basis of small-scale, village-level activities (Harrison 1983:17–19), the post-independence reality was very different. The model for Indian industrialisation was the Soviet Union, with an emphasis on the establishment of a range of heavy industries in the public (government) sector as the basis for 'import-substituting industrialisation'. This would result in India itself making many of the manufactured goods it previously bought from Britain, its former colonial ruler, and other countries. The Indian government set about establishing new industries producing a wide range of commodities—steel, fertilisers, machine tools, railway locomotives, heavy electrical equipment and other capital goods. In addition, the government established the conditions for increasing the supply of high-quality scientists and engineers, and provided funding for an extensive network of institutions engaged in scientific research and development (Chamarik and Goonetilleke 1994:17–49).

The concentration of resources on large-scale industrial undertakings was a feature of the post-war development policies of many newly independent countries, including China (see Ishikawa 1973), and such activities generated an initial optimism that industrialisation in the Third World might be achieved more rapidly, and with fewer social costs, than had been possible with the early industrial nations such as Britain and Germany. Third World countries would not have to 'reinvent the wheel' and, since the R&D costs of developing existing technologies had already been repaid many times over, it was believed that the Third World would be able to access these resources very cheaply. Observers such as Lord Blackett, a noted British physicist and chair of the Committee on Science and Technology in Developing Countries (set up by the International Council of Scientific Unions), suggested that the poor developing countries would be able to shop freely in the 'world's well-stocked supermarket [of] production goods and services' (Blackett 1963). In this, they would be further helped by the aid programs which the governments of the major industrial countries had established in order to provide assistance to poor countries seeking to industrialise (Jones 1971).

This sense of optimism concerning the benefits that Western science and technology could bring to the less-developed countries was especially influential within the United Nations, which organised the first of a series of conferences on the Application of Science and Technology for the Benefit of the Less Developed Nations, in Geneva in 1963. This conference resulted in the creation of a new UN body—the Advisory Committee on the Application of Science and Technology to Development (ACAST)—which was given the responsibility of preparing a World Plan of Action for Science and Technology (Clarke 1985:53). In addressing the proposals subsequently brought forward by ACAST, the then Secretary-General of the United Nations, U Thant, said that science and technology 'could be the most powerful force in the world for the achievement of higher living standards, [and] it was the task of the UN to harness it for that purpose' (ACAST 1970:1–3).

However, by the end of the UN's First Development Decade in 1970, a more sceptical view of the role of science and technology in development was emerging. Ironically, this new perspective was in some measure the result of the very work carried out by the United Nations and its agencies, in the search for policy measures that could be introduced to enhance the role of science and technology for development.

Towards a critical analysis

One of the most important documents contributing to this reappraisal of science and technology came out of ACAST, as it prepared the World Plan of Action for Science and Technology. This was a study prepared by the 'Sussex Group', consisting of a number of noted academics from the University of Sussex, in England. These researchers pointed out that not only did the Third World account for a mere 2 per cent of total world R&D expenditures, but that this expenditure was often uncoordinated and misdirected, and allocated to research projects which bore little relationship to the needs of the poor countries. Priority was accorded to 'pure' or 'basic' research rather than relevant applied research that would address critical problems

associated with energy, food and agriculture, health, housing and so on.
In other words, much science and technology activity carried out within
the Third World was 'marginal' or 'alienated from production', and was
not directly associated with the kinds of activities which would generate
economic growth or improve the quality of life. Instead, scientific R&D
stood apart as an 'enclave' activity which took its cue from the research
orientations of the Western scientific community, and which reflected
the priorities of Western science and technology (ACAST 1970; Cooper
1973; Herrera 1973; Sagasti 1975; Yearley 1988).

There were a number of reasons why this was the case. There was,
firstly, the orientation of local Third World scientists and institutions
towards the norms and values of the Western tradition in which they
were usually trained, and which judged success in terms of advances in
high-level basic research. Underwriting this was a system of education
and training which almost seems purpose-built to divorce the local
intellectual elite from the social and economic realities of their own
societies. For example, when the colonial authorities in Sri Lanka
established widespread local access to education in the nineteenth and
early twentieth centuries, the elite English-language schools adopted the
same curriculum as the British private schools on which they were
modelled. Sri Lankan school children sat the same exams as their UK
counterparts, namely the Cambridge Senior and London Matriculation
exams, which were intended to prepare British students for entry to
British universities. As a consequence, generations of Sri Lanka's elite
were educated with little reference to the local economic, social or
cultural context; instead, they learned about Britain's economy and
society, and about science in a Western context. This tendency was
reinforced with the establishment in 1921 of the University College of
Colombo, whose students were prepared for the degree examinations
of London University in the liberal arts and science. In the process,
Western norms and values in education were strongly inculcated into
those individuals who emerged after independence as the leading
decision-makers in government, administration, education and science
in Sri Lanka (Mendis 1952; de Silva 1977). The priority accorded this
Western world-view within the wider colonial context, and the neglect
of a focus on local problems and needs, was to contribute significantly to
the emergence of a marginalised and alienated scientific community in
the Third World.

Other factors were to add to this problem. In particular, it became
evident that the structure of the typical Third World economy was such
that it did not encourage local R&D, nor did it make significant
demands upon the local scientific and technological community for
innovative ideas and practices. Unlike the industrialised countries, most

Third World economies were (and are) largely based on agriculture and/or extractive industries (mining), and such activities are not especially research-intensive. Ranching and plantation agriculture also do not depend upon a process of continuing innovation, and much peasant agriculture is based on local knowledge systems which do not necessarily rely upon laboratory-based R&D in order to improve land and/or labour productivity. In the industrial sector as well, there was little to stimulate the local scientific and technological capabilities, given the reliance upon imported industrial technology in the immediate post-independence period (Herrera 1973). Both government and the private sector (usually foreign-owned companies) in the Third World tended to rely upon the transfer of known and reliable technologies, which often came in the form of a 'turnkey' project (for example, a complete fertiliser factory which required only local labour and management to begin operating).

As a consequence of all these factors (and in contrast to the situation in the industrialised countries), only weak links were established between science and production in the Third World. This, in turn, was to contribute to the phenomenon of the brain drain, as large numbers of trained and educated professionals, unable to find work in their own countries, left to take up jobs in the developed countries. In the post-war period, hundreds of thousands of scientists, engineers, doctors and other medical personnel, and professionals of all kinds, migrated to the United States, Canada, the United Kingdom, Western Europe and Australasia (Yearley 1988). The value of such personnel to the countries to which they migrated, which immediately benefited from their expertise without paying for their prior education and training, constituted a reverse form of foreign aid from the poor countries to the rich.

The marginalisation of the local scientific enterprise and the reliance upon Western technology as the basis for a country's development was to have even more profound impacts upon poorer groups, in particular the peasant farmers and poor urban workers who did not have the option of seeking well-paid employment overseas. A number of studies drew attention to the capital-intensive nature of much imported Western technology, which not only created few local jobs but also frequently destroyed thousands of existing jobs in agriculture and industry (see, for example, ILO 1971; Marsden 1973).

In addition to problems of unemployment resulting from Western technology imports, it was becoming clear that Blackett's (1963) expectation that the poor countries would be able to access Western technology at relatively cheap prices was not being fulfilled. As Vaitsos (1973) found, Third World countries were often over-charged for technology transferred from rich countries, especially when a trans-national corporation held monopoly rights over a piece of equipment, a process or an ingredient, via the patent system. In a study of a number of industries in the Andean Pact countries of Latin America, Vaitsos (1973) found that patented technology transferred from a parent company in the developed country to a subsidiary in the Third World was systematically over-priced, sometimes many thousand per cent. This practice, known as 'transfer pricing', was widespread and systematic, and represented a substantial hidden cost of Western technology.

In the rural sector too, the reliance upon Western science and technology was proving costly, with the rural poor often bearing a dis-proportionate share of the burden of innovation. Although there is no overall consensus on this issue, many observers believe that the program of agricultural improvement known as the Green Revolution may have improved the overall supply of food in some Third World countries, but at the same time made the situation of many of the rural poor much worse (Griffin 1974; Shiva 1991). The Green Revolution was the attempt to increase the output of rice and wheat in Asia particularly, through a systematic and large-scale program of plant improvement. This research was funded by the Ford and Rockefeller Foundations, which estab-lished the International Rice Research Institute at Los Banos, in the Philippines, in 1962. Soon after, the institute released the first of a series of high-yielding varieties of rice which held out the promise of a doub-ling of yields. But such increases were achievable only under certain conditions, in particular the application of regular doses of chemical fertilisers and an assured supply of water (which implied irrigated rather than rain-fed agriculture). The problem with this was that most small farmers could not afford to purchase chemical fertiliser, or the diesel fuel required to operate the pumps which made it possible to draw on groundwater resources. Under these circumstances, the Green Revo-lution was seen by many to have initiated a process whereby the benefits of the new technology were monopolised by larger, richer farmers, who experienced none of the financial problems of smaller producers. Subsequently, many peasant farmers were squeezed out of agricultural production because of debts incurred by borrowings to pay for the new technology, or because they were unable to compete with larger farmers for the resources needed to benefit from the new seeds. In addition, as larger farmers grew even richer, they began to invest in labour-saving technologies such as tractors, and thousands of agricultural labourers also lost their jobs. Many large landlords also took the opportunity to remove their tenant farmers (who paid a share of their rice output as rent), because such farmers could not afford the Green Revolution technology or were unwilling to invest heavily in a technology that would generate higher returns to the landlord (as a share of increased volume of output). Increasingly, landlords took to cultivating their land with tractors and small amounts of hired labour and, as a consequence, many thousands of tenants in India, Pakistan and elsewhere in the Third World were thrown off the land they farmed (George 1976). So, while the overall effect of the Green Revolution was to increase food production, at the same time it made it harder for many poor agricultural labourers to buy the food which was being produced in ever-greater volumes (because they lost their jobs), and harder for small farmers and tenants to produce their own food (because they lost their land) (ILO 1977).

Another important issue raised by the Green Revolution (and by other programs of development in general) concerned the plight of hitherto neglected women in the rural areas of the Third World, and the failure of Western technology and Western models of development to consider the gender effects of technological innovation. The Green Revolution, for example, resulted in the provision of improved inputs and the use of mechanised techniques for ploughing, but gave little thought to the consequences of greatly increased grain output for women, who were the traditional harvesters of rice. Moreover, at the same time as massive investments were being made in Green Revolution technology, little attention was paid to improving the small-scale backyard production carried on by women in home gardens. Nor were any attempts made to improve women's domestic technology (for food processing, cooking, cleaning, and for the collection of firewood and water), which occupied so much time and effort (Chambers 1983). Attention to these problems would have done much to improve and 'develop' the condition of poor rural women, as well as increasing output and efficiency, but they were accorded a low priority by politicians and bureaucrats everywhere.

The response to crisis

To some observers, the problems of the Green Revolution, and the issues associated with transfer pricing, unemployment, gender inequities and the structure and performance of Third World science and technology systems, were evidence of the structural inequality and exploitation that were symptomatic of the relationship between the developed and underdeveloped countries. To the school of thought known as 'dependency theorists', Western technology was just one more mechanism for extracting profits and resources from the Third World (Amin 1976). Other observers, though, argued that problems in the transfer of technology largely arose out of policy failure, and a lack of understanding concerning the 'inappropriateness' of Western technology in the less-developed countries. According to these observers, Western technology was designed for the conditions typical of the industrialised countries, where capital in the form of advanced technology had replaced much of the labour which had previously been utilised in production. When applied in the poorer countries, this technology not only utilised scarce capital resources but also failed to create new jobs in labour-abundant societies which desperately needed new and expanded employment opportunities. This was a key problem in the debate about transfer of technology which dominated much of the analysis of science and technology policy in the late 1960s and early 1970s.

The most significant Western analyst on this topic was E. F. Schumacher (1973), an economist who advocated the idea of 'intermediate technology' as an alternative to advanced Western technology. In Schumacher's view, traditional indigenous technology was not productive enough to generate high incomes for Third World producers and could not eliminate their poverty. At the same time, advanced Western technology was not only far too expensive for most Third World producers but would never generate the numbers of jobs that were needed to employ the large numbers of people who lived in rural areas. According to Schumacher, what was required was an intermediate technology which was mid-way between the local and the Western, and which would generate new employment and higher incomes in the villages and rural areas where new jobs were sorely needed. Schumacher gave practical expression to his ideas by founding the Intermediate Technology Development Group, which undertook many practical and appropriate projects in sectors such as health, rural development, building and other areas. A case in point concerns the production of bricks for improved construction of domestic buildings in the Third World. In the industrialised world, a typical brick factory might produce one million bricks per week, but it would be very expensive to build and operate; for this sort of factory, most developing countries would have to import spare parts and energy inputs. The ITDG developed small-scale alternatives which produced only 10,000 bricks per week, using hand-operated methods and simple machinery. Capital costs per workplace were only £400, compared with £40,000 for the modern brickworks, and the bricks produced in the small-scale ITDG factory were only half the price of the others. ITDG helped to set up such plants in Ghana, Gambia, Egypt, South Sudan and Tanzania (McRobie 1982).

While some Western researchers played a significant part in developing the conceptual framework and practical solutions for appropriate or intermediate technologies, the direct experience of Third World countries such as India and China was undoubtedly of the greatest importance. In India, the concept of appropriate technology owed much to Gandhian ideas about village self-reliance, which involved a bias towards small-scale technologies and a rejection of materialist and consumptionist philosophies which depended upon high rates of growth (Harrison 1983:17–19). In China's case, the roots of appropriate technology were to be found in the *gung ho* movement of the 1930s, which involved the creation of small-scale, labour-intensive and mobile production units designed to service the needs of the highly mobile guerilla force which was the Red Army (Burchett and Alley 1976). The relevance of Western science and technology to the needs of the Third World, and especially the problems of the rural poor, was also questioned by the many non-governmental organisations which emerged in the less-developed countries in the 1960s and 1970s. 'People's science' and environmental groups, such as the Consumers Association of Penang in Malaysia (1981; 1982) and the Centre for Science and Environment in India, provided a powerful critique of Western models of development. For most of these groups, appropriate technology was seen as providing an important alternative path of development which would not only ensure autonomy and self-reliance at all levels of society, but also maintain ecological integrity, and allow change and development to occur with minimal disruption to traditional lifestyles and values (Consumers Association of Penang 1981).

Typical of the kind of technology which came out of the Third World's own experience is the biogas fertiliser plant, which is an effective alternative to Western systems of energy and fertiliser production. Through a process of anaerobic microbial fermentation, a biogas plant is able to turn vegetable matter, animal manure and other waste materials into a nitrogen-rich slurry which can be used as a fertiliser. In addition, the process creates methane gas which can be used for cooking, heating water, and even driving generators for lighting and other purposes. All that is needed for a community to become self-reliant in fertiliser and energy is a cement-lined pit in which floats a large drum containing the gas, and the raw materials and labour to keep the biogas plant going. The biogas fertiliser plant and the conventional Western technology for fertiliser production are compared in Table 10.1.

Armed with such examples, many observers perceived in appropriate technology a model of technological development which would generate jobs, greater equality and enhanced self-reliance for the Third World. To this extent, it was a highly political agenda because it gave practical expression to the idea of 'de-linking' from the developed countries, thereby challenging the dependency relationship which, for many in the Third World, characterised their situation.

Table 10.1. Production of fertiliser by Western and alternative technologies (230,000 tonnes of nitrogen per year)

	Western technology (large-scale coal-based fertiliser plant)	Alternative technology (village-scale biogas fertiliser plant)
Number of plants	1	26,150
Capital cost	1200 million rupees	1070 million rupees
Foreign exchange	600 million rupees	nil
Employment	1000	130,750
Energy	about 0.1 million MWH *consumed* per annum	about 6.35 million MWH *produced* per annum

Source: Reddy 1975.

The appropriate technology movement was not without its critics, though. Many observers in the Third World itself saw it as an attempt to impose a second-best technology on the less-developed countries which, far from liberating them, would reinforce their situation of dependency and subordination (Harrison 1983:154–5). From a different perspective again, Burch (1981; 1982) argued that appropriate technology was unlikely to become a mass phenomenon in most Third World countries because it was not grounded in the then-prevailing social and political structures. Schumacher and others had argued in favour of appropriate technology as a means of generating employment and creating the basis of a more egalitarian society based on small-scale production in rural areas. But this ignored the effects of the pre-existing income inequality in most Third World countries, which skewed consumer demand towards the product choices—motor vehicles, luxury household products, fashion clothing, large houses and so on—favoured by the wealthier, dominant social classes. As Stewart (1977) noted, in many instances the choice of production technique was ruled out once a choice of product was made. In other words, there were no viable, labour-intensive techniques for making motor vehicles or other sophisticated products. As long as income was unequally distributed, then, the structure of production in Third World countries was in many respects pre-determined in favour of capital-intensive and inappropriate technology. To this extent, the appropriate technology movement was putting the cart before the horse. Rather than a more equal society emerging from the application of appropriate technology, the creation of a more egalitarian society was a precondition for the widespread utilisation of appropriate technology. Only with a prior redistribution of income would the structure of consumer demand shift from luxury products made by capital-intensive technology for upper-class consumption, towards the production of a range of basic items—bicycles, cookers, saucepans, farm implements, cheap building materials, simple energy systems and so on—made by local, labour-intensive technologies for consumption by poorer local groups. Only then would appropriate technology be firmly rooted in the social structure and be widely utilised in the creation of new industries and new jobs. As a practical demonstration of this, India's Planning Commission undertook a study which revealed that every 1 million rupees ($US120,000) of income transferred from rich to poor would create 20 new jobs (Harrison 1983:154).

Clearly, in order to solve India's massive problems of unemployment on the basis of prevailing assumptions, there would have to be an unprecedented shift in the distribution of income from rich to poor. Such a proposal was, of course, politically unlikely given the extent to which the state in India reflected the interests of wealthier social classes. As a consequence, the failure to redistribute income appeared to consign appropriate technology to a marginal position in the overall analysis of Third World development. It was to be rescued, however, when the focus in development thinking shifted from a strategy of import substitution to meet domestic demands, towards a strategy of export orientation as a way of serving global markets.

Structural transformation in the 1980s: from technology transfer to technological capabilities

The 1970s was a decade in which the limits to the social improvements that could be wrought by technology alone had come to be clearly understood. The problems of technological choice and transfer generated much analysis and data, but in the meantime the world was rapidly changing. By the mid-1970s, the long post-war period of stability had come to a close, along with the financial arrangements known as the Bretton Woods agreement, which had underwritten a period of significant and sustained growth in the global economy. Major increases in the price of oil in 1973 and 1979 fuelled a growing instability and a world-wide recession that lasted into the early 1980s. Out of this emerged a significantly different world order, which raised new and important questions about the relationship between science, technology and development.

One of the most significant outcomes of the 1980s was the emergence of a group of newly industrialising countries, which had apparently succeeded in overcoming the problems of underdevelopment and had industrialised on the basis of producing goods for export rather than the model of import-substituting industrialisation discussed earlier. Export-oriented industrialisation required the establishment of a productive capacity which emphasised the production of consumer goods for world markets rather than the production of capital and infrastructure goods for the domestic market. The implications of this shift were significant, for a number of reasons. First, producing goods for relatively wealthy consumers in the rich countries obviously opened up many new opportunities for large-scale production by a number of Third World countries. Second, by concentrating on exports a Third World country could build up a productive capability using relatively simple, labour-intensive technology. Products such as textiles, shoes, toys, plastic products and similar goods, which were among the significant products made and exported, did not require a heavy engineering capability. The production of garments for mass markets overseas, for example, relied on little more than large numbers of low-paid people skilled in the operation of sewing machines.

There was, of course, much more than this to the development of the newly industrialising countries. Countries such as Taiwan, South Korea, Singapore and Hong Kong (sometimes referred to as the 'tiger' economies) had diverse historical experiences, and these were important for their later industrialisation (Burch 1987). But they shared the experience of rapid industrialisation which, in the eyes of organisations like the World Bank, provided a model for other Third World countries to follow. If this was the case, it meant that Third World dependence and stagnation were not inevitable outcomes of colonial experience, as the dependency theorists argued. Third World countries could develop, not by rejecting capitalism and embracing some alternative, but rather by pursuing a capitalist model which made use of their cheap labour and other resources. The important elements in this were the need to maintain a comparative advantage in labour costs, as well as an open and unrestricted economy into which capital, skills, technology and new processes could flow in the pursuit of profits.

This shift of the focus of industrialisation from import-substitution to exports changed the focus of the debate about science and technology. It moved from issues of technological choice and transfer, towards an analysis of the ways in which Third World countries could establish and maintain an indigenous technological capability (Stewart and James 1982). There were numerous ways of building this new capability. Bell (1984:189), for example, focused on the concept of 'learning'—generally defined as an increasing capacity to manage technology and implement technological innovations. In the Third World, 'learning by doing' was an important way of acquiring this capacity. In one example of this, Bell (1984:192) reported on an Argentinian bakery firm which started out as a straightforward user of bakery equipment. In the course of making its bakery products, the company experienced problems with its equipment. In solving them, it undertook technical improvements which were later incorporated into the production of innovative bakery equipment, which was later exported.

While the analysis of the acquisition of indigenous technological capabilities was significant in increasing the understanding of the role of science and technology in development, it too was open to criticism. For example, Kaplinsky (1984) made the point that the focus on acquiring technological capability emphasised small-scale, incremental change. Such a focus failed to acknowledge the importance of large-scale technological leaps associated with major innovations such as biotechnology or information technology, which were science-based and not necessarily accessible to 'learning' as the basis for technology acquisition. Such developments were very important for some countries, such as India, which wanted to encourage the development of science-based industries as a way of catching-up with the industrialised countries. Where this was the aim, the acquisition of technological capability required much more than learning; it required the development of a significant capacity to do scientific research at an advanced level.

Another criticism of the concept of indigenous technological capability was the neglect of any significant level of discussion about the appropriateness or otherwise of the technology being acquired. This is not really surprising, since it was assumed that only those technologies that were appropriate would be acquired. 'Development' was being driven by the opening of global markets for products which found a niche on the basis of their competitive prices: that is to say, producers took advantage of low labour costs to locate labour-intensive activities in the Third World. If this was the case, then there was no specific need to address the issue of the appropriateness or otherwise of particular transfers of technology, since labour-intensive technologies went hand-in-hand with the utilisation of cheap labour. Similarly, there was also little interest in the 1980s in the role of the transnational corporation as a potential source of conflict and exploitation. If the question of the choice of technology was less of an issue than it had been in the 1970s, then the problems of transfer pricing (discussed earlier) and of technological dependence (largely associated with the decisions of transnational corporations) were also seen to be irrelevant. More importantly, perhaps, the success of the newly industrialising countries such as Singapore suggested that the benefits to be obtained from a partnership with the global corporations far outweighed the costs and, for that reason also, little attention was directed towards the issues which had engaged researchers in the 1970s.

While the focus on indigenous technological capability did shift

analysis towards an acknowledgment of the responsibility that the Third
World had for its own development, it did not offer any guidance about
the ways in which Third World countries could access the latest, science-
based technologies, and avoid the technological dependence of an
earlier period. One response to this was the emergence of the concept
of 'technology blending' which, in its most general formulation,
involves the adaptation of new and old technologies (without destroying
or replacing the latter) in order to meet the continuing needs of the
poor (Bhalla 1994).

Three main forms of technology blending have so far been identified:
the physical combination of old and new technologies (retorting); the
application of new technologies to market-oriented, traditional, small-
scale activities without displacing them; and the application of new
technologies to public goods and services (e.g. rural telecommunications, public health, education, and so on) (Bhalla 1994:431).

An interesting (and early) example of successful technology blending
was Cuba's program for the establishment of a local biotechnology
industry (Kenney and Buttel 1985). Importantly, this program was
highly focused and concentrated on a limited range of activities that
were important to Cuba's social and economic goals. These included
the commitment to health care, an acknowledgment of the importance
of agriculture (and especially sugar) to the economy, increasing the
level of animal protein content in local diets, and expanding the export
of biomedical products. Cuba did not seek to undertake basic research
at the leading edge of biotechnology, but instead applied existing
knowledge to these practical problems. Cuban scientists were sent to
Europe and the (then) Soviet Union for training, while technicians
were taught in Japan to maintain and repair equipment. A local technological capability in the production of biotechnology equipment, as
well as biotechnology products, was thus established (Kenney and
Buttel 1985).

The Cuban case is a good example of the third form of technology
blending, the application of new technologies to public goods and
services. It utilises new technology for practical purposes, while avoiding
the marginalisation of R&D capacities which might be associated with
the funding of large-scale basic research in this area. As Kenney and
Buttel (1985) noted, India's efforts in the biotechnology area were in
distinct contrast to those of Cuba, and were organised around a substantial industrial base, access to laboratories around the world, and a
core of researchers familiar with the latest global developments in
biotechnology. In short, India's efforts in this area were a reflection of
the priorities established in Western centres of excellence, and the
challenge to India was to ensure that the outcomes associated with a

similar high-technology orientation in the past—a brain drain and a lack of linkage between science and production—did not recur.

To some extent, technology blending re-establishes a focus on appropriate technology, which was in large measure overlooked by the literature on the acquisition of indigenous technological capabilities. But according to Bhalla (1994), the concept of technology blending is more than a variant of appropriate technology. Whereas appropriate technology was mainly concerned with incremental innovations (that is, small variations to existing technologies), the blending of new and old technologies implies a more significant level of innovation on the part of the less-developed country. There is also one other major difference which, according to Bhalla (1994), may not be in the interests of the Third World. While appropriate technology was designed to increase national and local self-reliance by stimulating local alternatives to Western technology, the concept of technology blending could erode such self-reliance and autonomy, relying as it does on the R&D resources of the industrialised world. Bhalla (1994:438) suggests this could be avoided if the consumers of new technologies (mostly the Third World countries) can ensure that the developed countries design these technologies with the special needs of the Third World in mind.

The evidence from the past suggests that the developed world's R&D system (most of which is located within private-sector facilities) is unlikely to respond to such concerns. Nevertheless, significant issues are emerging which will require the industrialised countries to address some of the problems associated with advanced technology, making it more energy-efficient, less wasteful of resources and, in a general sense, more appropriate. The global environmental problems which have emerged in recent years and which pose major dilemmas for the world community are forcing a major reconsideration of existing problems of production and consumption.

Sustainable development and industrialisation

To many observers, the environmental and resource costs of current and projected patterns of production and consumption raise important questions about the nature of economic growth, and whether it is possible to sustain such patterns of production and consumption indefinitely. This question becomes critical if we consider current levels of growth in countries such as India and China, with large and growing populations and a rapidly increasing demand for the kinds of goods and services associated with Western consumption patterns.

Can the increasing global demand for the products of advanced industrial society be satisfied without provoking an environmental catastrophe? In the view of many researchers, the answer to this question is no. After only 250 years of industrialisation, and with only one-third of the world's population having achieved a high level of consumption, the global environment is already showing signs of stress and possible collapse; global warming, ozone depletion, acid rain, desertification and soil erosion, species loss and diminishing biodiversity, deforestation, air and water pollution and resource depletion, are all regarded as possible indicators of an impending environmental disaster.

Such problems first began to be taken seriously by governments in the early 1970s. In 1972, the United Nations organised the Stockholm Conference on the Human Environment, which represented one of the first attempts to address global problems at the global level. Increasing concern at the situation led to the establishment in 1987 of the World Commission on Environment and Development, sponsored by the United Nations and chaired by Gro Harlem Brundtland, a former Prime Minister of Norway. The Brundtland report, entitled *Our Common Future*, advanced the concept of sustainable development, defined as 'development that meets the needs of the present without compromising the ability of future generations to meet their own needs' (WCED 1987:87).

The report analysed the role of science and technology in achieving sustainability, and suggested that new technologies—biotechnology, microelectronics, communications technology, new materials and so forth—offered major opportunities for improved productivity in agriculture and industry, increased efficiency in energy and resource use and more effective organisational structures (WCED 1987:182–3, 261–3). However, the report also noted that new technologies are not necessarily benign and may generate new environmental hazards, hitherto unknown health risks, or other negative outcomes. In the case of agriculture, for example, the Brundtland report referred to the substantial gains made from the application of Green Revolution technology (discussed earlier), but pointed to the problems associated with large applications of agrochemicals and a narrowing of the genetic base of wheat and rice production (WCED 1987:162–70).

The implementation of the concept of sustainable development advanced in the Brundtland report was the major concern of the UN Conference on Environment and Development (the Earth Summit), held in Rio de Janeiro in June 1992. At this meeting, 3500 diplomats and advisers, 700 UN officials and 120 heads of state met in order to 'elaborate strategies and measures for promoting sustainable development and reversing environmental degradation' (*The Ecologist* 1993:v). The meeting considered all of the major environmental issues facing humanity, and concluded with the adoption of a series of international agreements: the conventions on climate change and biodiversity; the

Rio Declaration on Environment and Development which laid down the principles of sustainable development; and *Agenda 21*, the action program designed to give effect to the decisions of the conference (United Nations 1993).

Agenda 21 was a detailed policy document running to over 450 pages, which addressed the social and economic dimensions of environment and development, issues in the conservation and management of resources for development, the role to be played by major groups (e.g. indigenous peoples, business and industry, farmers and so on), and the means of implementation. On the question of the role of science and technology, *Agenda 21* suggested (among other things) that improved access to environmentally sound technologies from the industrialised countries, combined with enhanced co-operation and support for new technological capabilities, would underwrite sustainable development by protecting the environment, reducing pollution, utilising resources more effectively, increasing the incidence of recycling, and improving waste handling.

The Commission on Sustainable Development, which was the body designated to follow up and implement the *Agenda 21* program, made only slow progress in the years following the Earth Summit. In the opinion of some observers, this was because the Earth Summit adopted a reformist approach to sustainable development, which attempted to solve major problems within the existing social framework. In this view, the objectives of the Earth Summit are unlikely to be achieved, because the main *causes* of the world's environmental problems—the commitment to growth, increasing consumption (especially by wealthy consumers in the industrialised countries), and the maintenance of pollution-intensive and energy-intensive production systems—are not being addressed. For the sceptics, a top-down approach to sustainable development, which targets the Third World as the main focus for ameliorative action, will serve only to maintain the *status quo* elsewhere. Sustainable development is not just something for the less-developed countries; the consumption patterns of wealthy consumers in the industrialised countries (and the production systems which serve them) also have to be targeted for action. If they are not, the privileged consumers in the industrialised countries (and their wealthy counterparts in the less-developed countries) will not only continue to consume resources and generate high levels of pollution, but may also deny existing and future generations everywhere a chance to enjoy a reasonable—and sustainable—level of consumption. Whether or not this happens depends on the effects of current processes of social change. Of particular significance is the process of transformation referred to as 'globalisation' which, as the twentieth century draws to a close, is profoundly affecting social, political and economic relationships everywhere.

New issues in the 1990s: science and technology in the global economy

At its simplest, the concept of 'globalisation' refers to the vast changes that have occurred in the international economy over the past two decades, and the effects that such changes have had on the production and consumption of goods and services. These changes include the decline of bureaucratic communist states and the spread of capitalist institutions to Eastern Europe and elsewhere; the increasing mobility of capital, labour, and goods and services across national borders as global corporations move to integrate and co-ordinate production and consumption on a world scale; the widespread acceptance of market forces in production and trade; a diminution in the effectiveness of trade unions; the emergence of new, flexible production systems in industry and the service sector; a new international division of labour as mass-production techniques spread to Third World countries; a diminished role for the state, in terms of delivering services to its citizens as well as regulating the activities of large-scale, global corporations; and rapid technological change in production (for example, in the use of computers and robotics), and in transport and communications.

All of these factors are resulting in a homogenisation of production, consumption and cultural values across the entire world (United Nations 1995). As McMichael has put it:

> The Japanese eat poultry fattened in Thailand with American corn, using chopsticks made with wood from Indonesian or Chilean forests. Canadians eat strawberries grown in Mexico with American fertilizer. Consumers on both sides of the Atlantic wear clothes assembled in Saipan with Chinese labour, drink orange juice from concentrate made with Brazilian oranges, and decorate their homes with flowers from Colombia. The British and French eat green beans from Kenya, and cocoa from Ghana finds its way into Swiss chocolate. [McMichael 1996:1]

The social consequences of such a global system of production and consumption are profound and far-reaching. In the case of a global product such as a McDonald's hamburger, for example, local agricultural systems and local diets may be radically changed, and sometimes in ways which are especially detrimental to poor people in the Third World. For example, the increasing consumption of hamburgers in the United States led to extensive deforestation in Central America in the period 1960–90, as forest land was converted to cattle pasture.

For the same reason, peasant farmers were displaced as land formerly used to grow food for local consumption came to be used to produce beef for hamburgers (McMichael 1996:7). Of course, the accelerating pace of globalisation will ensure that these and other far-reaching changes will continue to have a powerful impact on peoples and environments everywhere.

To some observers, then, globalisation is simply the latest manifestation of that process of exploitation which began in the colonial period and which created a dependent and subordinate 'Third World'. In this latest phase, such exploitation is not carried out by imperial nation-states such as Britain or France, but rather by the global corporations which control 33 per cent of the world's productive assets and 75 per cent of world trade in commodities, manufactured goods and services (United Nations 1995). These powerful corporations—the oil companies, food and drug manufacturers, car makers and others—exert a growing power and influence, reinforced by new global agencies such as the World Trade Organisation (Raghavan 1997). To other observers, globalisation is a much more positive development, and can be seen as a process whereby the world community is becoming more integrated and interconnected, with the expectation that this may lead to greater understanding and a reduction in conflict and division. From this perspective, globalisation has been accompanied by the spread of liberal democracy and the decline of authoritarian regimes which exercised arbitrary power and coercive measures against ordinary people. Such changes are positive and go a long way to making the world a safer and happier place.

While it is difficult to assess the overall impact of processes of globalisation at this early stage, it is nevertheless possible to ask questions about the extent to which such changes are compatible with the goals of sustainable development, appropriate science and technology, and Third World autonomy. For example, is it possible that the recommendations of the Earth Summit can be implemented by national governments who accept a need for smaller government and a greater reliance on market forces to solve the whole range of social and environmental problems that were previously considered the responsibility of the state? Similarly, are national governments whose power is declining relative to that of global corporations, able to regulate the behaviour of these large companies so that they adhere to acceptable environmental standards? Can sustainable development be established by the voluntary actions of transnational corporations whose main interests are served by continuing economic growth on a global scale? It is no exaggeration to suggest that the future of all humanity may depend upon the way in which these questions are answered over the next few decades.

Conclusion

This chapter has demonstrated that, while there is widespread agreement that science and technology are important in the development of the poorer countries of the world, there is no consensus on precisely how science and technology contribute to this, nor on the issue of what policies should be adopted to ensure the efficient and appropriate use of such resources. In this context, it is important to understand that science and technology are not independent of society; nor do they have the same social impacts in every situation. The example of the biogas fertiliser plant, discussed earlier, demonstrates this point. Biogas technology has been widely introduced in both India and China, but with very different social impacts. In India, many biogas fertiliser plants are privately owned, as are the cattle which provide the dung which fuels the plant. Before the introduction of these plants in India, dung was usually left lying on the ground, either because the animals' owners had no use for it, or because they left it where it fell for reasons of caste or status. However, poor people did collect the dung, and used it mainly as fuel for cooking. With the introduction of biogas plants into village India, animal dung become a valuable resource, and cattle-owners who also owned biogas plants then ensured it was collected. As a result, poor people were denied access to a previously free resource, and their social position was worsened as a result of what was said to be an 'appropriate' technology (Hanlon 1977). However, in China, where biogas plants were owned by the community rather than an individual or a family, and where the cattle were also a collective resource, there is no evidence that any individual's social position was worsened as a result of the innovation. Instead, it is likely that everyone in the commune shared in some benefits—some more than others, perhaps, but nevertheless, no one was worse off.

Biogas technology was the same in both India and China; what was different was the social context of innovation and the fact that the form of ownership differed. This point is crucial for our understanding of the impacts of science and technology in a wide variety of situations. The technology itself *is* important, but *what* technology is introduced, *where* and *under what conditions*, are also critical in determining the impacts— in short, who gains and who loses from technological innovation. Why, for example, was the Green Revolution technology introduced into Third World countries? In the view of many researchers, there were more appropriate and productive technologies available, based on small-scale agriculture and involving a range of labour-intensive activities such as transplanting rice, hand-weeding, crop rotation and so on (Dorner 1972; Griffin 1974). These techniques significantly increased yields at only a fraction of the capital costs of the Green Revolution, but the technology of the Green Revolution was preferred because the interests of the large farmers (who were the main beneficiaries) were given priority by governments which themselves contained many landowners and rich farmers. While acknowledging the need to increase agricultural output, many governments in the Third World rejected policies based on an intensive strategy of agricultural production organised around small farmers, because this implied extensive land reform which might see a landlord's property redistributed to landless peasants, tenants, labourers and others. Given this, the powerful social groups who dominated government decision-making in countries like India would only consider solutions to the problem of food production which did not challenge their power and take away their land (Griffin 1974:198–203). In this sense, the Green Revolution is an example of a 'technical fix', the attempt to use technology to solve social problems, while avoiding the need to identify and deal with the original causes of the problem.

These examples suggest that there is no single unequivocal answer to the question: what is the role of science and technology in development? Rather than continuing to seek answers to this question, perhaps it is time to ask a different one, namely, who wants to introduce what kind of technology, who owns and controls it, and who is going to benefit? Then, and only then, can we begin to get some idea of the policy options and solutions which will really benefit the poor of the Third World.

Further reading

One of the most comprehensive recent studies on this topic is the volume by Jean-Jacques Salomon *et al.* (1994), *The Uncertain Quest*, published by the United Nations University. The volume entitled *Technological Independence: The Asian Experience*, edited by Chamarik and Goonetilleke (1994) offers a wide-ranging analysis of the policies and outcomes associated with the scientific and technological development of some of the world's most dynamic economies. The survey by Clarke (1985), *Science and Technology in World Development*, although dated, still effectively covers a wide range of material. A good recent introduction to the issue of development in general is McMichael (1996), *Development and Social Change*.

References

Advisory Committee on the Application of Science and Technology to Development (ACAST) (1970), *Science and Technology for Development: Proposals for the Second UN Development Decade*. New York: United Nations.
Amin, Samir (1976), *Unequal Development*. Brighton: Harvester Press.
Bell, Martin (1984), '"Learning" and the Accumulation of Industrial Technological Capacity in Developing Countries', in Martin Fransman and Kenneth King (eds), *Technological Capability in the Third World*. London: Macmillan.

Bhalla, A. (1994), 'Technology Choice and Diffusion', in Jean-Jacques Salomon, Francisco R. Sagasti and Celine Sachs-Jeantet (eds), *The Uncertain Quest: Science, Technology and Development*. Tokyo: United Nations University Press.

Blackett, P. M. S. (1963), 'Planning for Science and Technology in Emerging Countries', *New Scientist*, 326, 14 February.

Burch, D. F. (1981), 'Development Through Appropriate Technology: The Limits of the Theory', *Social Alternatives*, 2, 1, March.

Burch, D. F. (1982), 'Appropriate Technology for the Third World: Why the Will is Lacking', *The Ecologist*, 12, 2, March–April.

Burch, D. F. (1987), *Overseas Aid and the Transfer of Technology*. Aldershot: Avebury.

Burchett, Wilfred, and Alley, Rewi (1976), *China: The Quality of Life*. Harmondsworth: Penguin.

Chamarik, Saneh, and Goonetilleke, Susantha (1994), *Technological Independence: The Asian Experience*. Tokyo: United Nations University Press.

Chambers, R. (1983), *Rural Development: Putting the Last First*. London: Longman.

Clarke, Robin (1985), *Science and Technology in World Development*. Oxford: UNESCO/Oxford University Press.

Consumers Association of Penang (1981), *Appropriate Technology, Culture and Lifestyle in Development: Declarations and Resolutions, from a seminar organised by the Institut Masyrakat Berhad and the Consumers Association of Penang*. Penang: Universiti Sains Malaysia, 3–7 November.

Consumers Association of Penang (1982), *Development and the Environmental Crisis: Proceedings of a Symposium organised by the Consumers Association of Penang, the School of Biological Sciences, Universiti Sains Malaysia, and Sahabat Alam Malaysia*. Penang: Regional Centre for Science and Maths, 16–20 September.

Cooper, Charles (1973), 'Science, Technology and Production in the Under-developed Countries: An Introduction', in Charles Cooper (ed.), *Science, Technology and Development*. London: Frank Cass & Co.

de Silva, C. R. (1977), 'Education', in K. M. de Silva (ed.), *Sri Lanka: A Survey*. London: C. Hurst and Co.

Dorner, P. (1972), *Land Reform and Economic Development*. Harmondsworth: Penguin.

Ecologist, The (1993), *Whose Common Future?* London: Earthscan Publications.

George, Susan (1976), *How the Other Half Dies*. Harmondsworth: Penguin.

Griffin, Keith (1974), *The Political Economy of Agrarian Change*. London: Macmillan.

Hanlon, J. (1977) 'Does Appropriate Technology Walk on Plastic Sandals?', *New Scientist*, 74, 1053, 26 May.

Harrison, Paul (1983), *The Third World Tomorrow*. Harmondsworth: Penguin.

Herrera, Amilcar (1973), 'Social Determinants of Science in Latin America: Explicit Science Policy and Implicit Science Policy', in Charles Cooper (ed.), *Science, Technology and Development*. London: Frank Cass & Co.

Hettne, B. (1990), *Development Theory and the Three Worlds*. White Plains, NJ: Longman.

International Labour Office (ILO) (1971), *Matching Employment Opportunities and Expectations: A Programme of Action for Ceylon*. Geneva: United Nations.

International Labour Office (ILO) (1977), *Poverty and Landlessness in Rural Asia*. Geneva: United Nations.

Ishikawa, Shigeru (1973), 'A Note on the Choice of Technology in China', in Charles Cooper (ed.), *Science, Technology and Development*. London: Frank Cass and Co.

Jones, Graham (1971), *The Role of Science and Technology in Developing Countries*. Oxford: Oxford University Press.

Kaplinsky, R. (1984), 'Trade in Technology: Who, What, Where, and When?', in Martin Fransman and Kenneth King (eds), *Technological Capability in the Third World*. London: Macmillan.

Kenney, M., and Buttel, F. (1985), 'Biotechnology: Prospects and Dilemmas for Third World Development', *Development and Change*, 16, 1, January.

Marsden, Keith (1973), 'Progressive Technologies for Developing Countries', in Richard Jolly, Emanuel de Kadt, Hans Singer and Fiona Wilson (eds), *Third World Employment*. Harmondsworth: Penguin.

McMichael, Philip (1996), *Development and Social Change: A Global Perspective*. Thousand Oaks, Calif.: Pine Forge Press.

McRobie, George (1982), *Small is Possible*. London: Sphere Books.

Mendis, G. C (1952), *Ceylon Under the British*, 3rd edn. Colombo: Colombo Apothecaries Co.

Raghavan, Chakravarti (1997), 'WTO Conference: How the Developing Countries Lost Out', *Third World Resurgence*, 77–78.

Reddy, A. K. N. (1975), 'Alternative Technologies: A Viewpoint from India', *Social Studies of Science*, 5, 3.

Sagasti, Francisco R. (1975), 'Underdevelopment, Science and Technology: The Point of View of the Underdeveloped Countries', in Eugene Rabinowitch and Victor Rabinowitch (eds), *Views of Science, Technology and Development*. Oxford: Pergamon Press.

Salomon, J. J., Sagasti, F. R., and Sachs-Jeantet, C. (1994), *The Uncertain Quest: Science, Technology and Development*. Tokyo: United Nations University Press.

Schumacher, E. F. (1973), *Small is Beautiful*. London: Blond and Briggs.

Shiva, Vandana (1991), *The Violence of the Green Revolution*. Penang: Third World Network.

Stewart, F., and James, J. (eds) (1982), *The Economics of New Technology in Developing Countries*. London: Frances Pinter.

Stewart, F. (1977), *Technology and Underdevelopment*. London: Macmillan.

United Nations (1993), *Report of the United Nations Conference on Environment and Development*. New York.

United Nations (1995), *States of Disarray: The Social Effects of Globalisation*. Geneva: United Nations Research Institute for Social Development.

Vaitsos, Constantine (1973), 'Patents Revisited: Their Function in Developing Countries', in Charles Cooper (ed.), *Science, Technology and Development*. London: Frank Cass and Co.

Wellisz, Stanislaw H. (1966), 'The Modernisation of Technology', in Myron Wiener (ed.), *Modernisation: The Dynamics of Growth*. New York: Basic Books.

World Bank (1993), *World Development Report*. Oxford: Oxford University Press.

World Bank (1996), *World Development Report*. Oxford: Oxford University Press.

World Commission on Environment and Development (WCED) (1987), *Our Common Future*. Oxford: Oxford University Press.

Yearley, Steven (1988), *Science, Technology and Social Change*. London: Unwin Hyman.

CHAPTER 11

Science, Technology and the Future

Ian Lowe

The world of today is undergoing rapid changes, many of them driven by advances in science and technology. Our world has been shaped dramatically by new technology. Think of the impact of the car, of television or of the personal computer. Many people see the current rate of change as bewildering, even disorienting. There is no reason to suppose that the pace of change will ease. Indeed, there are two reasons for expecting change to be more rapid in the future. More scientists are working today than ever before, so the pace of scientific advance is greater than ever (Jones 1982:179–80). Additionally, the power of information technology means that new techniques move much more rapidly from one part of the world to another. So we must expect continued rapid technological change, and associated social, economic and political changes (Kennedy 1993:344–9).

It is a key point that the future is not pre-determined. Many people behave as if it were an unknown land which we discover one day at a time. Just as the world of today has been shaped by the decisions and actions of our forebears, the future is being formed all the time by what we do, what we say and what we think. Japan has changed in forty years from a middle-rank economic power with a reputation for shoddy workmanship to the world's dominant economy with a reputation for excellent design and quality manufacture (Kennedy 1993:150–4). That is a clear demonstration that past trends are not future destiny. It is also a dramatic example of the crucial role of technology in building a better future, since there is no doubt that the rise of Japan to economic dominance has been a consequence of the way that nation has success-fully harnessed technology, especially in manufacturing.

Our scientific knowledge is an essential basis for planning the future. We need to understand as completely as possible the complex natural systems of the Earth. We also need to know as fully as possible the options available for meeting our needs and the impacts of those options. Thus science is an essential basis for understanding our future options, while technology is the means of achieving our desired future. This chapter discusses the complex problem of trying to use science and technology to develop a preferred future. It builds on the material in earlier chapters to show how crucially the social dimensions of science and technology influence the future of humanity. In those terms, it draws together the two main themes of this book: the importance of science and technology in the world, and the profound impacts of the choices we make about science and technology. I hope that this chapter will inspire you to think about your role in creating our shared future.

Forecasting

There are obvious problems involved in the exercise of attempting to determine the future. From time immemorial, humans have sought seers who claimed to be able to foretell the future. When I was Acting Director of the Australian Commission for the Future, I became accustomed to receiving requests for specific forecasts of particular aspects of the future. One telephone call, for example, asked me to estimate the year in which the first base will be established on the moon! It is implicit in any such prediction that the future is actually pre-determined, so that somebody who is sufficiently clever can work out what will happen. The past sweep of political events shows how difficult that can be. Imagine having tried to predict in advance the date of the dismantling of the Berlin Wall, or the end of the apartheid system in South Africa. We know that predicting the political future is compli-cated by the uncertainty of human behaviour; there is a widespread perception that we have a better chance of knowing the future of science and technology.

Our scientific knowledge does enable us to make some sorts of predictions with great accuracy. For example, calendars give the dates when the moon will be full, while tide tables give not just the time of high tide but also the depth of water to expect. Astronomers predict dates of eclipses and appearances of comets decades into the future. These predictions are possible because we understand the scientific laws governing the systems concerned. There has even been some success in predicting such events as earthquakes, based on analysis of the factors believed to cause tremors (Casti 1991:34–5). At the height of the scientific view that the entire world operated like a mechanical system, there was a belief that anyone who knew the positions and velocities of every particle in the universe would be able to predict the entire future by using the laws of mechanics. Of course, we don't have anything like that much information. More to the point, even if we did know the current state of every particle in the entire universe, we would still not be able to predict the future because it does not evolve along simple mechanistic lines.

The molecules of gas in an enclosed vessel might behave in an entirely predictable manner, but the humans in a city certainly do not; learner drivers, for example, are sometimes told that they must never assume they know what other road users will do. The future is, at least in part, shaped by the decisions and actions of humans, as individuals and as members of groups. We all make conscious decisions about how we will spend our time, in the expectation that we will influence at least our own future, if not that of other people. The act of reading this chapter is changing your life in at least two ways. It is, I hope, exposing you to some new ideas and approaches which you will be unable to erase completely from your mind. Equally importantly, the time and mental energy it is occupying cannot simultaneously be used to do other things, so the act of reading this chapter has meant you have forgone other opportunities for use of the time. In other words, just as I hope you are a better person for having read this chapter, you are also a different person because you didn't use the time to read something else, or listen to music, or walk in the park, or make love.

There is an old joke that it is difficult to make forecasts, especially about the future. The future cannot be foretold with any certainty. What we can do is look at present trends and see the consequences of those trends continuing—although by doing so, we are likely to alter those trends. That process can occur in either of two ways. A forecast can be made with the intention of reinforcing a trend. If a government leader says that the current positive economic trends are good and look like continuing, the statement is at least partially intended to persuade investors and consumers that the outlook is positive, thus stimulating activity and producing a stronger economy. In similar terms, a prediction by an acknowledged expert that the stock market is about to fall might stimulate a wave of selling, causing the overall market decline that was predicted. Thus a prediction can reinforce a trend, or even generate a new trend that fulfils the forecast. On the other hand, a forecast can have the opposite effect. If you saw somebody about to walk in front of a bus, you would probably shout a warning in the hope of forestalling a trend which would end in tragedy. The warning would be an attempt to prevent the likely outcome of present trends. If I counsel a student that she is likely to fail if she continues on her current course of action, I hope she will take the warning to heart. So the act of making a forecast can change the future, and sometimes that is a conscious aim. Just as an accurate forecast of rain can save you from a drenching, an accurate prediction of social, economic or environmental trends can allow us to prevent a serious problem.

Social and economic aspects of choices

The choices we make about science and technology determine which options are available in the future. In terms of the science budget, the balance of the research effort determines which questions can be answered. Putting resources into solar energy research does not guarantee success, but not putting effort into an area is an absolute guarantee that there will not be significant progress. If, for example, a country puts 22 per cent of its research effort into support of agriculture and 7 per cent into support of manufacturing, it is more likely to be economically competitive in farm produce than in manufactured goods. Those are the figures for Australia in the 1990s (Lowe 1991:184), so an outside observer would probably conclude that Australia has chosen to put its economic emphasis on agriculture rather than value-added products. Similarly, Australia spends about twice as much on research in the broad area of health as it devotes to support of manufacturing. In 1992–93, this amounted to $149 million, of which $143 million went to medical research and $6 million to health projects (McGauran 1996: 3.15, McCloskey 1993:98). So you might expect from the balance of the research effort that Australia would be a relatively unhealthy community with sophisticated high-technology medical services. When I analysed Australia's energy research budget about fifteen years ago, I concluded that much more effort was going into programs supporting nuclear energy than all forms of renewable energy put together (Lowe 1983). The balance of the research effort shapes the capability of a nation to make progress.

A similar argument can be made about technology. Imagine a city with a growing problem of traffic congestion. There might be two alternative solutions: to widen the roads, or to improve the public transport system. Widening the roads makes driving to the city a more attractive proposition, so it is likely to increase the number of vehicles heading to the city, thus producing congestion and a demand for more roads. By contrast, improving the bus service is likely to attract people out of their cars onto the buses, especially if there are also traffic arrangements such as dedicated bus lanes to give those vehicles a faster run to the city. So the choices made about alternative transport options—public transport services or roads to provide for cars—tend to shape the pattern of transport behaviour.

Decisions about science and technology therefore play a significant role in shaping our future society. That is the reason for arguing that those decisions should be informed choices of society as a whole, rather than being driven by the internal logic and priorities of the scientific community. It is entirely appropriate for scientists to choose between several competing research projects in a narrow field, such as electrochemistry. But the issue of the priority to be given to electrochemistry research in competition with other fields such as weed eradication, kidney failure or astronomy should be a social choice. The major foresight study by the Australian Science and Technology Council, discussed in Chapter 9, aimed to direct Australia's science effort toward emerging future needs (ASTEC 1996). The difficult political problem, as also discussed in that chapter, is that different people and different groups have their own views about priorities. A key task of the political process is to balance those competing interests.

Sustainability

There is a growing recognition that many of our practices are not sustainable. Depletion of the ozone layer, degradation of our soils, local pollution of air and water, deforestation and global climate change are all symptoms of this fundamental problem. While it has not been an issue in the public eye in recent years, depletion of our mineral resource base is an equally important problem. We need, as a matter of urgency, to find ways of satisfying our needs with less impact on the natural systems of the Earth. As the report of the World Commission on Environment and Development said, unless our pattern of economic development is ecologically rational we will be unable to maintain living standards, let alone improve them (WCED 1987:40).

Finding a mode of human development that is sustainable, at least in principle, is a complex task. It requires an understanding of physical, chemical, biological, social, political and economic factors. Indeed, it would be entirely understandable if we were all to conclude that the task is much too difficult. Until recently, most of our political leaders have behaved as if they hoped the problem would just go away. In the 1990s, however, the phrase *sustainable development* entered political discussion. Even those politicians who don't know what it means seem to feel obliged to say that they support it. Since various individuals are using the term to mean things which obviously differ, it is important to be clear about what I think it means. Development means a process of change, usually with connotations of approval. It is sustainable only if it can be continued, or sustained, for the foreseeable future. Thus sustainable development is a pattern of development which can be continued. I think the best short definition is that sustainable development is a pattern of activity which meets the needs of the present generation without reducing the opportunities available to future generations (WCED 1987:8). Thus an activity can be regarded as sustainable only if it does not foreclose options to future generations. It must not deplete natural resources or have unacceptable impacts on the natural environment.

Both those criteria seem obvious; depletion of the resource base reduces the opportunities available to future generations, as does degrading the natural environment. There are value judgements implicit in these criteria. There is no absolute standard for determining whether a rate of depletion of any particular resource is unacceptable, any more than there is an agreed standard for acceptable impacts on the natural world. I will return to these two issues below. While these are necessary, they are not sufficient. For an activity to be sustainable, it must also not threaten social stability either locally, nationally or internationally. It is possible to envisage, for example, two groups each basing their plan for sustainable development on the same resource, leading to inevitable conflict. There is real potential for international conflict in the resource demands of the future.

Resources

The issue of depletion of resources is a complex one (Meadows *et al.* 1972; Cole *et al.* 1973). The size of the resource base is influenced, for example, by economics. A price increase, whether driven by scarcity or achieved by control of the market, is likely to make marginal resources economic and so expand the stock of available resources. New technologies can also extend the resource base; a new extraction technique may turn deposits which were previously inaccessible into useful resources. The most obvious example in recent decades is the expansion of the useful oil resources by development of techniques for exploiting oil beneath the sea. The political culture of the time also has an influence. The question of whether the minerals under the frozen ground of the Antarctic should be regarded as useable resources was the subject of active international debate until the early 1990s, when an international treaty effectively prohibited exploration and mining in Antarctica (Davis 1992).

Energy is another factor affecting resources. When a high-quality resource is depleted, there are usually lower-grade resources which can be used if money and energy are available in sufficient quantity. In that sense, energy can be regarded as the key resource. With sufficient energy, quantities of almost any other resource can be produced. Poorer grades of ore can be exploited, land can be farmed more intensively and potable water can be produced from the ocean, if we have abundant energy. For that reason, the availability and price of energy influence the issue of which mineral deposits can be regarded as resources. If we are moving into an era in which scarcity or environmental concerns are likely to limit the use of energy, the resource base will be constrained (Lowe 1989:109–16).

There is one obvious exception to the general assertion that there is no shortage of resources. For the best part of thirty years now, it has become steadily more difficult to find oil. The drilling per unit of proven resource has gone up and up. We are now getting oil from such unlikely places as the North Sea and Alaska. There is pessimism about the chance of ever again finding the sort of massive deposits which have fuelled the expansion in transport since 1950. The current rate of using petroleum fuels does not just threaten the global atmosphere, it also risks depleting the oil fields within the life-time of today's young people. We are not likely to run out of oil, in the sense of there literally being none left, but we may well decide (for example) that its value as a chemical feedstock rules out using it as fuel for cars (Fleay 1996: 131–4). This inevitably raises the inter-generational issue of whether we are unreasonably foreclosing options for future generations by our profligate use of oil.

Even when we are not depleting resources in absolute terms, we usually exploit the richest and most easily accessible deposits, thus inevitably limiting the options available to our descendants. Thus our use of copper is very unlikely to deprive future generations of that mineral but it is certainly exhausting the best grades of ore, ensuring that it will be either more scarce or more expensive in future times. As the average ore grade being worked gets poorer, the quantity of rock which must be dug up and crushed for a kilogram of copper steadily increases, as do the fuel energy needed for extraction and the amount of waste produced (Chapman 1975:91–4). Thus our activities may well be condemning future generations to a greater economic or environmental cost for their minerals, even where there is not a level of depletion that is itself unreasonable in absolute terms.

Environment

We also need to consider what have been called environmental issues. I prefer to describe these as ecological issues, as the word *environment* alludes to surroundings. Natural eco-systems are more than just our surroundings; we are actually part of the natural systems of the planet. We are developing a broader awareness of the impacts of our actions on those systems. The whales of the Southern Ocean, the rainforest of the Amazon and the Great Panda of China are certainly not parts of our immediate environment; our concern for the loss of whales or Amazon rainforest represents an awareness of the ecological impacts of human actions.

There have always been some local impacts of productive activity, as reflected in the old Yorkshire saying 'Where there's muck, there's brass', roughly translated as saying that making money always makes a bit of a mess. These local problems have been tolerated, either because the pollution was seen as an acceptable price for the economic activity, or because those who derived the benefits were not the people who bore the brunt of the pollution. In recent years the scale of the human population and the nature of our technology have broadened the range of impacts, affecting whole regions in the case of acid rain, and the entire globe in the cases of climate change and ozone depletion. These problems cannot be resolved, even in principle, by any one group or nation; if they are to be resolved, it will require global co-operation of an unprecedented kind (WCED 1987:2–11).

Take the example of the enhanced greenhouse effect, mainly due to the release of carbon dioxide from the burning of fuels. Because carbon fuels like oil and coal have been cheap to obtain, we have evolved a lifestyle which depends on massive use of these compounds. The world burns thousands of millions of tonnes of these fuels each year; in other words, your lifestyle requires the burning each year of more than a tonne of carbon fuels. The process of withdrawal will be difficult, expensive and possibly even painful, at least in economic terms. The scale of the problem is truly formidable. World leaders recently agonised over the question of whether we should adopt a target suggested by the Framework Convention on Climate Change: the reduction of the rate of emitting greenhouse gases by 2005 to the 1990 level. The Australian government took the official position that such a commitment would do unacceptable economic damage! While adoption of the target would be a useful step forward, the science says that the level of emissions which would allow global concentrations to be stabilised is about 40 per cent of the current figure (IPCC 1996). Given that there is a perfectly reasonable expectation in Third World countries that they will improve their standard of living—if not to that currently enjoyed by the industrialised countries, at least to something closer to human dignity than the conditions under which many people now live—the level of carbon dioxide production that will eventually be seen as reasonable for countries like Australia, the United Kingdom and the United States is probably about 20 per cent of the present value. Thus dealing with global warming will require not minor cosmetic changes but a fundamentally different approach to the use of energy. That is an inescapable conclusion (Lowe 1989:155–62).

It is a fundamental principle of sustainable development that the integrity of ecological systems should not be threatened. *Ecological integrity* is a short-hand term for the general health and resilience of natural systems. This includes the ability of eco-systems to assimilate wastes through basic natural cycles, such as the water cycle and the carbon cycle. It also includes the capacity of eco-systems to withstand other stresses, such as climate change or depletion of the ozone layer. The effects of a growing human population, with increasing production of a range of wastes, are putting severe pressure on the ability of natural systems to maintain their integrity. For future development to be sustainable, we need to reduce the pressure on natural systems by improving the efficiency of using energy and resources, as well as imposing rigorous upper limits on the emission of pollutants (SoEAC 1996:10.5).

Bio-diversity refers to the variety of species, populations, habitats and eco-systems existing on this planet. There are sound practical reasons for seeking to maintain bio-diversity through such means as the reservation of representative eco-systems and habitats, or the protection of endangered species. Such protection provides a stockpile of genetic diversity for potential use in medicine and agriculture; this is especially important in the face of expected changes in climate. It also enables scientific study of species and properties we do not yet understand, as well as improving the chances of natural eco-systems being stable under changing conditions. Thus bio-diversity enhances human welfare and is therefore desirable in those practical terms. There is also a moral argument for protecting bio-diversity; this rests on our recognising that other life-forms have some right to exist, whether they have obvious direct value to humans or not (SoEAC 1996:10.4).

Finally, it is a sound general principle to try to avoid unnecessary risks, but under conditions of uncertainty the risks may not be quantifiable or even known. This strongly suggests a need to adopt a cautious approach, especially when there is a risk of irreversible change. In the environmental sense, irreversible changes are such events as the loss of a species or a wilderness area. It is equally true that damage to the national economic structure or to the well-being of the community can be difficult or impossible to reverse. This *precautionary approach* differs fundamentally from the traditional principle of applying environmental constraints to energy use only when serious irreversible effects could be proved. Since the need for caution arises particularly from conditions of uncertainty, there is a general need for basic research on ecological systems to improve the level of our understanding of these systems (SoEAC 1996:10.24–10.26).

Population

We should not ignore the impact of population growth on the problem. About two-thirds of the current rate of increase in the emissions of greenhouse gases can be attributed to increasing populations, with associated demands for increasing food production and preparation, for housing, for transport and so on. Whatever the lifestyle of a country, its resource demands and its environmental or ecological impacts are directly proportional to the number of people enjoying that lifestyle. Unless we are able to stabilise the human population, we cannot hope to achieve a sustainable way of life (Lowe 1996).

Deforestation arising from increasing population in developing countries is a double burden. It both releases carbon dioxide into the air and also reduces the capacity of natural systems to absorb carbon dioxide from the atmosphere. When media commentator Phillip Adams was chairing Australia's Commission for the Future, I told him that we are losing forest globally at the rate of about a football field each second. He revealed that he was a founder member of the Anti-Football League, a semi-serious lobby group trying to reduce the level of attention given to football, and suggested that the solution to the global problem might be to reafforest football fields, preferably at the rate of one per second! While that remark was not meant to be taken literally, there is no doubt that we could do much to slow down climate change by a determined restoration of the level of forest cover. New Zealand has proposed increasing the area of forest as a contribution to slowing climate change (Upton 1996). We could reafforest land that has been cleared for farming if we were prepared to reduce the amount of meat in our diet; turning vegetable matter into meat is inefficient, uses enormous quantities of land, and produces a range of troublesome waste products.

The social difficulty of implementing such a strategy illustrates the inherent complexity of the task of shaping a sustainable future. Any change of substance will produce winners and losers; in a pluralistic democracy, the losers can be expected to campaign against the proposed changes. The likely losses to particular interest groups will often be greater than the gain to society as a whole, so there will often be much more emotional energy in the campaign to forestall the proposed changes. I have suggested that there is now a political equivalent to Newton's third law of motion, which says that every action has an equal and opposite reaction: any proposal for major change will generate a pressure group which is committed to preventing that change.

It has been estimated that the human population in our year AD 0 was about 250 million, that it doubled to about 500 million by about 1650, doubled again to about 1 billion by 1850, reached 2 billion in 1930 and

4 billion about 1975. It is clear from these figures that the doubling-time has been shrinking. The human population is now approaching 6 billion and growing by more than 90 million each year (or three extra humans every second). The current rate of growth represents a doubling time of about 40 years. If such a rate of growth were to continue, the next 120 years would see three more doublings. That would give an eightfold increase in the population. Some people believe that the planet is already over-populated; while that is arguable, it seems unarguable that the current rate of increase cannot continue for long into the future without posing unacceptable strains on natural systems. Concern about the scale of the human population is compounded by the issue of 'pipe-line growth'. Recent growth means that children make up a significant fraction of the human population; their development to ages at which they are able to reproduce means continued future population increase. Even if the average net reproduction rate were to stabilise now at the replacement rate (one child per adult), the human population would increase to over 8 billion. After the 1994 United Nations conference on population in Cairo, it was concluded that the optimistic scenario for the future is one in which the human population is stabilised somewhere in the region of 10 to 15 billion. There is real concern about whether it will be possible to provide a civilised lifestyle for that many humans (Brown *et al.* 1996:3–20).

For hundreds of years there has been concern about the eventual implications of population increase. The British clergyman Thomas

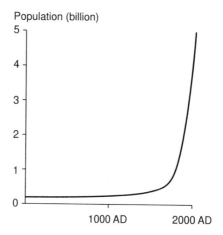

Figure 11.1 Human population during the last 2000 years.

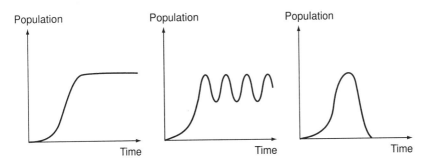

Figure 11.2   Three models of population growth in a closed system.
Left: stability; *centre:* fluctuation; *right:* extinction.

Malthus argued that human population was growing geometrically while food production was only increasing arithmetically, so the demand for food must outstrip our capacity to produce it. This grim prediction has been avoided by technological change which has dramatically increased agricultural productivity, allowing our food production to be increased at about the same rate as the population for the last two hundred years. This cannot go on for ever. There are only three naturally occurring models of population change in a closed system. Sometimes the population increases until it reaches an equilibrium level at which it stabilises. In other cases, the population exceeds the sustainable level, collapses to a reduced level, increases again and oscillates about the equilibrium. In the third model, the population grossly exceeds the level that is sustainable and collapses completely, with extinction the result (Lowe 1996:9–11). There would be general agreement that the first of these future patterns of population change is the most desirable. As a thinking species, we should (at least in principle) be able to devise ways of organising our future development so that our population will reach a stable equilibrium at a sustainable level.

Modelling the future

In 1968 a group of people met in Rome at the invitation of an Italian economic consultant, Dr Aurelio Peccei. Their discussion of the human condition led to the establishment of a body which became known as the Club of Rome. This group was responsible for the first serious modelling study of global futures, conducted by a team led by Dennis Meadows. The report of this work, published in 1972 as *The Limits to*

Growth, caused a storm. While many of the critics of this work have clearly never read it, the strength of the reaction reflects its fundamental challenge to basic assumptions about the future of human society in general and our economic system in particular. It has been said that 'only lunatics and economists believe in perpetual growth', but that belief is still widespread! *The Limits to Growth* was based on the results of a complicated world model. Some excerpts from that report illustrate the strengths and limitations of the work.

> Our world model was built specifically to investigate five major trends of global concern—accelerating industrialisation, rapid population growth, widespread malnutrition, depletion of non-renewable resources, and a deteriorating environment. These trends are all inter-connected in many ways, and their development is measured in decades or centuries, rather than in months or years. With the model we are seeking to understand the causes of these trends, their inter-relationships, and their implications as much as one hundred years in the future.
>
> The model we have constructed is, like every other model, imperfect, over-simplified and unfinished. We are well aware of its shortcomings, but we believe it is the most useful model now available for dealing with problems far out on the space-time graph. To our knowledge it is the only formal model in existence that is truly global in scope, that has a time horizon longer than thirty years, and that includes important variables such as population, food production and pollution, not as independent entities but as dynamically interacting elements, as they are in the real world. [Meadows *et al.* 1972:21–2]

Having spelled out the advantages of a formal mathematical model, such as the assumptions being open to inspection and criticism, the report set out its broad conclusions:

1. If the present trends in world population, industrialisation, pollution, food production and resource depletion continue unchanged, the limits to growth on this planet will be reached *sometime within the next hundred years* [my emphasis]. The most probable result will be a rather sudden and uncontrollable decline in both population and industrial capacity.

2. It is possible to alter these growth trends and to establish a condition of ecological and economic stability that is sustainable far into the future. The state of global equilibrium could be designed so that the basic material needs of each person on earth are satisfied and each person has an equal opportunity to realise [their] individual human potential.

3. If the world's people decide to strive for this second outcome rather than the first, the sooner they begin working to attain it, the greater will be their chances of success. [Meadows *et al.* 1972:23–4]

It is difficult to believe that it could have been regarded as con-tentious to suggest that the continuation of current trends would see limits reached within a hundred years. We are already seeing global problems which suggest that we are stretching the capacity of natural systems to absorb our wastes, while there are serious studies foreseeing the end of the age of plentiful oil (Fleay 1995:13–30). Criticisms of the modelling study can be classified as: general reservations about the method; claims that it is too optimistic; and claims that it is too pessimistic. In the first category, there were legitimate concerns about the aggregation of data to give global figures when there are clear differences between nations and between regions, as well as the unified treatment of pollution (Cole *et al.* 1973). Assumptions that there would be widespread use of nuclear power and the implicit idea that the United States would be a model for world development were seen as unrealistically optimistic. The 'stabilised world model' in which population stabilised with low pollution levels, despite greater food production and industrial output per head than the 1970 values, was based on the following heroic assumptions:

- an average family size of two children achieved through 100% access to totally effective birth control measures
- industrial output per head maintained constant after 1975
- the average life of industrial plant increased through better design
- resource use and pollution per unit of output reduced to 25% of 1970 levels
- capital diverted to food production to give adequate nutrition for all
- programs of soil preservation and enrichment used to maintain agricul-tural productivity. [Meadows *et al.* 1972:163–4]

The strongest criticism came from those who regarded the work as unduly pessimistic, usually because they felt it took insufficient account of the possibility of salvation through technological innovation or economic growth (Cole *et al.* 1973). This line of argument suggested that shortages would inevitably stimulate the development of alterna-tives, and that strong economic growth would surely create the wealth which will be needed to clean up the environment. Thus conventional economists dismissed the whole study as 'unrealistic'. Reflecting on this criticism, the Club of Rome said in its second report, *Mankind at the Turning Point*:

we have found that technological optimism is the most common and the most dangerous reaction to our findings ... Technology can relieve the symptoms of a problem without affecting the underlying causes. Faith in technology as the ultimate solution to all problems can thus divert our attention from the most fundamental problem—*the problem of growth in a finite system*—and prevent us from taking effective action to solve it ... we would deplore an unreasoned rejection of the benefits of technology as strongly as we argue here against an unreasoned acceptance of them. Perhaps the best summary of our position is the motto of the Sierra Club: not blind opposition to progress but opposition to blind progress.

Taking no action to solve these problems is equivalent to taking strong action. Every day of continued exponential growth brings the world system closer to the ultimate limits of that growth. A decision to do nothing is a decision to increase the risk of collapse.

The way to proceed is clear ... [we possess] all that is necessary to create a totally new form of human society ... the two missing ingredients are a realistic long-term goal ... and the human will to achieve that goal. [Mesarovic and Pestel 1975:88]

The second report of the Club of Rome endeavoured to meet some of the legitimate criticisms of the degree of aggregation in *The Limits to Growth*. It divided the world into ten inter-dependent regions, treating them as linked sub-systems of the global system. This approach showed that the most serious medium-term problem is the demand for food to meet the rapidly growing population of South Asia.

Even with a strong population policy to achieve equilibrium within fifty years, all potentially arable land cultivated, fertiliser use per hectare at the American level, and all needed technological inputs being made available, there would still be a need for food imports to prevent mass starvation. The conclusion was: 'The only feasible solution to the world food situation requires a global approach to the problem; investment aid; a balanced economic development for all regions; an effective population policy; worldwide diversification of industry ... a truly global economic system' (Mesarovic and Pestel 1975:127).

The broad conclusions of the modelling studies conducted by the Club of Rome are:

1. the current crises are not temporary
2. solutions of these crises can only be developed in a global context
3. solutions cannot be achieved by traditional faith in economics
4. resolution of the crises requires co-operation, not confrontation.

This was a call for a new global ethic, involving an identification with future generations that affects our attitude toward use of material resources and environmental impacts of our actions. Underlying this call for a global ethic was an even more basic appeal: that we should develop an attitude toward nature based on harmony rather than conquest. This point is developed much more completely in the most recent report of the Club of Rome, *The First Global Revolution*, which concludes that recent technological changes have given us the capacity to solve our problems if we have the political will to do so. On the other hand, it warns, there are new complications such as the threat of climate change, 'the precarious nature of global food security', and growing tension between rich nations and poorer countries (King and Schneider 1991:xv). Recent specific studies also point to the likelihood of a serious food shortage in South and East Asia in the early decades of the twenty-first century (Brown 1995:13–19).

Political will to change

At any given time, there are usually a range of technological solutions to any problem. Each solution has its particular strengths and weaknesses (Gale and Lowe 1991:44–57). There are various technologies which can be used to reduce the carbon dioxide emissions currently associated with our energy use, especially such renewable energy forms as solar thermal, wind power, geothermal energy and photovoltaic cells directly producing electricity from sunlight. It should also be noted that no renewable energy form is entirely free of undesirable impacts on the natural environment. Given that there is no such thing as a totally benign source of energy, the highest priority should be improving the efficiency of the end use of energy. In terms of the cost of avoiding carbon emissions, efficiency improvements are by far the best investment.

If we want to achieve a sustainable future, the issue of equitable distribution of resources needs to be addressed. At the moment, those in the industrialised countries account for about 20 per cent of the human population, but together we consume over 80 per cent of the natural resources being used. Dr Lester Brown, director of a Washington organisation called the Worldwatch Institute, has calculated that a crash program to provide the entire human population by 2000 with basic shelter, clean drinking water, adequate nutrition and reasonable health care would cost a massive $US200 billion per year. This is only about 15 per cent of the global arms budget (Brown *et al.* 1989:174–94)! In other words, the problems could potentially be resolved by a more sensible distribution of the resources currently in use. It would not require peace breaking out in all parts of the globe; all it would take would be a 15 per cent cut in the present level of military spending, a level which can be said to be truly obscene. Every dollar spent on weapons could be considered a crime against those who cannot be fed, or who are inadequately sheltered, or who do not have access to clean drinking water. That is almost a paraphrase of a famous

statement by Dwight Eisenhower, who was President of the United States
from 1952 to 1960 after a distinguished military career, in a speech he
made at the end of his term of office, warning his country about the
emergence of a military-industrial complex.

There is a growing public mood for change. A regular poll conducted by the *New York Times* and CBS News asks Americans if they agree
with the statement that 'Protecting the environment is so important
that requirements and standards cannot be too high, and continuing
environmental improvements must be made regardless of cost.' This
quite strong statement was being asked in the early 1980s, when there
was a small majority in favour. The level of support has grown steadily
throughout the 1980s. By mid-1989, over 80 per cent of Americans
sampled agreed with this statement, with only 13 per cent disagreeing
(Ruckelshaus 1989:117). Dr Mostafa Tolba of the UN Environment
Program has said that people the world over want their political,
scientific and industrial leaders to be doing far more about ecological issues. He said that people want action, and show every sign of
being prepared to pay the price of acting to secure a better future, but
governments are lagging behind public opinion (Noyce 1989). There is
evidence from particular opinion polls in various countries and from
patterns of voting that the general public may be more prepared to face
change than those who lead us; in a 1994 survey, 18 per cent of
Australians rated the environment more important than economic
growth, while 71 per cent said they were equally important (SoEAC
1996:10.11). It has been said that when the people lead, the leaders
eventually follow. Some appear to have heard the message, and have at
least given their rhetoric a green tinge. A conservative Australian
political power broker recently said:

> The most important question we now face is whether we collectively have the
> foresight and courage to make the necessary changes. ... Meeting the
> challenge will require unprecedented co-operation and vision. ... There is
> no quick technological fix. The critical issue is, and will always remain, the
> need to plan for a more secure and sustainable world. It will require a long-
> term commitment from all of us as individuals and a fundamental change in
> our attitude to the use of resources. [Richardson 1990:68–76]

Despite this greener shade of rhetoric, the political agenda is still
dominated by economic issues in general, and a belief in the benefits of
growth in particular. We need to make a clear distinction between
development, a pattern of change which is seen as being desirable, and
growth, an increase in flows of material goods. We continue to need
development, innovation and improvement of our technologies, but

there is a brisk debate about the role of economic growth. Some see it as essential to a sustainable society (WCED 1987), while others see it as the main problem (Daly 1991). The State of the Environment report for Australia argued that we need to see the economy as part of society, and society in turn as a part of the natural ecology of Earth (SoEAC 1996: 10.12). While most political decisions appear based on the implied view that the first priority is a healthy economy which will provide the wealth to solve environmental problems, no amount of wealth will recover an extinct species, and the cost of repairing degraded areas may prove impractical (SoEAC 1996:10.12). Economic decisions need to be set within a framework of the ecological limits.

In evaluating our economic performance, we should move away from such primitive measures as the gross domestic product, or GDP. As the sum of all economic activities, it includes problems such as road accidents as well as productive activity such as growing apples. Using this measure encourages the absurd belief that community welfare is helped by road accidents and natural disasters, since these unfortunate events stimulate economic activity which would not otherwise have occurred. It is equally problematic that the current GDP calculation also ignores things for which we do not pay money: spectacular sunsets, clean air, the company of friends, housework and volunteer work.

The late Senator Robert Kennedy once said that the GDP measures all things except those which make life worthwhile. We need to develop measures of community well-being that incorporate the effects of our actions on the stock of natural capital, on bio-diversity and on ecological integrity. It is no longer acceptable to operate as if we were a business in liquidation, getting rid of our stock of assets at bargain-basement prices to any passer-by to produce cash flow. We need to behave instead as if we intend to be long-term inhabitants of this planet. I believe that we would generally make much wiser decisions if we were always to ask ourselves what our descendants will think of our actions in fifty or a hundred years' time. If you reflect on that issue, I am sure you would prefer to be seen as prudent and far-sighted, rather than greedy and short-sighted.

The future of the human species is critically bound up with the recognition that we are part of a complex eco-system. We still have only a primitive understanding of that system. We share this planet with millions of other species, so many that we have only a vague idea of how many there actually are. Our destiny is inextricably intertwined with the overall health of that eco-system. This Earth is the only home we have and the only home we are ever likely to have. There is no prospect of rescue by friendly aliens or mass migration to another part of the cosmos. The future of your nation and the entire human species is something you and others are in the act of creating. Shaping a satisfactory future depends critically on our recognition of the ecological realities of life on this planet. We will determine whether the human species has the sort of future we will find acceptable. That is a great challenge and an awesome responsibility.

Special responsibility of scientists and technologists

There is a growing view that scientists and technologists have to take responsibility for their actions. Putting this into practice is not simple, however, as discussed in Chapters 3 and 4 of this book. Many people would now agree that the scientists who worked on the Manhattan Project were responsible for the production of the fission bomb, since that was the aim of the exercise. It might be considered harsh to extend the blame to the physicists whose basic research in the first four decades of the twentieth century made the bomb project possible, since they were only trying to understand the structure of the atom and the basic relationship between energy and matter. So one approach to this issue of responsibility is to judge it by the motive of the individual. A scientist who is trying to build a bomb or synthesise a chemical weapon is clearly responsible for the use of the device, but it is possible to argue that no blame (or credit) attaches to those whose basic research was used to make the weapon.

I discussed earlier in this chapter the crucial role of science and technology in shaping our future. In those terms, each of us has some freedom to choose the field in which we work. Easlea (1973) argues that we have a responsibility to use our individual talents to try to build a better world. Whether you accept that argument or not, you can no longer claim that you are unaware of the social consequences of science and technology. Just as anyone who fires a gun must take responsibility for where the bullet goes, so those who develop new knowledge or apply it to specific tasks have some responsibility for the consequences. In fact, the responsibility goes further than this accountability for our actions. A case discussed in Chapters 4 and 5, that of cervical cancer patients in the National Women's Hospital of New Zealand, suggested that scientists may be held responsible for their inaction if that is held to do unnecessary harm, even if the inaction was a consequence of sincerely held belief in a particular theory. Increasingly, society expects its technical experts to be aware of the broader consequences of their work.

During most of the twentieth century, people trusted the technical experts to make decisions on technical issues. The obvious reason is that this approach allows use of technical expertise. If a nuclear power station were being built near where you live, you would presumably want the best technical expertise to be used to make it as safe as possible. That is an appropriate area to leave to the experts. However, the prior question of whether a nuclear power station should be built, rather than a coal-burning unit or a wind farm, is not one for technical experts in nuclear technology. Indeed, a better answer than any of those energy supply options might be to use the existing energy sources more effectively. Technologists are now expected to realise that any proposal has costs as well as benefits (Gale and Lowe 1991:44–57). If you work in a technical field, you will probably be asked to explore the advantages and problems of a range of options, rather than being left to make the choice on technical criteria alone. There is a whole emerging field of multi-criteria decision-making, recognising that choices of technology in the modern world have to consider social, political, economic and environmental aspects as well as questions of technical performance (Mills *et al.* 1996).

Confession of an optimist

What are the prospects for using science and technology to produce a better world than the one in which we now live? I am unashamedly optimistic. I do not underestimate the scale of the problems; the decisions to be made in the next ten or twenty years are probably more critical than any in the previous history of the human species (Brown *et al.* 1996:1–20). The grounds for hope are that we are better informed than ever before, have a greater technological capacity than ever before, and have an emerging sense of responsibility for the shaping of our future. Whenever I discuss these sorts of issues with young people, I am always impressed by their knowledge and commitment to a better future. As I said at the start of this chapter, the future doesn't just happen; it will be the product of our decisions and actions, as individuals and in groups. We have the capacity to shape a better world, one which is genuinely sustainable, if we have the imagination and the collective will to do so. If we don't move in this direction, our descendants will justifiably be angered by our failure to give them the sort of opportunities we have had. We should never doubt the capacity of determined people to change the world for the better; it is the only force that ever has.

While there are grounds for a determined optimist to be hopeful, there remains the legacy of our reluctance to plan a better future. A few years ago, as a result of the determined advocacy of Barry Jones who was at that time Minister for Science, the Australian government established

a Commission for the Future. Its charter consisted of three tasks: to
monitor those developments in science and technology which are likely
to have significant social, economic or political impacts; to spread
information about those developments and their possible impacts; and
in those ways, to make it possible for people to play a greater role in
determining their future (CFF 1988). Despite these stated aims, it would
be hard to make a case that the Australian government has ever been
really committed to a serious evaluation of future options. The same
comment could be made about most national governments, and would
probably be made about the globe as a whole if we were observed by
witnesses from another galaxy. We spend billions of dollars each year on
science and technology, but devote only a tiny fraction of those resources to evaluating its consequences. At its high point the Commission
for the Future was costing each Australian about five cents a year; that is
a trifling sum in the overall scheme of things, but even that commitment
was opposed by economic fundamentalists who believe that decisions
about technology should be left to the market. The Commission for the
Future has since ceased to receive regular government funding.

Hostility toward planning is not rational, but is nevertheless widespread in English-speaking nations. Other industrial societies in Europe
and Asia are generally less naive about the magic of the market. We
urgently need the sort of projects which allow us all to be better
informed about future options. There is a growing tendency for scientific conferences to include a component aimed at public education;
recently David Suzuki, Paul Ehrlich and some Australian speakers
participated in a public day at the end of a Sydney conference on
renewable energy technology, and several hundred people gave up their
Saturday and paid good money to listen to them. A new profession of
science communicators has developed, with professional bodies and
international conference.

Creating the future

To plan the future we want, we need a solid base of information and the
exploration of a range of options. That exploration is complicated
because it has to go beyond narrowly technical issues and also investigate the social, political and economic feasibility of the various alternatives. I recently spent some time working with the Green Independents
in the island state of Tasmania on an alternative blue-print for the future
development of that state. Since it became a plan for a green future, we
called it the green-print. It explored options for a sustainable future.
The interesting conclusion was that a green future might be better, in

economic terms, for Tasmanians than the historic approach of assuming they will keep finding more minerals to dig up and more forests to chop down, and it will also provide more employment (Lowe 1990).

In the context of a proposed hydro-electric project in north Queensland, I looked at the option of using more solar energy for hot water. As a legacy of past policies, only about 5 per cent of households in that part of Australia use solar energy for water heating, even though the economics are very attractive. I was so impressed by the data that I put solar panels on my own roof in the Queensland city of Brisbane fourteen years ago, after which it only cost $10 per year for the water heating needs of a family of four! A ten-year program to bring Queensland up to the level of the state of Western Australia, where solar has 25 per cent of the market, would on my estimation create about 1500 permanent jobs. Given that the use of solar panels replaces electric water heating in most homes, such an approach would also save more electricity than the proposed power station would have supplied. This case study is a specific example of one general theme developed in this book: that technological choices affect our future.

That example illustrates a general point. The debate about contentious proposals, such as nuclear power stations or genetic manipulation, is often a surrogate debate about what sort of society we want to have in the future. We argue about the specific issues, rather than that broad general question. It would be better, at least in principle, to have a general debate about the sort of future we want. We would then have a firm base for taking the specific decisions that will move us toward that desired future, as can be seen from a final analogy. Very few people go on holiday by loading the members of their household and some clothes into a car or public transport vehicle and then moving randomly around the road or rail system. Most people going on holiday have a broad idea of where they want to go and what they want to experience, while perhaps retaining the flexibility to vary their plan if problems arise or unforeseen opportunities become apparent. I believe that our future is at least as important as a family holiday, and so deserves at least the same level of planning. We should have a general idea of where we want to go, while keeping the flexibility to respond to things we cannot foresee: new problems, new opportunities.

The current strategy of industrial civilisation is effectively one of bumbling randomly in whichever directions we are carried by market forces, the patterns of investment and international politics. This has little to commend it as a long-term strategy. After all, this is not a dress rehearsal or an out-of-town try-out, it's the real show. We only get one future to build; we should be trying to make it a good one! In those terms, we need to keep developing our scientific knowledge base and our technological capacity to change the world. But we also need, as a matter of some urgency, to adopt the overall goal of moving toward a pattern of development that would be sustainable, at least in principle. I hope the themes developed in this book have shown you how important science and technology are in the modern world, and how much our future will be affected by the choices we make. I also hope that it has inspired you to play an active role in using science and technology to help make the world a better place. Milbrath (1989:1–6) argues that we need to learn the techniques for making society stable and sustainable. I hope this book has been a useful step along that path for you.

Further reading

Charles Birch's excellent book *Confronting the Future*, first published in 1976, was a ground-breaking overview of the issues involved; the revised edition is a perfect extension of the ideas introduced in this chapter. Brian Easlea's *Liberation and the Aims of Science* is a classic analysis of the social responsibility of scientists. The printed version of the 1991 Boyer Lectures by Fay Gale and Ian Lowe, *Changing Australia*, discusses the role of education and technology in shaping the future. The report of the World Commission on Environment and Development, *Our Common Future*, documents the links between economic development and the state of the natural environment; it is an important and optimistic statement by a group of world leaders. Lester Milbrath's book *Envisioning a Sustainable Society* is a hopeful discussion of a possible path to allow sustainable human development. Paul Kennedy's *Preparing for the Twenty-first Century* has a strong economic emphasis, but is a very readable account of the situation facing the global community at the end of the twentieth century.

References

Australian Science and Technology Council (ASTEC) (1996), *Matching Science and Technology to Australia's Future Needs*. Canberra: Australian Government Publishing Service.

Birch, C. (1976), *Confronting the Future*. Harmondsworth: Penguin.

Brown, L. R. (1995), *Who Will Feed China?* Washington, DC: Worldwatch Institute.

Brown, L. R. *et al.* (1989), *State of the World 1989*. Washington, DC: Worldwatch Institute.

Brown, L. R. *et al.* (1996), *State of the World 1996*. Washington, DC: Worldwatch Institute.

Casti, J. L. (1991), *Searching for Certainty*. London: Abacus.

Chapman, P. F. (1975), *Fuel's Paradise*. Harmondsworth: Penguin.

Cole, H. S. D. *et al.* (ed.) (1973), *Models of Doom: A Critique of 'The Limits to Growth'*. New York: Universe Books.

Commission for the Future (CFF) (1988), *Annual Report*. Melbourne: Commission for the Future.

Daly, H. (1991), *Steady State Economics*. Washington, DC: Island Press.

Davis, B. W. (1992), 'Antarctica as a Global Protected Area: Perception and Reality', *Australian Geographer*, 23:39–43.

Easlea, B. D. (1973), *Liberation and the Aims of Science*. London: Chatto and Windus.

Fleay, B. (1996), *The Decline of the Age of Oil*. Annandale: Pluto Press.

Gale, F., and Lowe, I. (1991), *Changing Australia*. Sydney: ABC Books.

Inter-governmental Panel on Climate Change (IPCC) (1996), *Second Assessment Report*. Geneva: United Nations.

Jones, B. O. (1982), *Sleepers, Wake!* Melbourne: Oxford University Press.

Kennedy, P. (1993), *Preparing for the Twenty-First Century*. London: Harper Collins.

King, A., and Schneider, B. (1991), *The First Global Revolution*. London: Simon and Schuster.

Lowe, I. (1983), 'Who Benefits from Australian Energy Research?', *Science and Public Policy*, 10:278–84.

Lowe, I. (1989), *Living in the Greenhouse*. Newham: Scribe Books.

Lowe, I. (1990), *A Sustainable Development Strategy for Tasmania*. Report to Department of Premier and Cabinet, Hobart.

Lowe, I. (1991), 'Science Policy for the Future', in R. Haynes (ed.), *High Tech: High Co$t?* Chippendale: Pan Macmillan.

Lowe, I. (1996), *Understanding Australia's Population Debate*. Canberra: Australian Government Publishing Service.

McCloskey, I. (1993), 'Funding of Medical Research in Australia by the National Health and Medical Research Council', in F. Q. Wood and V. Meek (eds), *Research Grants Management and Funding*. Canberra: ANUTECH:97–104.

McGauran, P. (1996), *Science and Technology Budget Statement, 1996–97*. Canberra: Australian Government Publishing Service.

Meadows, D. H., Meadows, D. L., Randers, J., and Behrens, W. W. (1972), *The Limits to Growth*. New York: Universe Books.

Mesarovic, M. D., and Pestel, E. (1975), *Mankind at the Turning Point: The Second Report to the Club of Rome*. London: Hutchinson.

Milbrath, L. (1989), *Envisioning a Sustainable Society*. Albany: State University of New York Press.

Mills, D., Vlacic, L., and Lowe, I. (1996), 'Improving Electricity Planning: Use of a Multicriteria Decision-making Model', *International Transactions in Operational Research*, 3:293–304.

Noyce, P. (1989), personal communication.

Richardson, G. (1990), 'Greenhouse: The Challenge of Change', in K. Coghill (ed.), *Greenhouse: What's to be Done?* Leichhardt, NSW: Pluto Press.

Ruckelshaus, W. S. (1989), 'Towards a Sustainable World', *Scientific American*, 261, 3:114–22.

State of the Environment Advisory Council (SoEAC) (1996), *State of the Environment Australia, 1996*. Melbourne: CSIRO Publishing.

Upton, S. (1996), *New Zealand's Response to Climate Change*. Wellington: Department of Environment.

World Commission on Environment and Development (WCED) (1987), *Our Common Future*. Oxford: Oxford University Press.

APPENDIXES

1. Surviving in the Information Jungle

In Chapter 2, reference was made to Derek J. de Solla Price's book, *Little Science, Big Science* (Price 1965). Price pointed out that the number of scientists has expanded about a million-fold since the time of Galileo. Naturally, this huge growth has led to an enormous increase in the amount of literature, in science and in related subjects.

Given the sheer scale of publication today, it is reasonable to ask: is important information going to be lost? The short answer is, not necessarily. To someone who knows their way about the information jungle, it is not difficult to locate any information you want. In parallel with the growth of the scientific literature, the means of navigating around it has developed. In our view, it is essential for any person who wants to be informed to understand these techniques, and this appendix outlines some of the most important methods.

In almost any library, the books are treated separately from the journals and magazines. The latter are usually referred to as 'periodicals'. The means of finding your way around the books are usually better known, and more and more libraries are resorting to computer catalogues.

The computer catalogue

Computer catalogues vary, but they enable you to find out far more than the older card catalogues. Searches by author and title can be carried out, but perhaps the most important improvement is the use of keyword searching. Selecting a keyword option (however it is named) and then typing in a word or two can produce a cascade of book details. Indeed, in a large library, literally thousands of books can be listed, making the search almost useless.

The answer to this problem is to use multiple keywords, refining the object of your search so precisely that a manageable list of books emerges. Figure A1.1 shows how one of the authors (Martin Bridgstock) coped with a couple of unmanageable-looking topics in the Griffith University Library.

In this case, the researcher wanted to find any books in the library concerning water power, which played a large part in the Industrial Revolution. Typing in either *water* or *power* separately produced thousands of items, including ones on hydro-electricity and control of water supplies, far too many to look through. However, typing in the two words together produced a list of only thirteen items, and five of these were useful.

This type of searching is often termed 'Boolean' searching, as it derives from the work of mathematician George Boole, who invented set theory. Different computer systems require different types of command, and you may find yourself having to use commands such as *and, or* and others. However, the logic of Boolean searching is so useful that it is well worth investing a little time in seeing how it works. No other piece of

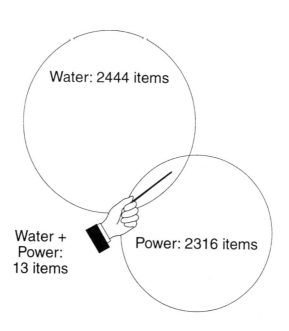

Figure A1.1. Results of a Boolean library search using two headings.

knowledge is more useful in harnessing library computers to your own special needs.

An important point to remember is equip yourself with a list of alternative keywords before starting a search. For example, the researcher in the case above started by using the terms *water* and *wheels* and found nothing useful. It would have been frustrating to have stopped there, when a change in one word yielded the information needed. Therefore, it is always a good idea to give a few minutes' thought to possible different words which can be tried.

Navigating through the periodicals: the principle of indexing

Locating relevant books is relatively easy, once the catalogue is understood. The periodicals section of a library is more difficult. A major journal—such as *Science* or *Nature*—takes up tens of metres of shelf space, which is intimidating to contemplate: perhaps somewhere in all that paper is exactly the information you want, yet there seems to be no way of getting to it. Within the thousands of pages of a large periodical, how can you find what you want?

The answer lies in a series of items known as abstracts and indexes. These used to be published in bound form—and many still are—but they are increasingly appearing in electronic form. Used properly, they render the periodical section of a library as accessible as the books.

Perhaps the simplest and most useful of the abstracts and indexes is one known as APAIS—the Australian Public Affairs Information Service. This is published monthly by the National Library in Canberra. Its principle is worth explaining in some detail, as most indexes are similar. Each month, the APAIS compilers work through all the papers and articles in several hundred Australian publications. They attach several keywords to each and then, by computer, sort the published items under the keywords. Thus, turning to APAIS for, say July 1997, one can look up keywords such as *banking* or *science* and find the items published in that month on that topic.

Naturally, APAIS is also published in annual volumes. So, by looking up a keyword in ten volumes, one can locate everything written on, say science in Australia in all those publications over ten years. An additional feature is that each APAIS volume has an index of authors in the back. Thus, one can locate all the work written by, say, Charles Birch, Paul Davies or Ian Lowe simply by looking up their names.

Using APAIS enables one to ransack the Australian periodical literature for relevant items very easily. APAIS is also on CD-ROM, so that it can be searched on computer, making it even more valuable. Many people concerned with Australian current affairs find that APAIS is all they need to keep abreast of developments. However, for those who want more, APAIS is only the beginning.

The United States has a counterpart to APAIS, called, logically enough, PAIS. It is organised in a similar way, though it is somewhat larger. Of course, from the non-American viewpoint is has the exasperating drawback that many of the periodicals it refers to are not easily available.

A good many other indexes exist, organised on the same lines as APAIS and PAIS. They differ in the types of periodicals upon which they focus. For example, the major American indexes, *Social Sciences Index* and the *Applied Science and Technology Index*, work by taking in several hundred relevant magazines and journals from those particular fields. As with APAIS, there are annual volumes and major author indexes in the back. In addition, both indexes are on CD-ROM, which can greatly speed up the searching.

At least two major newspapers have indexes devoted entirely to them. These are the London *Times* and *New York Times* index. Each index covers one year of one of these great newspapers and, for any given topic, shows exactly where stories can be found: not only the date and page is given, but also the column. For example, it might seem hard to find where, in the *Times* of 1991, Marilyn Monroe was reported to be having trouble with imitators. However, looking up Monroe's name soon yields the information that a story about this appeared in the *Times* of 29 April, on page 12 in column a.

On a recent trip to the United Kingdom, Martin Bridgstock was impressed by a further development. For at least two major newspapers, the *Times* and the *Guardian*, the full text of stories is now on CD-ROM. As a result, one can not only look up references in a computer index, but also obtain the full text. In some Australian libraries, many Australian newapers are also on-line. This varies from place to place, and it would be a good idea to find out which publications are accessible in this way.

Indexes using other principles

There is a large range of indexes using the keyword principle, and each library has its own selection. Rather than working through all of them— when a brief conversation with a librarian will reveal more—it is more useful to look at abstracts and indexes which use different principles.

The largest index of all is not really relevant to Science, Technology and Society. This is the *Biological Abstracts*, which takes in over 7000 journals and magazines. It provides not only references, but also a brief summary of the papers, In addition, one can look up biological species (such as *Homo sapiens* or *Rattus rattus*) in a separate index.

An intriguing alternative to keyword-type indexes are the citation indexes, published by the Institute for Scientific Information in Chicago. There are three of these large indexes, devoted to Science, Social Science and the Arts and Humanities. The major difference from other indexes is that the entry for each paper lists not only the paper's details, but also the books and papers to which it refers.

As we saw in Chapter 2, scientists place great stress upon acknowledging sources of information and ideas in the papers they write. The three citation indexes take advantage of this: in the index, each book and paper referred to in a given year is indexed, and the papers referring to them are listed below.

What is the point of this unusual arrangement? The citation indexes are most valuable when one has found an old piece of work, and wishes to update one's knowledge of the area to which it refers. For example, a researcher who finds a paper dated 1980 relevant to her interests will probably want to know what recent work has been done. This can be found using the citation indexes: work is indexed under the name of the author cited. For example, if one wants to know who, in 1997, has referred to the work of Thomas Kuhn (1970), one can look up 'Kuhn, T. S.' in the appropriate 1997 citation index, and obtain a list of papers which referred to Kuhn's famous work.

The citation indexes also allow keyword searching, based on words in the papers' titles, and one can look for articles by specific authors. They are therefore versatile, and since each citation index draws on several thousand publications, they have a wide coverage.

The citation indexes are now published on CD-ROM, which makes them a good deal easier to use. The old bound volumes were large and heavy, and the print minuscule. Even so, for researchers outside the United States, the citation indexes present both great advantages and substantial problems. Their scale, and their unique structure, make it possible to find references which escape other indexes. On the other hand, many references made in the literature are not important ones. Often, one hunts down a paper and then finds that a 'token reference' has been made, perhaps of the form 'Smith has also done research in a related area'. This is maddening and time-wasting.

As an example which worked well, Martin Bridgstock took the CD-ROM for the *Social Science Citation Index* of 1995 and looked for recent work concerning the Auckland cervical cancer scandal (described in Chapters 4 and 5). Selecting the citation option and typing the name 'Coney, S.' produced four references. One of these was a review of a book by Sandra Coney, *Unfinished Business: What Happened to the Cartwright Report*. It is hard to imagine a more useful follow-up to Coney's original account of what happened.

Many other abstracts and indexes exist. These are too numerous to list, and more are appearing all the time. The reader is urged to locate indexes which are available, and to use them in any research project. They greatly increase the researcher's ability to locate important information.

References

Kuhn, T. S. (1970), *The Structure of Scientific Revolutions.* Chicago: University of Chicago Press.

Price, D. J. de Solla (1965), *Little Science, Big Science.* New York: Columbia University Press.

Ziman, J. (1976), *The Force of Knowledge.* Cambridge: Cambridge University Press.

2. Referencing

From your reading of Chapter 2, you will know that many scientists—and academics generally—are concerned about receiving due recognition for the information, ideas and arguments which they have contributed. Often this is the only direct reward they receive for their work.

A key feature of this acknowledgment is the use of references in written work. Therefore, the proper understanding of referencing is important in making sense of much scientific and scholarly writing. In addition, you will have noticed that this book itself is referenced, and you may wish to understand the system used.

There are excellent—and lengthy—guides to the different referencing systems. The Australian Government Publishing Service (1988) for instance, devotes about thirty-five pages to explaining how to reference. We will give an outline of the two most important systems, and suggest you consult the Australian government if your thirst for knowledge is greater. Since the best way to learn something is by doing it, imagine that you are writing a piece of text, and you wish to reference it. What are you trying to do?

A reference should enable the reader of your text to find the passage which you have reproduced, or the ideas which you have used, by looking up the relevant page in the book or article from which it came. Therefore your reference must identify the book or article and state the relevant page number. To identify a book, you need to say at least who wrote it, where it was published, and in what year it was published. In addition, you should normally give the name of the publisher. In the case of a journal article, you need to say who wrote the article, which journal it appeared in, which issue it appeared in, and which year it appeared.

Just how this information is set out depends on which convention you adopt. The two most widely used are the Modern Languages

Association of America (MLA) system and the Harvard system. They both have other names; the MLA system is sometimes simply called the note system and the Harvard system is also called the author–date system.

There are other systems, such as the Vancouver (Australian Government Publishing Service 1988: 153), and journals often have the irritating habit of modifying existing systems to suit themselves. Generally, though, most systems resemble one or other of the two main ones, and if you understand these, you can follow the others.

MLA system

In this system a reference is indicated in the text by a number, normally as a superscript (like this[5]), at the end of the passage which is to be acknowledged. This number refers the reader either to a *footnote*, which is found at the foot of the page, or to an *endnote*, which is found at the end of the text. Footnotes are generally more difficult to organise unless you have a word processor, so it is probably better to use endnotes for your references. What is said here about endnotes applies equally to footnotes, and it is also worth mentioning that a lot of people talk about footnotes even when the notes are placed at the end of a piece of writing.

For example, suppose you have written:

A scientist, whether theorist or experimenter, puts forward statements, or systems of statements, and tests them step by step.[3]

At the end of the text, you place a third endnote:

1. .....
2. .....
3. Karl R. Popper, *The Logic of Scientific Discovery* (New York: Harper, 1959), p. 27.

Please note the punctuation: the book title is italicised. In *every* system, book titles are italicised (or, if you cannot do this, underlining is an acceptable alternative). Generally, the place of publication comes before the name of the publisher.

Now, suppose you go on to refer to an article by Popper, and that this is your fifth reference.

4. .....
5. Karl R. Popper, 'A Note on Berkeley as a Precursor to Mach and Einstein', *British Journal for the Philosophy of Science*, 4, 1953, p. 84.

Titles of articles are *never* italicised, but names of journals always are. The number after the journal name is the volume number. In many instances there is one volume per year, so it is not strictly necessary to have both year and volume number. Still, it is the convention to include both.

Suppose in your next reference you want to refer to that same article and the same page in an endnote: do you have to write the whole thing out again? No, indeed; you just write:

7. *ibid.*

This term means 'the same as above'. And if the next reference is to a different page of the same work, then you write:

8. *ibid.*, p. 88.

The term *ibid.* is an abbreviation (which is why it is followed by a full stop), for a Latin word (which is why it is italicised; *always* italicise words from other languages). The full word is *ibidem*, meaning 'in the same' book, chapter, etc.

If your next reference is to Popper but to the book, you can write:

9. Popper, *op. cit.*, p. 33.

The term *op. cit.* means 'in the work already cited'. This saves writing everything out again, but take care that you have not previously cited two works by the same author. Another method, which avoids this problem, is to give the title of the work, e.g.:

9. Popper, *The Logic of Scientific Discovery*, p. 33.

Some articles are in books, rather than journals. The convention here is that you give the editor(s) as well as the author. Let's use someone besides Popper:

10. Merrilee H. Salmon, 'Explanation in the Social Sciences', in Philip Kitcher and Wesley C. Salmon (eds), *Scientific Explanation* (Minnesota: Minnesota University Press, 1989), p. 309.

These, then are the main conventions for referencing that you will need if you follow the MLA system. If you use endnotes rather than footnotes, as we have advised, then list them consecutively on a separate page at the end of your text, under the heading *Endnotes*. Alternatively, you may, if you prefer, collect them under the heading *References*. You may like to include another kind of endnote, what is called a *discursive* endnote. Here you do not just give a reference, you make some additional comment. For instance:

11. *ibid.* Salmon's view on scientific method expressed here is very similar to that of Popper.

It is unlikely that a first-year university student will be in a position to make comments like this. In later years, however, you may come to see the value of discursive endnotes. Since these are more than references, the heading *References* is misleading.

Believe it or not, you are not finished with the MLA system yet! In addition to your references and discursive endnotes, you must provide a bibliography. This is an alphabetical list by author's name, of all the books you have consulted. It is placed at the end of your text. Why do you need a bibliography as well as references? Because you may have read a book or article, but not referred to it. By listing it in your bibliography you indicate that you took the author's ideas into account, but you chose not to refer to them directly. In the MLA system, the bibliography will look like this:

Popper, Karl R., *The Logic of Scientific Discovery*. New York: Harper, 1959.
Popper, Karl R., 'A Note on Berkeley as a Precursor to Mach and Einstein', *British Journal for the Philosophy of Science*, 4, 1954.
Salmon, Merrilee H., 'Explanation in the Social Sciences', in Philip Kitcher and Wesley C. Salmon (eds), *Scientific Explanation*. Minnesota: Minnesota University Press, 1989.

For articles, the page numbers in the journals are sometimes listed, but we won't insist on that here.

Harvard system

The Harvard system is more compact because it includes references in the body of the text itself, rather than in footnotes or endnotes. Using the same examples, the first reference to Popper is:

According to Karl Popper, the method of science is conjecture and refutation ... (Popper 1959: 27).

The same style is used for a direct quote:

A scientist, whether theorist or experimenter, puts forward statements, or systems of statements, and tests them step by step. In the field of the empirical sciences, more particularly, he constructs hypotheses, or systems of theories, and tests them against experience by observation and experiment (Popper 1959: 27).

It is no longer necessary to give references in endnotes, so it is no longer necessary to put superscript numbers in the text to mark where the reference applies. You may, of course, still use discursive endnotes in which you amplify or comment on something in a way which is not appropriate for the main text, and here you will need to use superscript numbers in the text. But if the same text is written out twice using each of the conventions, the one that uses the Harvard system will normally have fewer endnotes. The terms *ibid.* and *op.cit.* are not used in the Harvard system: you have to keep mentioning the author, date and page number.

The Harvard system was designed to be simple and to save space in science journals. Nowadays, many non-science journals require submissions to be made in the Harvard style. (You have probably noticed already that this book uses the Harvard system.)

As in the MLA system, the bibliography is listed at the end of the text. However, the form of the bibliography is different from that of the MLA system, in that the year of publication is inserted just after the author's name.

Salmon, Merrilee H. (1989), 'Explanation in the Social Sciences', in Philip Kitcher and Wesley C. Salmon (eds), *Scientific Explanation.* Minnesota: Minnesota University Press.

One last point. If by chance you are using two works by the same author published in the same year, you can distinguish them by adding letters to the year: Salmon 1989a: 307; Salmon 1989b: 42, etc. It is then clear from your bibliography which books are referred to.

References

Australian Government Publishing Service (1988), *Style Manual*, 4th edn. Canberra: AGPS Press.

Index

industrial R&D, 16, 23–6, 29, 172–3, 176,
    201
military R&D, 16, 26, 36, 140–1
public policy, 15–17, 146, 181–2, 185,
    187–93, 196–202, 252; *see also*
    Australian Science and Technology
    Council; Commission for the Future
research funds, 20; *see also* Australian
    scientific activity, 15–17
Australian Academy of Science, 202
Australian National Technology Strategy,
    198–9
Australian Research Council, 20
Australian Research Grants Committee,
    182
Australian Science and Technology
    Council (ASTEC), 23, 25, 37, 146,
    182–3, 200–1, 204, 236
authority, attitudes towards, 68, 78

Bacon, Francis, 7–8
Baltimore, David, 102
basic research, 201–4, 211–12, 222, 250
benefits versus risks, 95–6
Bernal, J. D., 8–10
Bethe, Hans, 51
BHP, 27, 140, 197
Big Bang theory, 4, 86, 105
bio-diversity, 224, 240, 249
biogas plants, 217–18, 228
biological control, 139
biological sciences, 202–3, 260
biotechnology, 175, 221–2, 224
Blackett, P. M. S., 92, 211, 213
brain drain, 213, 223
Bretton Woods agreement, 219
British Empire, 6, 135, 209, 212, 227
    Australia as part, 24, 135–8, 142, 144,
        155, 188
    see also United Kingdom
Brown, Lester, 247
Brundtland, Gro Harlem, 224
Bush, Vannevar, 9, 13
Button, John, 145
Buxtun, Peter, 60, 62

Canada, 137, 189, 213, 226
cane toad, 139
capital
    economics, 164–5, 167, 168–70, 195,
        197–200, 210
    Industrial Revolution, 116–18, 123–4
    Third World, 213, 216, 218, 220, 226,
        228, 245
Cardwell, D., 119, 123, 126, 128–30
cars, *see* motor vehicle industry

Cartwright, Silvia (Royal Commissioner),
    63, 100–1
cause and responsibility, 48–50
cervical cancer scandal, *see* National
    Women's Hospital case
chemical and biological weapons, 33, 35
chemical industry, *see* alkali industry
Chernobyl disaster (1986), 10, 95
China
    ancient technology, 6
    economy, 161–2
    science and technology in development,
        12, 208, 210, 217, 223, 226, 228
    World War I, 148
    World War II, 58, 78
choice
    collective choice, 183–6
    freedom, 47–8, 50, 101
    social and economic aspects, 235–6
Clark, Norman, 159, 161, 169–70, 176, 178
climate change, 239–41, 247
Club of Rome, 243, 245–7
coal, 113, 124–5, 137, 143, 152–3, 169
codes of conduct, 68–9, 76–7, 78, 80–2
cold fusion, 84
Cold War, 9, 35–6, 55
Cole, Stephen, 20, 85–7
Collins, Harry, 84
commercialisation, 183
Commission for the Future, 233, 241, 252
Commission on Sustainable Development,
    225
Committee on Science and Technology in
    Developing Countries (ICSU), 211
Commonwealth Scientific and Industrial
    Research Organisation, *see* CSIRO
community, scientific, 15–39, 79
computers
    R&D, 26–7, 29, 34, 38, 127, 153, 169,
        173–5, 200, 221, 226
    social and economic impacts, 4, 159,
        161, 232
Coney, Sandra, and Bunkle, Phillida, 63,
    99–102, 105
confidentiality, 75–6
conflict, *see* controversies
consequentialism, 55, 64–5; *see also*
    utilitarianism
consumption, *see* demand and supply
continental drift, 4, 11, 83, 87, 88–94, 105
contractarianism, 65
controversies, 11, 71, 83–107
    continental drift, 4, 11, 83, 87, 88–94,
        105
    closure, 87–8, 91, 93–4
    scientific, 83–7, 105